Card Games

for
dummies®
A Wiley Brand

Card Games

3rd Edition

**by Barry Rigal
Card Game Writer, Journalist,
and World-Famous Bridge Author**

Card Games For Dummies®, 3rd Edition

Published by: John Wiley & Sons, Inc., 111 River Street, Hoboken, NJ 07030-5774, www.wiley.com

Copyright © 2022 by John Wiley & Sons, Inc., Hoboken, New Jersey

Published simultaneously in Canada

For general information on our other products and services, please contact our Customer Care Department within the U.S. at 877-762-2974, outside the U.S. at 317-572-3993, or fax 317-572-4002. For technical support, please visit https://hub.wiley.com/community/support/dummies.

Wiley publishes in a variety of print and electronic formats and by print-on-demand. Some material included with standard print versions of this book may not be included in e-books or in print-on-demand. If this book refers to media such as a CD or DVD that is not included in the version you purchased, you may download this material at http://booksupport.wiley.com. For more information about Wiley products, visit www.wiley.com.

Library of Congress Control Number: 2022936113

ISBN 978-1-119-88042-4 (pbk); ISBN 978-1-119-88043-1 (ebk); ISBN 978-1-119-88044-8 (ebk)

SKY10059971_111523

Contents at a Glance

Table of Contents

Introduction

C ard games offer the most fascinating challenges that you may ever encounter. In most games, you can manipulate the 52 pieces of pasteboard into infinite permutations and combinations. Working out those combinations is the fun part of cards — in almost every game, you don't know what the other players have in their hands. During the course of play, you use strategy, memory, cunning, and a whole host of other qualities to put together the best hand possible (or to bluff with the worst hand out there).

All in all, figuring out the fundamentals of a new card game can bring untold satisfaction. At the same time, you don't have to play cards all that well in order to enjoy yourself. Card games allow you to make friends with the people you play with and against.

About This Book

If you've never played a card game before, you may wonder why you need to buy a book about the subject. All your friends say the games are easy to pick up, so can't you just sit down and start playing, picking up a few rules here and there? Obviously, I wouldn't advise that!

Many card games have been in circulation for hundreds of years, generating scores of variations. A reference book not only explains the core rules of a game but also lists the main variations, to let you choose the rules you and your friends want to play by.

Card Games For Dummies, 3rd Edition, is different from every other card-game book on the shelf. So many books on cards simply don't talk about the games people play today. The writers are experts in one or two of the games about which they write, but they remain novices at others. They rely on authors of other books to help them out, who were themselves dependent on previous authors. As a result, the games they describe may not be popular any more, or perhaps the games now have different rules. Many books, in other words, have lost touch with reality. *Card Games For Dummies, 3rd Edition,* has one or two introductory games in it such as

Whist, but for the most part actually focuses on the games that people play today all around the world, especially newer crazes, such Texas Hold 'Em and Omaha.

Of course, I'm not an expert in every game, so this book has benefited enormously from a great deal of input from a host of game players who have answered my questions about the rules of the games in this book and about regional variations. The net result is that I've captured most of the popular variations to the standard games.

This book also differs from other gaming books because I wrote it in plain English. I eliminate as much card jargon as possible and concentrate on telling you how to get up and going. Of course, for games that do involve technical terms that may be new to you, I tell you exactly what each term means so that you can easily understand it.

Regardless of how much experience you've had with card games, you'll find something here for you. Absolute beginners will appreciate that I discuss each game in this book starting at the very beginning, before a card hits the table. If you've played a few card games before, maybe you'll try out a new game or pick up a variation on one of your favorites. (I can tell you that I've become hooked on several new games since I began researching this book. I'm sure you'll have the same experience.)

However, I don't limit my coverage of the games in this book to a description and a summary. Instead, each chapter offers hints on strategy, so even experienced players can pick up something new.

And in line with the wave of technology sweeping up the card game world, I tell you where to find information about a game on the Internet and point out places where you can play games online. (If you don't have a computer, or you can't tell the Internet from a hairnet, you won't miss out on anything; I tell you everything you need to know about how to play a game right here in this book.) I've placed all the computer-related stuff in sidebars, where you can find the information easily if you want to read it or skip over it quickly if you have better things to do.

Just to show that one can improve on perfection, the third edition of *Card Games For Dummies* has an expanded section on Poker, Children's Games, Solitaire, and a host of added variants on the traditional games.

Conventions Used in This Book

Throughout this book, I talk quite a bit about specific cards. Instead of constantly saying "the king of hearts" or "the 7 of spades" every time I refer to those cards, I abbreviate the cards and suits by using the following symbols:

>> **The suits:** I represent each of the four suits in a standard deck of cards with spade ♠, heart ♥, club ♣, and diamond ♦ symbols.

>> **The card values:** I use the following abbreviations to refer to specific card values: ace (A), king (K), queen (Q), jack (J), 10, 9, 8, 7, 6, 5, 4, 3, and 2.

When I refer to a specific card in the text, you see ♥K and ♠7 rather than "the king of hearts" or "the 7 of spades."

I show you entire hands of cards in figures to help you see what a set of cards looks like when you're actually holding it in your hand.

During the printing of this book, some Web addresses may have broken across two lines of text. If you come across such a situation, rest assured that we haven't put in any extra characters (such as hyphens) to indicate the break. So, when using one of these Web addresses, type in exactly what you see in this book, pretending as though the line break doesn't exist.

What You're Not to Read

For the most part, I've tried to avoid using more technical jargon than is absolutely necessary. However, the book does include some sidebars that give you historical perspective on how certain games were created or about where you can go online for additional information about specific games. These are asides and not critical to the text. You can spot them easily enough — the text is on a shaded background.

Foolish Assumptions

I'm not going to assume that the average reader will have all that much technical knowledge. Frequently, the most challenging bit of mathematics you have to perform is to count up to 1! The book is aimed at serving as an introduction to many card games. If you get hooked after reading it, you can access many other

Dummies publications that can provide advanced knowledge of the games. For example, if you want to focus on Bridge, I recommend *Bridge For Dummies* by Eddie Kantar (Wiley). I also urge you Poker fiends out there to check out *Poker For Dummies* by Richard D. Harroch and Lou Krieger (Wiley) and *Winning at Internet Poker For Dummies* by Mark Harlan and Chris Derossi (Wiley).

Icons Used in This Book

In each chapter, I place icons in the margin to emphasize the following types of information:

With this icon, I point out the wrong way to play a game. Pay special attention to these icons so that you avoid finding things out the hard way.

This reinforces a point of the game that may be less obvious (or intuitively right) than meets the eye. You should keep these points in mind as you play the game.

I've been playing cards for quite some time, and I use these icons to emphasize some insights born of experience that will help make you a sharper player.

Next to this icon, you'll find a list of all the stuff you need to play a game — I tell you how many players you need, what type of cards you play with, and if you need any other special equipment, such as something to keep score with.

Most of the games in this book have so many variations, I'd have to write a whole library to include them all. Instead, I cover the most popular variations of a game and tag them with this icon.

Beyond This Book

In addition to the material in the print or ebook you're reading right now, this product comes with some goodies on the Web that you can access anywhere. Simply go to www.dummies.com and type in "Card Games For Dummies, 3rd Edition Cheat Sheet" in the Search box. You'll find handy tips and tricks on picking the best games, card game do's and don'ts, and more!

Where to Go from Here

Each game in this book is a self-contained chapter. If you want information on a particular game, consult the appropriate chapter and discover everything you need to know in order to get started.

Along with the Table of Contents at the front of the book, the index at the back of the book can help you locate the game you want to play without too many diversions. Having said that, one of the more interesting ways to experience this book may be to open it at random and discover a game that you've never heard of before.

1

Discovering Card Games

IN THIS PART . . .

After I explain some of the basics of cards (along with some tidbits about the history of cards and the etiquette of card games), I introduce a diverse range of games for you to deal out. If you don't have anyone to play cards with, don't worry. I provide an entire chapter of Solitaire card games. And if you're a beginning card player, teaching children to play cards, or just a kid at heart, check out the chapter on popular children's games, including War and Go Fish. Enjoy!

IN THIS CHAPTER

» Speaking card game lingo

» Following the rules and etiquette of card games

» Hand-picking the best card game

Chapter 1

Card Game Basics

I'm sure that if you've ever played cards at all, you don't need me to explain what fun 52 pieces of pasteboard can be. But just in case, here goes . . .

Because you don't know what the other players have in their hands in almost every card game, playing cards combines the opportunity for strategy, bluffing, memory, and cunning. At the same time, you don't have to play cards all that well in order to enjoy yourself. Cards allow you to make friends with the people you play with and against. A deck of cards opens up a pastime where the ability to communicate is often of paramount importance, and you get to meet new faces and talk to them without having to make the effort to do so.

If you want to take the plunge and start playing cards, you encounter a bewildering range of options to choose from. Cards have been played in Europe for the last 800 years (see the sidebar "Card Games Through the Ages" for more details), and as a result, you have plenty of new games to test out and new rules to add to existing games.

One of the features of *Card Games For Dummies, 3rd Edition,* is the diversity of card games covered in it. I can't hope to list *all* the rules of every card game within the chapters, so this chapter discusses the general rules that apply to *most* card games. Get these basics under your belt so you can jump in to any of the games I describe in detail later in the book.

Talking the Talk

Card gamers have a language all their own. This section covers the most common and useful lingo you encounter as you get to know various card games.

REMEMBER

When card games come together, the players arrange themselves in a circle around the card-playing surface, which is normally a table. I describe it as such for the rest of this section.

Getting all decked out

You play card games with a *deck* of cards intended for that game, also referred to as a *pack* in the United Kingdom. The cards should all be exactly the same size and shape and should have identical backs. The front of the cards should be immediately identifiable and distinguishable.

A deck of cards has subdivisions of four separate subgroups. Each one of these subgroups has 13 cards, although the standard deck in France and Germany may have only 8 cards in each subgroup. The four subgroups each have a separate identifiable marking, and in American and English decks, you see two sets of black markings (spades and clubs) and two sets of red markings (hearts and diamonds). Each of these sets is referred to as a *suit*.

CARD GAMES THROUGH THE AGES

Some form of playing cards existed in China, at least 80 years and maybe as much as 250 years before they surfaced in Europe. The earliest known Chinese cards had four suits, described in mid-15th-century sources, and featured 38 cards: 9 each in three suits and 11 in the fourth. Similar cards are used in parts of China and Southeast Asia to this day, though the deck composition and designs are not identical.

Although some scholars claim the Saracens or the Persians invented card games (the Persians certainly seem to have invented Poker), the Mamelukes of Egypt appear to be credible ancestors of modern card games. A Mameluke deck from around 1400 A.D. consists of 52 cards with suits of swords, polo sticks, cups, and coins.

National standard designs appeared in the late 15th century. Swiss decks (with shields, flowers, bells, and acorns) and German decks (with hearts, leaves, bells, and acorns) appeared by 1475. The French deck (with spades, hearts, diamonds, and clubs) first appeared by 1480.

In Great Britain, The Worshipful Company of Playing-Card Makers was set up in 1628 to produce cards, and a tax was introduced on every deck. Laws were also enacted to ban the import of cards; from then on, you could only play with cards of domestic origin. The year 1862 was very significant for the rise in popularity of playing cards. Along with a fall in the duty charge of playing cards, printer Thomas de la Rue patented the process for mass-producing cards. From then on, well-designed playing cards were in plentiful supply.

Ranking card order

Each suit in U.S. and U.K. decks has 13 cards, and the rankings of the 13 vary from game to game. The most traditional order in card games today is ace, king, queen, jack, and then 10 down to 2.

VARIATION

As you find throughout this book, the ranking order changes for different games. You see numerous games where 10s or perhaps jacks get promoted in the ranking order (such as in Pinochle and Euchre, respectively), and many games have jacks gambol joyfully from one suit to another, becoming extra trumps (as in Euchre).

Also, Gin Rummy and several other games such as Cribbage treat the ace exclusively as the low card, below the two.

Preparing to Play

Before you can start any card game, you need to ration out the cards. Furthermore, in almost every game, you don't want any other players to know what cards you have been dealt. That is where the shuffle and deal come into play.

Shuffling off

Before the dealer distributes the cards to the players, a player must randomize, or *shuffle*, them in such a way that no one knows what anyone else receives. (Shuffling is particularly relevant when the cards have all been played out on the previous hand.)

The shuffler, not necessarily the player who must distribute the cards, mixes up the cards by holding them face-down and interleaving them a sufficient number of times so that the order of all the cards becomes random and unpredictable. When one player completes the task, another player (frequently in European games, the player to the right of the dealer) rearranges the deck by splitting it into two halves and reassembles the two halves, putting the lower half on top of the other portion. This is called *cutting the deck.*

Getting a square deal

In most games, one player is responsible for distributing the cards to the players — this player is the *dealer.* For the first hand, you often select the dealer by having each player draw a card from the deck; the lowest card (or, perhaps, the highest) gets to deal. After the first hand is complete, the rules of most games dictate that the player to the dealer's left deals the next hand, with the deal rotating clockwise.

REMEMBER

Before the deal for the first hand, a process may take place to determine where the players sit. In games in which your position at the table is important, such as Poker or Hearts, you often deal out a card to each player and then seat the players clockwise in order from highest to lowest.

The player to the dealer's left, frequently the first person to play a card after the deal, is known as the *elder* or *eldest hand.* The *younger hand* is the player to the dealer's right. These players may also be known as the *left hand opponent* and *right hand opponent* (which you sometimes see abbreviated as *LHO* and *RHO*). The dealer may also refer to the player sitting opposite them — their partner in a partnership game — as the CHO, or *center hand opponent.*

VARIATION

You may have been brought up on the sober concept that the right way to distribute the cards to each player is to pass them out one at a time, face-down, in a clockwise manner. However, that style is by no means the only possible, or indeed acceptable, way to deal. Games from south and eastern Europe and Switzerland, as well as tarot games, feature counterclockwise dealing and playing. And in Euchre the cards are dealt clockwise, but in batches of two or three, rather than one at a time.

The due process of a deal involves the dealer taking the deck in one hand and passing a single card from the top of the deck to the player on their left, in such a way that nobody can see the face of the card. The dealer then does the same for the next player, and so on around the table. The process continues until everyone receives their due number of cards.

WARNING

Players generally consider it bad form for any player to look at their cards until the deal has been completed.

In several games, only some of the cards are dealt out. In such games, you put a parcel of undealt cards in a pile in the middle of the table. This pile is known as the *stock* or *talon*. Frequently, the dealer turns the top card of the stock face-up for one reason or another, and this card is known as the *up-card*.

The cards dealt out to a player, taken as a whole, constitute a *hand*. It's normal practice to pick up your hand at the conclusion of the deal and to arrange the hand in an overlapping fan shape; if you like, you can sort the cards out by suit and rank, as appropriate for the game you're playing, to make your decision making easier. Make sure, however, to take care that no one but you can see your cards. Similarly, you shouldn't make any undue efforts to look at any one else's hand.

Most card games need not only a dealer (a job that changes from hand to hand) but also a scorekeeper — not normally a sought-after task. The least innumerate mathematician may be landed with the task — or the soberest player. The good news is that scientific studies have shown that the scorer generally wins the game. I wonder why!

Exposing yourself (or someone else)

In general, any irregularity in a deal that leads to a card or cards being turned over invalidates the whole deal, and the normal procedure is for the dealer to collect all the cards and start over.

However, some minor exceptions to this principle exist, and these tend to result in the dealer getting the worst penalty if they exposes cards from their own hand. But most casual games call for leniency.

Bidding fair

Some, but by no means all, the games in this book include another preparatory phase of game play during which players have to estimate how much their hands will be worth in the latter stages of the game. The game may call for a silent esti-mate (as in Ninety-Nine), an announcement (Oh Hell!), or an *auction* (Euchre or Bridge), in which whoever makes the highest bid wins a right to form a prediction. The process may offer the option to make a single call (Euchre) or a competitive auction (Bridge). Either way, these phases of the game are known as the *bidding*.

Frequently, a contested auction results in one player or partnership winning the chance to determine the boss, or trump, suit. This right is also known as *determin-ing the contract*. One player or side essentially promises to achieve something in the play of the cards in exchange for being allowed to determine which suit has special powers.

The bidding at games such as Euchre, Pinochle, or Bridge should be distinguished from the *betting* at Poker or Blackjack. At Pinochle or Bridge, players must predict how many points or tricks, respectively, they can take, with penalties if they over-estimate their hands' values. In games such as Spades or Oh Hell!, underestimation is similarly penalized. However, at Blackjack, you have to pay to play, without seeing your hand. At Poker, by contrast, although you must put up a stake in order to stay in the game and receive cards, the real expenditure comes after the initial bet, when you have to pay to stay in the game.

Making a declaration

Are you the impatient type? Want to score points even before the game play begins? Well, some games have a *declaration* phase, in which you score points for combinations of cards that are worth certain amounts based on a predetermined table of values unique to the game. You can accumulate these points in a game like Pinochle, and sometimes an exchange of cards is permitted to improve your score on the hand.

Having a number of consecutive cards in the same suit is called a *run* or *sequence*. Having three or four cards of the same rank (obviously in different suits, unless you have more than one deck of cards in play, in which case there are no such restrictions) is called a *set or book*.

Playing the Game

The most important phase of most card games resides in the *play* of the hand. In many of the games in this book, the objective is to try to accumulate points — or, in a game like Hearts, to try to *avoid* accumulating points.

The standard way of accumulating or avoiding points derives from the concept that a game is made up of several distinct phases; in each phase (except for certain games like Poker and Blackjack), players detach cards from their hands and put them face-up on the table, in order. Whoever plays the highest card in the suit led usually gets to collect all those cards and stack them face-down in front of them. This unit of playing cards is called a *trick* — your success in many competitive card games hinges on how many tricks you win during the course of play. (Again, however, some games in the book, such as Setback, feature trying to win specific valuable cards rather than simply trying to obtain the majority of the tricks.)

So the high card takes the trick. But how do you get to that point? Here are the steps that get you there:

1. **The first player to act makes the *opening lead,* or the lead to the very first trick.**

   Depending on the rules of the game, the elder hand (the player to the dealer's left), the dealer, or the player who selected the contract during the bidding process makes the opening lead.

2. **The player who wins the trick generally leads to the next trick and so on throughout the hand, until everyone plays all their cards.**

   The order of play nearly always follows a clockwise or occasionally counter-clockwise pattern in relation to the deal or the winner of the trick.

The player who wins the trick makes the next lead and scores or avoids points. But it doesn't always take the high card to win the trick, and sometimes you make mistakes during the course of a hand. The following sections detail tricks and penalizing treats.

Winning with high cards or trump

The concept that the highest card played on a trick wins the trick is a simple one, but it doesn't do justice to the rules of most games in this book. Each has more complex rules than that. For example, in most games, it isn't simply the high card that wins the trick; it's the highest card in the *suit led.*

My point is that most games (but not all!) state that when a player leads a suit — say, spades — all subsequent players must play spades if they still have one in their hands. This concept is called *following suit.*

So what happens if you can't follow suit? Well, here is where the concept of the trump suit comes in. Many of the trick-taking games have a trump suit, which has special powers. You may like to think of this as the "boss" suit, which outranks all the other suits. In games such as Whist, you select the boss suit at random. In other games, such as Euchre, the initial suit is random, but the players have a chance to select another suit if they want to. And in some games, such as Bridge, the choice is entirely up to the players playing individually or acting in a partnership.

REMEMBER

So, what do trumps do? Well, if you have no cards in the suit led, you can put a trump on the lead (or *trump it*). This action is also called *ruffing the trick.* Consequently, the importance of the trump suit lies in the fact that the smallest trump can beat even the ace of any other suit. So, if a trick doesn't have any trumps in it, the highest card of the suit led takes the trick; however, if one or more trumps hit the table on a trick, the highest trump takes the trick.

Failing to follow suit

Most games have rules that require you to play a card in the suit led if you can; and indeed, that is your ethical requirement. However, if you can follow suit but don't, you incur no penalty — you only face a penalty for being *caught* failing to follow suit! The penalty varies from game to game but is generally a pretty severe one.

In failing to follow suit, you have three terms to bear in mind:

» **Revoke:** The sinful failure to follow suit when you're able is known as *revoking* or *reneging*. (The latter term seems to be exclusive to the United States and is now synonymous with the revoke.)

» **Trump:** Putting a card from the trump suit down when a suit is led, in which you have no cards. If you play a trump, you stand to win the trick — so long as no one else subsequently plays a higher trump.

» **Discard:** The laying down of an off-suit card when you're unable to follow suit is called a *discard* or *renounce*, although the former term is more common these days. Discarding implies that you're letting go a card in a plain, non-trump suit rather than trumping.

Say your hand consists solely of clubs, diamonds, and hearts, and you're playing out a hand where hearts are trump:

» If another player leads a club and you play a diamond or a heart on the lead, you revoke.

» If a player leads a spade and you play a heart, you trump the spade.

» If you play a diamond on the lead of a spade, you discard.

Playing out of turn

For one reason or another, players occasionally lose track of who won the previous trick. If a player neglects to remember that they are supposed to lead, a potentially long and embarrassing pause ensues until someone plucks up enough courage to ask that player whether they're thinking about what to do next or if they're spacing out.

More frequently, however, somebody *leads out of turn*, under the false impression that the action is on them. If this happens, the general rule is that the next player can accept that lead by following to the trick, if they want to do so. Alternatively, they may be so hypnotized by the sight of the card that they may genuinely think it's their turn to play, so they follow suit innocently.

Either way, the general rule is that the next player's following legitimizes the original mistake. However, some games state that up until the faulty trick is completed, if anyone spots the error, you still have time to pick the whole trick up and correct the error.

Exposing yourself to public ridicule

The rules about exposed cards (accidentally dropping a card on the table as opposed to playing it) tend to vary, depending on whether you're playing a partnership game or playing on your own:

» In an individual game, the rules tend to be fairly lax; you can normally pick up your exposed cards, and the game continues. (Of course, your opponent benefits from seeing part of your hand, which is considered punishment enough for the error.)

» In a partnership game, the consequences of exposing a card are much more severe because you simultaneously give unauthorized information to both your partner and your opponents. Often, the rules of a game require you to play the exposed cards at the first opportunity, or your partner may be forbidden from playing the suit you let slip. These are the Draconian rules in place with games such as Bridge, for example.

MISS MANNER'S GUIDE TO CARD-GAME ETIQUETTE

Some elements of card-game etiquette relate to basic good manners and polite behavior, and some deal with areas that come perilously close to cheating. On the etiquette front, for example, you shouldn't pick up your cards until the deal is finished — if for no other reason than you may cause the dealer to expose a card if your fingers get in the way.

After you pick up your hand, avoid indicating in any way whether you're pleased or unhappy with its contents. This is particularly important in a partnership game where you can't divulge such potentially useful information.

The idea that you should play card games in silence may give the impression that you can't enjoy yourself — that you should focus on winning to the exclusion of having fun. That isn't the case, but you should avoid conversation if it gives away information that

(continued)

(continued)

you're not entitled to pass on or if the sole purpose of your remarks is to upset or irritate your partner or opponents. (The rules in Poker are a little different. Conversation during a poker game is one way for players to influence their opponents.)

The tempo of the way you play your cards can also be very revealing. You can make it clear by the way you play your card that you have doubt or no doubt at all as to what to do. You can't eliminate doubt altogether, but you can try to make your mind up before playing a card so that you avoid conveying information by your tempo to your partner and opponents. Again, though, in Poker, anything goes!

Selecting the Best Card Game

All the card games in this book are excellent, of course — I provide only the cream of the crop. However, depending on the number of players and your collective experience and expectations, some games are more suitable than others. Depending on your needs, the following lists recommend certain games for various situations.

As a general point, though, the best card game to play is probably the one that some of your players already know. You pick up strategies of the game, as well as its customs and traditions, much faster by playing with experienced players rather than in a group consisting entirely of beginners.

If you have a specific number of players:

>> **Solitaire games:** Accordion and Poker Patience if you're short on space; La Belle Lucie if you can spread yourself out. (See Chapter 2 for Solitaire games.)

>> **Two-player games:** Gin Rummy (Chapter 4), Spite and Malice (Chapter 2), and Cribbage (Chapter 16).

>> **Three-player games:** Pinochle (Chapter 14) and Ninety-Nine (Chapter 9).

>> **Four-player games:** Bridge (Chapter 12), Euchre (Chapter 10), Hearts (Chapter 13), and Spades (Chapter 11).

>> **Five- to eight-player games:** Hearts (Chapter 13) and Oh Hell! (Chapter 9).

>> **Eight or greater player games:** Eights (Chapter 6) and President (Chapter 17).

If you're picking the game based on time constraints:

>> You can play Setback (Chapter 15), Whist (Chapter 8), and Euchre (Chapter 10) to specified target scores, which you can adapt to reflect the time you have available.

>> You can play Ninety-Nine (Chapter 9) for a specified number of hands.

>> If you have a few years at your disposal, I recommend an ongoing battle of Spite and Malice (Chapter 2).

If you're selecting your game based on the type of play:

>> Serious, competitive types tend to enjoy Whist (Chapter 8) and Bridge (Chapter 12).

>> If you're playing in a cramped space (on a plane, train, or bus), Hearts (Chapter 13) and Eights (Chapter 6) work well.

>> In a bar, Cribbage (Chapter 16) goes well with alcohol.

>> For large groups in a social setting, Poker (Part 6) and Blackjack (Chapter 18) are ideal.

>> For games that combine bidding and play, Pinochle (Chapter 14) and Spades (Chapter 11) are good choices.

>> The best partnership games are Bridge (Chapter 12), Whist (Chapter 8), and Euchre (Chapter 10).

>> If your deck of cards is defective, you want to play a game that doesn't deal out all the cards. You can play Oh Hell! (Chapter 9), Spite and Malice (Chapter 2), and Setback (Chapter 15) with a deck that has missing cards.

If you're selecting the game based on the experience level of the players:

>> **For beginners:** Oh Hell! and Ninety-Nine (both in Chapter 9) have simple, easy-to-understand principles.

>> **For children:** Go Fish and Cheat (both in Chapter 3) are simple, but they require younger players to think in order to win. Whist (Chapter 8) is the best introduction to trick-taking games for children.

>> **For groups with mixed experience levels:** Whist (Chapter 8) and Fan Tan (Chapter 7) rely heavily on luck, which gives everyone a sporting chance. Rummy (Chapter 4) also comes easily to inexperienced card players.

>> **For experienced card players:** Pinochle (Chapter 14) and Cribbage (Chapter 16) offer new thrills and challenges.

Chapter **2**

Solitaire

You see many different versions of Solitaire in this chapter. The different games don't have all that much in common, except that you can play them with a single deck of cards (and they happen to be my favorite Solitaires). Some Solitaires need more than one deck, but not the ones included in this chapter (apart from the two-player, Solitaire-like game Spite and Malice at the end of the chapter). These games range from *automatic* Solitaires, where you can make every move immediately without thought or forethought, to Solitaires where you can plan your game strategy for at least 10 minutes if you want to. These games aren't easy, so if you win any of them, you'll feel a sense of achievement. In fact, I have never managed to win some of the Solitaires that I discuss in this chapter.

BEFORE HAND

To play Solitaire, you need the following:

» **One player**

» **One standard 52-card deck of cards** (you usually don't need jokers in games of Solitaire)

» **Space to spread out the cards**

Acquainting Yourself with Solitaire Terms

Before you start enjoying the various games of Solitaire, you need to know a little technical vocabulary:

» When you initially deal the cards, the pattern is known as a *layout* or *tableau*. The layout can consist of *rows* (horizontal lines of cards), *columns* (vertical lines), or *piles* of cards (a compact heap, frequently of face-down cards, sometimes with the top card face-up). Sometimes the pile of cards is all face-up, but overlapping. Accordingly, you can see all the cards in the pile, even if you can only access the top, uncovered card. You can move tableaus under the correct circumstances, which are dictated by the rules of the particular Solitaire you're playing.

» *Building* involves placing one card on top of another in a legal move. The definition of a *legal move* varies according to the individual rules of the Solitaire.

» In games where the objective is to build up cards on some of the original cards, the base cards are known as *foundations*. As a general rule, after you place cards on a foundation pile, you can't move them. You may build on a tableau in some cases.

The tableau and the foundation may sound like very similar items, but they differ in a few important ways. The object of a Solitaire is to build up the foundation; a tableau is just an intermediary home for the cards as they make their way to the final destination: the foundation. You use tableaus to get the cards in the right order to build on the foundation.

» When you move a complete row or column, you create a *space* or *gap* into which you can often move whatever card(s) you like.

» Frequently, you don't use all the cards in the initial layout; the remaining cards are called the *stock*. You go through the stock to advance the Solitaire.

» When working through the stock, you frequently have cards that you can't legally put into the layout. In such cases, the unused cards go into the *waste pile*.

» *Redeals* take place in the middle of a Solitaire when you've exhausted all legal moves. The rules of the Solitaire may allow you to redeal by shuffling and redistributing the unused cards in an attempt to advance the game.

» Many Solitaires permit one cheat — you can move an obstructing card or otherwise advance the game. This process is also known as a *merci*.

After you build your own foundation of Solitaire knowledge, you can begin to explore the many variations of the game. The following sections detail some of the specific types of Solitaires.

Putting the Squeeze on Accordion

The game Accordion is also known as Methuselah, Tower of Babel, or Idle Year (presumably because of the amount of time you need to keep playing the game to win it).

Accordion is a charmingly straightforward game that can easily seduce you into assuming that it must be easy to solve. Be warned — I've never completed a game of Accordion, and I don't know anyone who has! This challenge, I can only assume, makes success at the game doubly pleasurable.

Accordion also takes up very little space — a major benefit because you tend to play Solitaire in a cramped space, such as a bus station or an airport lounge.

The objective of Accordion is to finish up with a single pile of 52 cards. Relative success is reducing the number of piles to four or fewer. Your chances of complete victory may be less than 1 in 1,000, based on my experiences, but don't let that deter you from giving this game a try! The fact that it is a very fast game to play means that you can abandon unpromising hands and move on to another, without wasting much time.

Looking at the layout

The layout for Accordion is simple. Follow these steps to begin your long journey:

1. **Shuffle the deck well, and then turn over the top card in your deck and put it to your left to start your layout.**

2. **Turn over the next card.**

   If the card is either the same suit (both clubs, for example) or the same rank (both jacks) as the first card, put the second card on top of the first. If you don't have a match, use the card to start a new pile.

3. **Turn over the third card and compare it to the second card.**

   Again, if the suits or ranks of the cards match, put the third card on top of the second card; if not, start a third pile with the third card. You can't match the third card with the first card. However, when matching cards (of suit or rank) are three cards apart, you can combine them as if the cards were adjacent. In other words, you can build the fourth card on the first one.

4. **Continue by going through every card in the deck in this way.**

   I told you it was easy! The game ends after you turn over the last card. To win, you must assemble all the cards into one pile.

TIP

Shuffling the deck well is important because you work your way through the deck one card at a time, so you don't want to make the game too easy by having all the diamonds coming together, for example. That would spoil your sense of achievement, wouldn't it?

Your initial cards may look like one of the examples in Figure 2-1 after you lay out three cards.

FIGURE 2-1:
At the start of
Accordion, your
cards may fall in
this manner.

In the first example, you must create three different piles because the cards are unrelated in rank or suit. In the middle example, you can put the ♦4 on top of the ♦Q (because they share the same suit), leaving you with only two piles. In the bottom example, you can put the ♦7 on top of the ♦Q, which allows you to combine the two 7s, resulting in a single pile.

To see how you can combine cards placed three piles away from each other, look at Figure 2-2.

FIGURE 2-2:
You can match
cards that are
three places away
from each other
to further your
game progress.

After you turn up the ♣Q, you can place it on the ♦Q (because they're three apart and match in rank) and then put the ♣K on the ♣Q (same suit). The ♥J then moves to the first row.

TIP

Laying the cards out in lines of three helps ensure that you properly identify the cards that are three piles apart.

Choosing between moves

When moving the cards, you frequently have to be careful to make the plays in the correct order to set up more plays. You may have a choice of moves, but you may not be sure which move to execute first. Look at a possible scenario in Figure 2-3.

After you turn up the ♥4, you can place it on the ♥9, which opens up a series of moves that you can play. The best option is to move the ♥4 onto the ♠4 and then move the rest of the cards into their new spaces.

Because the ♠K is three cards away from the ♣K, you can combine the two cards and then move the ♥4 onto the ♥J. Now the ♦9 is three cards away from the ♦Q, so you can combine those two cards.

WARNING

If you move the ♥4 before you move the ♠K, you miss out on two possible moves.

REMEMBER

Making an available play isn't always mandatory. When you can choose between possible moves, play a couple more cards to help you decide which move is superior.

Figure 2-4 shows you how waiting can help you make up your mind when you have a choice.

FIGURE 2-3: Look ahead to see which move to make first.

At this point, you may not know whether to put the ♠A on the ♣A or on the ♠K because your piles don't indicate whether you should keep aces or kings on top of your piles.

FIGURE 2-4:
Playing the
waiting game can
help you make up
your mind.

TIP

If several piles have kings on the top, you may want to avoid hiding the ♠K. Instead of jumping the gun, you turn over another card to see what happens, which turns out to be the ♠J.

Now you can see daylight: Put the ♠J on the ♠A and then on the ♠K, and then you put the ♠J on the ♥J. Now you can combine the 9s. Next, put the ♣4 on the ♠J, allowing the ♣A to go on the ♣K and the ♦9 to go on the ♦Q. Put the ♣4 on the ♠7 to move down to three piles. Wasn't that fun? Getting a series of moves to come together like that makes up for the hundreds of unexciting plays you go through.

Play continues until you end up with one pile of cards — good luck!

Piling It On in Calculation

Different people have different criteria for what makes a good game of Solitaire. The version called Calculation should satisfy most tests, because you can solve it in a fair amount of time (so long as you work at it), it takes up little space, and you can devote your full attention to it or play without thinking — depending on your mood. However, unless you plan your plays carefully, the game will likely stymie you fairly early on.

In this game, only the card rankings matter — the suits of the cards are irrelevant. The object of the game is to build up four piles of cards on the foundation, from the ace on up to the king.

You begin by taking out an ace, 2, 3, and 4 from the deck and putting the four cards in a row from left to right, horizontally. These cards are the foundation on which you build — you hope — using the rest of the cards in the deck. Underneath those four foundations are precisely four waste piles, where you put cards that do not immediately fit on the foundation. Determining which pile to put those cards on is the challenging part of the game.

You build on each of the foundation piles one card at a time; however, you build up each pile in different sequences:

>> On the ace pile, you can only put the next ranking card — that is, the play sequence must go A, 2, 3, and so on.

>> On the 2 pile, you go up in pairs: 4, 6, 8, and so on.

>> On the 3 pile, you go up in intervals of three: 6, 9, Q, 2, 5, and so on.

>> And you shouldn't be surprised that on the 4 pile, you go up in fours: 8, Q, 3, 7, J, 2, and so on.

For each of the four piles, you have 13 moves available. After the last move, you reach the king, and your piles are complete.

You turn up cards from the stock one at a time. If the card you turn over has no legal place, you put it directly on top of one of the four waste piles that you create below the foundation. As soon as the card becomes a legal play on a foundation pile, you may take the card from the top of the waste pile (but not from the middle of the waste pile) and move it up.

TIP

When you have a legal move (you can put a card on one of the foundation piles), go ahead and make it. Don't wait to see what other cards you may turn up, because you may end up burying a card you could have played.

REMEMBER

You can't move cards from one waste pile to another. After a card is on one pile, you can move it only to the foundation. And just because a waste pile is empty doesn't entitle you to move cards from another waste pile into the gap.

You arrange the waste piles so that you can see all the lower cards in them to maximize your strategic planning.

Kings are exceptionally bad news in Calculation. They're always the last cards to go on each of the foundation piles, and when you put them on the waste pile, they can easily block everything beneath them. In a strange way, it's good to turn up kings at the beginning of the game — you can put them on the bottom of each of the waste piles or put them all together in one pile.

TIP

As a general rule, try to keep one waste pile reserved for the kings. However, if two or three kings appear early, it's a reasonable gamble to use all four piles and not keep one for the kings.

Figure 2-5 shows an example of the start of a game. Having selected your ace, 2, 3, and 4 from the deck, you start turning over the cards one at a time.

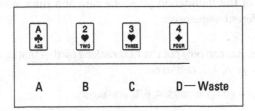

FIGURE 2-5:
A sample game of
Calculation.

TIP

Try to construct lines in the waste piles in reverse. For example, if your 4 pile is lagging because you're waiting for a queen, and you put a 7 on a jack on a waste pile, put a 3 on top of the 7 if it comes up. You hope that when the queen emerges, you can put the 3, 7, and jack on at one time and advance matters efficiently.

Reserving Your Time for Canfield

Canfield is one of the most commonly played Solitaires in the Western world. People often erroneously refer to this game as Klondike, which also appears in this chapter (see the following section, "Striking Gold with Klondike"). To further complicate matters, Canfield is also known as Demon Thirteen in the United Kingdom.

To set up Canfield, follow these simple steps:

1. **Place 13 cards in a pile, with only the top card face-up; this pile is called the *reserve* or the *heel*.**

2. **To the right of the reserve, spread out four cards, called a *tableau,* on which you can build by using the cards from the reserve or the *stock* (the remaining 34 cards in the deck).**

3. **Above the tableau, place a single face-up card, which acts as the base card of a foundation from which each suit will be built up.**

The object of Canfield is to get rid of all 13 cards in the reserve pile. You get rid of these cards by placing them in legal positions in the tableau.

You build on the tableau by placing a card that's one rank lower and of the opposite color of the uppermost card. For example, you can legally put the ♣2 on either the ♥3 or ♦3. After the ♣2 is on the top of the pile, you can place either the ♥A or ♦A on it. If you place the ♦A on the ♣2, you can place either the ♣K or the ♠K on the ♦A, and so on.

Take the remaining 34 cards, the stock, and work your way through them in threes, taking the top three cards at a time and flipping them over into a waste pile (make sure you preserve the order of the three cards). You have access to only the top card in the three, but if you use the top card — that is, you put it on the tableau or foundation — you gain access to the second card, and so on. After you go through the stock in threes, you turn up the last card out of the 34; this card is accessible. When the stock comes out in threes, you treat the last three cards as a regular group of three. If you have two cards left over at the end of the stock, you get to look at and use them both separately. .

After you work your way through the stock, pick it up and start again; continue until you either finish the game or get stuck and can't move any further.

As soon as a card equivalent in rank to the foundation base card emerges from either the reserve pile or the stock, pick the card up and put it in a separate pile in the foundation, above the tableau. You can build only the next higher card of the matching suit, and no other card, onto the foundation.

TIP

The cards (even a whole pile of cards) in the tableau can be moved onto other cards in the tableau, so long as you observe the opposite-color rule, and also onto gaps in the tableau. And you have the option of placing the top card in the reserve pile on the foundation or in the tableau.

Take a look at an example layout of the start of a game in Figure 2-6.

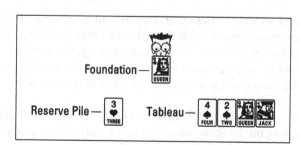

You're in luck! This layout is a very promising start. The ♣Q joins the ♦Q at the top of the foundation, in a separate pile. This move creates a gap in the tableau where you can place a card from the reserve pile.

The red 3 goes on the black 4, and the black 2 goes on the red 3. Another card from the reserve pile fills the gap in the tableau left by the black 2.

VARIATION

One variation that makes Canfield more difficult is to build up the foundation from the ace, meaning that you don't give yourself a random foundation card to start with. To compensate, some players use a reserve pile of only 11 cards.

Striking Gold with Klondike

Klondike, frequently misnamed Canfield (see the previous section), is by far the most frequently played Solitaire that I know. You need only a little time and a little space. In addition, you have a good chance of winning at Klondike — you may find yourself winning half the games you play.

Klondike requires little tactics or strategy. It's an ideal game for children, perhaps for that very reason, and I think that Klondike was the first Solitaire that I ever played. Klondike is also an ideal Solitaire for a spectator, who can lean over the player's shoulder and say things like "Put the red 7 on the black 8" until the player loses patience and punches the spectator in the shoulder.

The object of Klondike is to build up piles of the four suits from the ace (the lowest card) to the king on the foundation. You don't start with any cards in the foundation; you collect cards for it during the course of play.

To build the initial layout, or *tableau*, you deal seven piles, with one card in the first pile, two in the second pile, three in the third, and so on. Turn over the top card of each pile as you deal out the cards.

REMEMBER

When dealing out the piles, place seven cards face-down to form the seven piles; deal the next six cards to form the second layer of each row (except the row on the far left), and then the next five cards to form the third layer, and so on. If you lay out the cards in this way, you avoid any problems caused by imperfect shuffling.

You build on the top cards of each pile by putting the next-lower numbered cards of the opposite color on the top cards. Your building cards come from the stock.

To start the game, you play the cards in the stock, which should consist of 24 cards. Go through the stock three cards at a time, putting the cards into a waste pile, while preserving the order of the cards in that pile. You have access to only the top card of each set of three. If you use that top card, you gain access to the card below it, and so on. When you finish going through the stock, gather it up and go through it again.

You may go through the stock only three times. If you can't persuade the Solitaire to work out after the three turns, you lose the game. However, most people that I know ignore the three-times rule and continue with the Solitaire until it works out, which it does a fair percentage of the time.

VARIATION

As an alternative, you can go through the stock one card at a time and only one time. I haven't concluded whether you're more likely to get the Solitaire to work out with this rule or not, but instinctively, I feel that it must help. Some people go through the deck one card at a time on three separate occasions before calling the whole thing off.

You can move the turned-up cards around (leaving the face-down cards in place), and whenever you move all the face-up cards from one pile of the tableau, you turn over the new top card.

When you use all the cards in a pile, you create a space. You can move any king, or pile headed by a king — but only one headed by a king — into the space, and then you turn another face-down card over on the pile from which you moved the king pile.

Whenever you turn up an ace in the tableau (or in the stock), move that card to the foundation and start a new foundation pile. You may then take any top card from the tableau and move it onto the foundation, where appropriate. For example, after you put the ♦A in the foundation, you can take the ♦2 when it becomes available to start building up the diamonds.

Living La Belle Lucie

As far as I'm concerned, La Belle Lucie (which is also known as Midnight Oil, Clover Leaf, the Fan, or Alexander the Great) is the best Solitaire that I've played. Every move is critical. The game requires great planning and forethought and rewards the player with a healthy chance of success.

I've been known to take more than 10 minutes to make a move while I plan the intricacies of competing strategies. It's certainly not unusual for players to take a few minutes at a time to plan a move.

The objective of La Belle Lucie is to build up all four suits from a foundation of the ace through to the king.

Getting started

You start by dealing all the cards face-up in piles of threes, making sure that each card in every trio is visible (you fan each trio so that you can see a top, middle, and bottom card, hence its alias, Fan). The last four cards go in two piles of two. Your aim is to move cards around the tableau to free up cards that can build up the foundation.

Whenever you expose an ace on the top of a pile, you move it to start a foundation pile, and can start building the suit up from there. The next card to go on the ace is the 2 of that suit, and you keep going up to the king of the suit. If you don't expose an ace, you have to uncover one by moving the cards around.

You get three tries (or *cycles*) to move all the cards into suits. At the end of each cycle, you pick up all the cards off the foundations, shuffle them well, and distribute them in trios again.

Making your moves

You can move cards in the tableau onto the card of the same suit one higher in rank, but beware! You can move each card only once, and you can only move one card at a time, which is critical. For example, as soon as the ♦7 goes on the ♦8, you can't move the ♦8 again unless both cards go onto the foundation in the diamond suit. You can't move the ♦7 and ♦8 onto the ♦9 because of the one-card-at-a-time rule. You have thus "buried" the ♦8. You can't move this card until the next redeal, unless the ♦A through the ♦6 go into the foundation, whereupon the ♦7 and ♦8 can also go onto the foundation.

However, this rule doesn't matter if the ♦8 is at the bottom of a pile; no cards are trapped by the move. The rule does matter if the ♦8 covers something else. Note that kings never move; therefore, you want them at the bottom of piles.

TIP

Bear in mind that the purpose of the game is to build up all the suits in order, starting with the ace, so you try to get the aces out from their piles. If the aces are at the top of their piles already, so much the better. If not, you have to excavate them, but at the same time, you have to plan the sequence of moves that brings the cards to the top. It isn't a good idea to play five moves to get out the ♦A and then discover that the ♦2 got permanently buried in the process. Of course, sometimes burying a card may prove inevitable. The skill of the game is to bury as few cards as possible by making your moves in the right order, and to bury only cards that seem less relevant at the moment, such as jacks and queens. Kings automatically trap everything below them, so if you're worried about burying the ♦J by putting the ♦10 on it, and the ♦Q is below the ♥K, relax! You cost yourself nothing — you were never going to get to move the ♦J anyway.

Another example of a potentially bad holding is seeing something along the lines of the ♦Q ♦10. Even if you get to put the ♦10 on the jack, doing so freezes the jack. You can't move the ♦J again, because you can't move the ♦10 and the ♦J onto the ♦Q.

Sometimes you get mutually impossible moves, as shown in Figure 2-7. With the base shown, you can't move the ♦6 until you clear the ♥2, and you can't move the ♥2 until you free the ♦6 to get at the ♥3. Neither card moves until the ♥A is free, when the ♥2 can go to the foundation.

FIGURE 2-7:
Only one series
of moves can
get you out of
this mess.

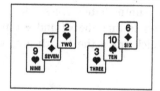

Certain moves are risk-free at the start of the game:

>> You can always move any queen onto the king of the same suit (because kings are stuck anyway).

>> After you move the top two cards of a pile of three and expose the card at the bottom of a pile, you can put the relevant card on top of it without worrying about the consequences. (When a card is at the bottom of a pile, it stands to reason that you can't trap anything underneath it if you should render it unable to move.)

>> Whenever a card is stuck (for example, if you put the ♦7 on the ♦8, you make both cards immobile), you can build more cards, such as the ♦6 and ♦5, on top of it. In fact, doing so can only help your chances of getting more cards out.

The initial layout for a sample hand appears in Figure 2-8 (the top card in each trio appears on the right).

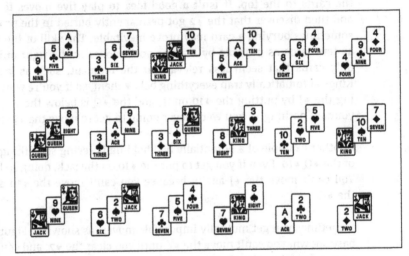

FIGURE 2-8:
Starting a game
of La Belle Lucie.

The figure layout has some encouraging features: All the kings are reasonably placed (they either appear at the bottoms of their piles or at least don't trap too many cards), and three of the aces are immediately accessible — a very fortunate combination of events. The bad news is that the ♥J and ♥9 are on top of one another, ensuring that the ♥10 (which traps the fourth ace) won't move this cycle.

Start by making the automatic moves:

1. Take off the ♠A and start a foundation pile for spades.

2. Put the ♦9 on the ♦10 (because the ♥10 can't move, and the ♦J can't come free, so you may as well build on the ♦10).

3. Take off the ♣A, the ♣2, and the ♦A.

4. The next card to go for is the ♠2; you can get it easily by putting the ♠J on the ♠Q.

But before you do that, can you put the ♠Q on the ♠K? To make that move, you need to put the ♥3 on the ♥4, and to do that, you need to move the ♦4 onto the ♦5. That last move is impossible, because the ♦5 is trapped below the ♥A, so put the ♠J on the ♠Q and take up the ♠2, ♠3, and ♠4.

Figure 2-9 shows an interesting combination of piles.

FIGURE 2-9:
Your game begins
to take shape
after you make
the automatic
moves.

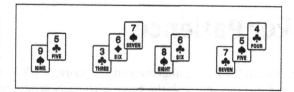

You want to clear the ♣4 away to get the ♠5 out, and you want to clear the ♠7 away to get the ♠3 out. Should you put the ♣4 on the ♠5, or should you put the ♠5 on the ♣6 and then put the ♣4 on the ♠5? The answer is that you need to keep the ♠8 (below the ♣6) free. Here's how to progress:

1. **Put the ♣4 on the ♠5 and free the ♠5 for the foundation.**

2. **Now put the ♣6 on the ♠7, the ♠7 on the ♠8, and the ♦6 on the ♦7.** (Because the ♦8 is under a king, it's stuck for the duration, so you can't move the ♦7.)

3. **The ♦3 is now free, which allows you to move it through the ♣8 onto the foundation.**

The preceding example shows a relatively simple problem, but the degree of interaction can get considerably more convoluted. This element of trading off one move against another is what makes La Belle Lucie such good fun.

The ♣9 is stuck (you can't move the ♦4), the ♠6 is stuck, and the ♥A is stuck, which leaves only diamonds. The ♦2 comes out easily enough by putting the ♣J on the queen. However, the ♦3 is under the ♠Q and the ♠J, so you take the ♦2 out, which ends the first cycle.

Starting the next cycle and ending the game

You keep your foundations, but now you pick up the cards left in the tableau, shuffle them well (they were in sequence, so an imperfect shuffle can restrict your mobility), and deal them out in threes again. If you have two cards left over, make one pair; if one card is left over after you put the cards out in threes, as at the start, make two pairs out of the last four cards.

You have three cycles to get out, and if you fail at the last turn, you're allowed one cheat, or *merci*, by moving a single card in the tableau; whether you want to pull one card up or push one card down is up to you.

Practicing Poker Patience

Poker Patience is, in theory, an undemanding Solitaire. It takes only a minute or two to play, and you can approach the game frivolously or seriously. I do both in this section.

To start, you need to know the ranks of Poker hands (in other words, what beats what). In ascending order, the ranks are as follows:

>> **One pair:** Two of a kind

>> **Two pair:** Such as two 5s and two 10s

>> **Three of a kind:** Also known as trips

>> **Straight:** Five cards in consecutive order; for example, ace through 5 or 7 to jack

>> **Flush:** Five cards of the same suit

>> **Full house:** Combination of three of a kind and a pair

>> **Four of a kind:** Also known as quads

>> **Straight flush:** A straight with all the cards in the same suit

REMEMBER

Aces can be either high or low — your choice.

The objective of the game is to lay out 25 cards to form a square, five cards by five cards. In the process, you want to make ten poker hands (five across and five down) and score as many points as possible.

Scoring 200 points (using my scoring system) counts as a win. Various scoring systems are shown in Table 2-1.

The U.S. scoring system has a major flaw (which has been corrected in the U.K. scoring method), based on the fact that although flushes are rarer in Poker, they're considerably easier to play for in Poker Patience than straights. To fix this problem, you can reverse the scoring table, as in the version that I recommend.

TABLE 2-1

Scoring Systems for Poker Patience

Poker Hand	U.S. Scoring	U.K. Scoring	Barry's Scoring
A pair	2	1	2
Two pair	5	3	5
Three of a kind	10	6	10
Straight	15	12	25
Flush	20	5	15
Full house	50	10	50
Four of a kind	70	16	70
Straight flush	100	30	100

To start, turn over one card face-up and then go on to the next, building your grid in any direction you like — up and down or right and left.

REMEMBER Although you can put any card anywhere you like in the grid, and you can expand the cards out in any direction you like, each card must touch another card. Whether you put it adjacent to another card or link it diagonally by touching the corner of another card is up to you.

TIP After many years of playing Poker Patience, I've decided that the best way to play (particularly when using my scoring table) is for straights to be set out in one direction (vertically or horizontally) and full houses or four of a kinds in the other direction. If you take my advice and decide for straights to go in the horizontal rows, you have excellent reasons to put the cards in columns either with themselves or with numbers five less than or five more than themselves. By making this separation, you help the formation of straights.

When playing Poker Patience, sooner or later you run into a useless or unplayable card. When this happens, don't panic; all you have to do is start a junk row or junk column. Inevitably, at least one row or column won't score as much as you want it to.

Look at the layout in Figure 2-10 to see the game theory at work. The matrix is updated after every two cards, although each card is turned over individually. After ten cards, the basic structure is going well. The nucleus of the straights is fine on the horizontal lines, and all the pairs are matched up.

In Figure 2-11, you can put the ♠9 on the bottom row, but completing the straight and collecting points always produces a warm, fuzzy feeling.

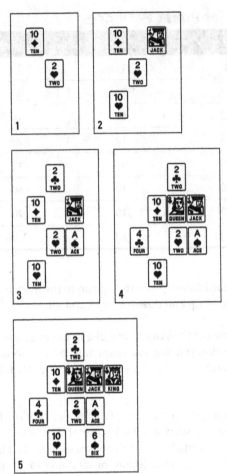

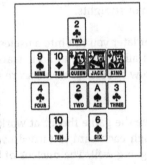

FIGURE 2-10:
A hand of
Poker Patience
after ten cards.

FIGURE 2-11:
Don't be
tempted by the
bottom row. Go
for the points!

Play continues in Figure 2-12. The ♥8 could've gone under the ♣3, but it seems premature to abandon the right-hand column. The ♠Q scores the full house, so abandon the straight in the fourth row.

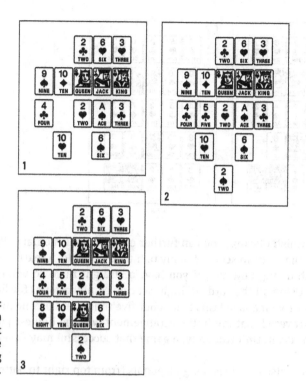

FIGURE 2-12:
Dumping a
straight
to go for the
higher-scoring
full house.

In Figure 2-13, the bottom row has become a junk pile. One row or column normally does.

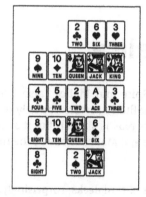

FIGURE 2-13:
Creating a junk
pile is a normal
thing for Poker
Patience.

In Figure 2-14, a lucky last card allows you to scramble to respectability; two straights, two full houses, and a three of a kind are 160, and having three pairs takes you to 166.

FIGURE 2-14:
Sometimes you
have to get lucky
to make
something out of
this big mess.

After you finish playing, you can further exercise your mental agility by trying to rearrange the cards to score as many points as possible. A rearrangement is really only worth doing, however, if you have a straight flush so you can rack up big numbers. Using all the cards in high-scoring combinations (flushes or higher) is a real coup. I've managed this feat about five times, and on one memorable occasion, I discovered that my initial arrangement was the highest possible with the cards I was dealt. Unfortunately, a game that successful may never happen again.

VARIATION

Some people also count the long diagonals (from top right to bottom left and vice versa) in the scoring. Planning the scores on the diagonals too carefully is pretty difficult, but it can be done — or you can just regard any score on them as a bonus. You can also play Poker Patience as a competitive game for two players or more. One player calls out the cards they draw at random, and then both players try to arrange their own grids to maximize the scores. The highest score wins.

Befriending Spite and Malice

You may legitimately grumble that Spite and Malice (also known as Cat and Mouse) is wholly out of place on the Solitaire roster. Not only does it technically not count as a Solitaire, even though its play is similar, but it also doesn't feature a single deck of cards. No matter: Spite and Malice is one of the finest competitive card games I know.

You can play the game with any number of card decks; surprisingly, it really doesn't matter whether the decks are complete or not. The alternative is to play with just two decks, but that leads to unnecessary reshuffling. You generally play the game with two players, although in theory there's no player limitation. It works for three or four players equally well or as a partnership game with four.

The object of Spite and Malice is very similar to Canfield (see the section "Reserving Your Time for Canfield," earlier in this chapter): You have a reserve pile that you want to get rid of before your opponent can.

Getting started

The preliminaries are very straightforward. Each player shuffles the decks very thoroughly, and you cut for deal, with the lowest card dealing. The dealer gives their opponent and themselves 26 (or 20 if you want a shorter game) cards face-down. These cards are your reserve, or *pay-off pile*, which both players try to dispose of; you always turn the top card face-up, and it remains available for play during the game. The dealer takes the remainder of the cards, the stock, and deals five cards to each player, which form the player's hand. The remaining stock cards sit in the middle of the table for the players to replenish their hands in due course. You can dispose of the reserve cards by putting them onto four communal foundation piles, built up from ace to queen, at the right moment. Each player can put cards onto the foundation piles, or onto waste piles, to which they each alone have access.

Putting the moves on

The nondealer is first to play. If you find yourself in this position, you have a series of options:

>> You can start off building on the communal foundation piles (or center stacks), which work their way up, always starting from the ace and going all the way through to the queen. Suits are irrelevant for this game, and kings are wild cards that you can use for anything you like (some people don't allow a wild card to represent an ace).

>> You can build onto the foundation with the five cards in your hand or from the waste pile, but you should prefer to use your reserve — remember, the object of the game is to get rid of your reserve. Suits are irrelevant for building on the foundation. A maximum of four open foundation piles are allowed at any one time. When a pile is complete from ace to queen, you set it aside and create a new space. You can put out cards from these three locations in any order at any time during your turn.

Some people play kings as normal cards and use two jokers per deck. In this version of the game, you keep the two decks of cards separate. The dealer uses one deck (without jokers) in full to give to each player for the reserve, and the other deck (with four jokers) provides everything else. This variation may be slightly unsatisfactory for you if you don't want to deal with constant reshuffling.

>> Each player can throw one card from the personal hand onto one of four personal waste piles. Each player sets up the waste piles, to which only the individual has access. The maximum number of cards you can discard is one per go, and you can only put a card on the waste pile that's equal to or one lower than the previous card. The discard is always the last element of any go. At the end of your turn, you replenish your hand back up to five cards from the stock.

REMEMBER

You can't play from your reserve onto your waste pile.

If you manage to get rid of all your five cards mid-turn, you get to fill up your hand to five cards again from the stock and continue your go.

VARIATION

You can set the number of center stacks at three rather than four, or you can use unlimited stacks, if you prefer. If you don't set a limit, some people also dictate that you must play an ace from your hand as soon as you pick it up to start a new foundation pile.

Figure 2-15 shows how a typical game may progress. At this point, it's Player A's turn, and they picked up a jack at the end of their previous turn.

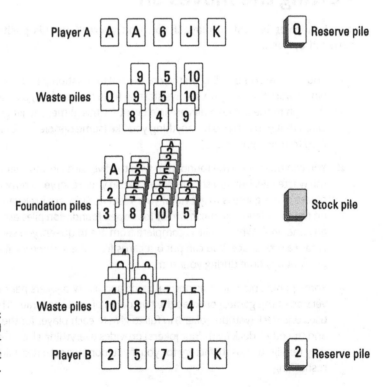

FIGURE 2-15:
Spite and Malice. Player A's excellent adventure.

Player A's main objectives are to get rid of their queen from the reserve and to try to prevent their opponent from playing the 2 from their reserve. They put out the jack from their hand onto the foundation 10 and the queen from their reserve. They clear this foundation pile away, because they completed it with the queen. They turn over a 7 on their reserve and play the 6 from their hand onto the 5 on the foundation pile. That move lets them put the 7 from their reserve onto the foundation, and they turn over a 2 (which is rather irritating for Player B, who had hoped they could use their own 2 from the reserve on an ace in a new foundation pile at their next turn).

Because they cleared a foundation pile earlier in the turn, Player A puts out one of the aces from their hand to start a new pile; now they can play the 2 from the reserve onto that ace (turning over another queen). They take the 9 and 10 back off waste pile D and onto the 8 in the foundation, and they use the king as a wild card to represent a jack. These moves allow them to take the queen from their reserve and put it on the jack to complete another set on the foundation. Now they can take that pile away. They turn over another 2 on the reserve, which is perfect: It allows them to play the second ace from their hand, and the 2 from the reserve goes on that. They turn over a new card on the reserve pile. And because they used up all five cards in their hand, Player A draws five new cards and can continue if they want to.

If they have no moves they want to make, they can end their turn by making one discard to any of their waste piles and picking up a replacement card from the stock.

TIP

But Player A should process one other thought — and this is where the malice in Spite and Malice comes in. The target of the game is to take the foundation piles just past the upcard on your opponent's reserve pile. However, you also want to stop your opponent from being able to easily get rid of the cards from their waste pile. In our featured game, because Player A has a 4 on top of a waste pile, they should play it onto the 3 to prevent their opponent from clearing away one of their waste piles. However, they should not put up the 5 from the waste pile — that would let their opponent clear away the 6 and 7 from another one of their waste piles. Make their work to clear their piles!

REMEMBER

One of the crucial moments in the game comes when your opponent chooses not to play; you always have the option of not making a move (announced as *passing with five*), but if you don't, your opponent can voluntarily pass also, which compels you to make a legal move if you can. The game has no forced moves, except when you pass and your opponent passes, too. In that case, you must play if you can.

Manipulating your stoppage time

Say your opponent in this game, Player B, indicates that they can't play, and you can see that the top cards on their waste piles are 10, 9, 6, and 2. You now know that whatever they have in their hand isn't one of the following cards: K, 10, 9, 8, 6, 5, or 2. If they had any of these numbers, they would have to discard onto their waste pile (remember, the only cards you can put onto a waste pile are cards of the same value, or one lower, than the top card there).

Similarly, you can look at the foundation piles, see that one pile has a 3 on it, and infer that your opponent doesn't have any 4s. So what you must do is ensure that you never leave the foundation piles in a position to allow them to put a Q, J, 7, 3, or ace up — the only cards they can have in their hand. If you can do that, you stop them playing for the duration, which has to be a good idea.

VARIATION

A less demanding version of the game allows you to discard anything you like to your waste piles. Of course, if you play this variation, you never get stuck for a move, but it does cut down on the opportunities for spite and malice!

If both players can't move, you collect all the waste piles and hands, shuffle them up, and redeal new hands. You leave the reserve piles as they are.

Spite and Malice is an excellent competitive game; you have to watch your own cards, plan how best to get rid of them, figure out how to use up your reserve pile, and strategize how to discard onto your waste pile. But equally important is spoiling your opponent's strategy, blocking their reserve pile, preventing them playing from their waste piles by taking the foundation piles past convenient numbers, and generally making yourself a nuisance.

TIP

Try to keep your waste piles as empty as possible; within a single pile, you may want to duplicate cards to preserve flexibility. Occasionally, however, you can see that by (for example) duplicating jacks in a single pile, you may prevent yourself from having access to the queen below the jack. If your opponent has a queen on the reserve pile, that duplication is a very bad idea.

The game ends when one player gets rid of their reserve pile, and the other player records how many cards they have left. The game is ideal for an ongoing struggle (say 20 years or so), as is the case for two of my friends who've been playing it for that long.

SOLITAIRE ON THE WEB

The Web offers a wide variety of sites for the Solitaire enthusiast. You can find tons of Solitaire games to play online for free; for example, you can go www.247solitaire.com.

Chapter **3**

Children's Games

J
ust because this chapter refers to children, adults should not pass it by and ignore the contents. The games in this chapter are suitable for a range of players — younger players, new players, adults playing with younger players, or players who just like fast-action card games that are easy to pick up and fun to play. (All the most enthusiastic Spit players I have met have been adults: It is more a question of attitude than age.) So, whoever you are, you sure to find a game in this chapter to enjoy.

Additionally, several games in other chapters of this book are just as suitable for children as the ones described here. Eights, also known as Crazy Eights (Chapter 6), President (Chapter 17), and Whist (Chapter 8) come to mind.

Beggar My Neighbor

Beggar My Neighbor, also known as Beat Your Neighbor Out of Doors and Strip Jack Naked, requires no strategy or planning at all, making it a great game for kids and for social situations. The objective of the game is to win all the cards from the other players.

To play Beggar My Neighbor, you need the following:

>> **Two to six players:** You can play with more than six players in a pinch.

>> **A standard deck of 52 cards:** With four or more players, add a second deck of cards. A great advantage of this game is that you don't really need a complete deck of cards — a card or two gone missing is almost irrelevant. Don't forget to remove the jokers!

To begin, one player deals out the whole deck in a clockwise rotation, dealing the cards face-down and one at a time so that each player gets about the same number of cards. You don't look at your cards; you form them into a neat pile, face-down in front of you.

The player to the left of the dealer turns over the top card from their pile and places it in the center of the table (or floor, if you want to sprawl out).

Different things can happen now, depending on what card the first player turns over:

>> If the value of the card is between 2 and 10, it has no special significance, and the play goes on to the next player.

>> If the card is a *court card* (an ace, king, queen, or jack), the game becomes a little more exciting. The next player has to pay a *forfeit*, meaning that they has to turn over some of their cards and place them onto the central pile:

- If the first card up is an ace, the second player must turn over four cards one by one onto the middle pile.

- If the first card is a king, the next player has to pay three cards.

- If the first card is a queen, the second player must pay two cards.

- If the first card is a jack, the second player turns up only one card.

If all the cards the second player turns over are between 2 and 10, the first player who turned over the court card takes up the whole pile and puts it under their personal pile, face-down. If the second player turns over another court card during the course of the forfeit, they pay the debt off, and the second player doesn't have to turn over any more cards. Instead, the third player must pay the forfeit dictated by the second court card and either turn over a court card in the process, or allow the second player to pick up the whole central pile if no court card comes.

When you have no more cards left, you're out, and the game continues without you. If you run out of cards in the middle of paying a forfeit for an ace, king, or queen, you are out of the game. In games of more than two players, the previous player picks up the pile of cards, and the next player starts afresh. The last player in the game — the one who accumulates the whole deck — wins.

Your success at Beggar My Neighbor depends on the luck of the draw; if you get a good smattering of court cards, you have a good chance to win. If someone feels bad because they lost, you may want to remind them of the luck factor. But don't forget to congratulate them if they win!

Because Beggar My Neighbor can go on for a long time — making it ideal for long car journeys, waiting for planes, or similar situations — you can agree that the player with the most cards at a certain predefined time is the winner.

KIDS AND CARD GAMES

These days, most children seem to be born with a remote or video-game controller in their hands. However, some children are lucky enough to receive decks of cards when they're young (as was the case with me).

Teaching children how to play cards is fun — both for them and for you! Children get an opportunity to interact with others, revel in the challenge of a game, and enjoy a sense of mastery. Card games also foster a strong sense of belonging and a connection to the family or social group.

In a more tangible sense, card games can enhance a child's skills. To play card games, children must master rules, develop mental strategies, understand objectives, evaluate their (and their opponents') strengths and weaknesses, and make plans. The games also force them to respond quickly and to deal socially with others.

Some studies suggest that card players develop better problem-solving and lateral-thinking skills (the ability to "think outside the box"). Developing competence in one field can improve a child's self-confidence to learn in other areas. Therefore, cards can increase a child's scores in math and critical thinking, as well as improve their social skills.

Finally, card games — like other cognitively engaging activities, including chess, backgammon, and crossword puzzles — are being cited as excellent activities for keeping the brain supple and engaged throughout life, potentially delaying the onset of Alzheimer's disease and other memory disabilities.

Snap, Animals, and Slapjack

Snap, Animals, and Slapjack are close cousins in the family of games that focus on acquiring your opponents' cards (such as Beggar My Neighbor; see the previous section). For these games, speed is the key to victory. The player with the quickest reactions wins. Snap, Animals, and Slapjack are among the few card games that depend almost entirely on physical dexterity.

Snap

Get ready for a fast and furious game! Snap is all about mental reaction time, and one of the few games in which luck plays no part at all.

BEFORE HAND

To play Snap, you need the following:

>> **Two or more players.** There is no formal upper limit, but if you play with more than six players, the neighbors may complain about the noise.

>> **A standard deck of 52 cards.** Play Snap with a single deck of cards if you have fewer than four players; add a second deck if more players compete. Playing this game with a used deck is a good idea — the cards can take a beating (literally).

You don't need a full deck of cards — a card or two can be missing from the deck. You can also play Snap with special cards designed for another game (such as an Old Maid deck), as long as most of the cards have backs identical to other cards in the deck.

The dealer deals out the whole deck of cards face-down, one card at a time to each player, in a clockwise rotation. It doesn't matter if some players get more cards than others. What does matter, however, is that you don't look at the cards you get.

Each player, starting with the player to the left of the dealer, takes a turn flipping over the top card of their pile and putting it face-up in front of them. After a few turns, each player has a little pile of face-up cards.

When you turn over all the cards into the pile in front of you, you pick up the pile and use it again without shuffling them.

The flipping process continues until one player turns over a card of the same rank as the top card on another player's pile. As soon as the matching card is revealed, the first person to call out "Snap!" takes the two piles with matching cards and puts them face down under their own pile.

Frequently, two players make the Snap call simultaneously. In this case, you put the two piles with the same card together, face-up, in middle of the table. Everyone continues to turn over the top cards on their piles until someone turns over a card that matches the card on the pile in the middle of the table. The first person to shout "Snap pool!" wins the middle pile. The new piles that are being created are still up for grabs in the usual way, of course. Whenever a pairing is created, the first to shout "Snap" wins them.

WARNING

When a player mistakenly calls out "Snap!" their pile goes into the center of the table; the first player to call "Snap pool!" at the relevant moment gets their pile. You have to operate with what you have left, and if you run out of cards, you are out of the game.

The player who ends up with all the cards wins the game.

For some reason, Snap brings out the worst competitive instincts in people, myself included. Establishing several informal rules can avoid Snap-induced bloodshed:

>> **Set rules about the proper way to turn over your card.** You can't turn over the card so that you see it first, which means that you must flip over the card in a continuous, fast motion onto your pile.

>> **Get an impartial witness to decide on all close calls.** If you can, choose someone who isn't playing the game, preferably an authority figure such as an adult.

TIP

A devious, cunning player remembers the order of their pile (or of another player's pile) when the pile gets small so they gain a big edge in the calling. Keep an eye on the cards as the game draws to a close; if you don't, you put yourself at a disadvantage. If you want to avoid this situation, you can agree to shuffle your pile when you've worked your way through it.

VARIATION

You can play a couple of variations to basic Snap to make the game more appropriate for the age range of the players:

>> In Simplified Snap, which is suitable for three or more players, all the players put the turned-over cards on a single pile in the middle of the table. You call "Snap!" whenever the top card on the pile matches the last card played. This method allows you to focus on only one place.

>> Speed Snap provides a challenge, which makes it better for older players. All players turn over their cards at the same moment so that the reaction process speeds up. To make sure that all the players turn over their cards simultaneously, the umpire (or one of the players) must say "One, two, three!" with all players turning over the cards on three.

Animals

Animals is a much louder version of Snap. To understand the basics of Animals, see the preceding section, "Snap." The major difference between Snap and Animals is the way you call out for the cards.

BEFORE
HAND

Make sure that you have the following items to play Animals:

>> **Two or more players**

>> **A standard deck of 52 cards**

>> **Pencils and scraps of paper**

At the start of the game, each player selects an animal, preferably one with a long and complicated name, such as *duck-billed platypus* or *Tyrannosaurus Rex*. Each player writes the name on a piece of paper and puts it in the middle of the table.

You shuffle the papers around, and every player takes one and then announces the name of the animal. Play can then begin.

When two players turn up matching cards, those players are the only ones who can win the cards. They must each try to call out the other person's animal name first, and whoever succeeds wins both piles.

VARIATION

One Animals variation (sometimes called Animal Noises) calls for everyone to select common animals, such as a cat or dog. To win the cards, the two players who turn up matching cards must make the noise of their opponent's animal before they do the same. Whoever makes and finishes the noise first wins the opponent's pile of cards.

WARNING

If you call out a name at the wrong moment, you concede all your played cards to the player with the animal (or animal noise) you call out. Making the wrong call or naming the wrong animal at the appropriate moment costs you nothing but loss, because the other player is likely to beat you to the punch.

Slapjack

Slapjack involves physical agility rather than verbal dexterity and memory, so make sure the players involved are active and eager. Young children can play this game if they can tell the difference between a jack and a king or queen.

BEFORE
HAND

Assemble the following items to play Slapjack:

>> **Two or more players.** A maximum of six is probably sensible or too many collisions may result at home plate.

>> **A standard deck of 52 cards:** Slapjack can totally wreck a deck of cards, so don't break out the collector cards you bought in Las Vegas.

The dealer deals out the entire deck, face-down and one card at a time, to each player in a clockwise rotation. At the end of the deal, each player should have a neat stack of cards in front of them. Make sure you don't look at your cards.

Beginning on the dealer's left, each player takes a turn playing a card face-up onto a single stack in the center of the table.

Play continues peacefully until someone plays a jack. Whoever slaps the jack first wins all the cards in the middle of the table and adds them to the bottom of the pile in front of them. The player to the slapper's left starts the next pile by placing a card face-up in the center of the table.

Spirits run high in Slapjack, so you may need to define some rules before the game starts:

>> You turn over a card by turning it away from you so that you can't peek at it in advance. (This puts the turner at a slight disadvantage, but the luck evens out things eventually.)

>> Rest your slapping hand on the table. Make the player who puts out the card slap with their other hand, which must also rest on the table.

>> When you can't decide who slapped first, the hand closest to the jack always wins the day.

WARNING

If you slap the wrong card, you must give a card from your face-down pile to the person who played the card you slapped.

After all your cards are gone, you aren't automatically out of the game; you stay in for one more chance, lying in ambush and waiting to slap the next jack that gets turned over. At that point, if you fail to slap the jack, you're out. The first player to get all the cards wins.

War

War is a great game for young children. The object is to acquire all the cards, which you can do in different ways.

To play War, you need the following:

>> **Two players**

>> **A standard deck of 52 cards**

Start by dealing out the deck one card at a time, face-down, so that each player gets 26 cards. Keep your cards in a pile and don't look at them. Each player turns over one card simultaneously; whoever turns over the highest card picks up the two cards and puts them face-down at the bottom of their pile.

The cards have the normal rank from highest to lowest: ace, king, queen, jack, and then 10 through 2 (see Chapter 1 for card-playing basics).

The game continues in this manner until both players turn over a card of the same rank, at which point you enter a *war*. A war can progress in one of three ways. I start with the most benevolent version and work my way to the most brutal:

>> Each player puts a card face-down on top of the tied card and then one face-up. Whoever has the higher face-up card takes all six cards.

>> Each player puts three face-down cards on the table and one face-up card, so the competition is for ten cards. This option speeds up the game, which often drags a little — especially for children!

>> Each player puts down cards depending on the rank of the tied cards. If the equal cards are 7s, you each count off seven face-down cards before turning a card over. If the equal cards are kings, queens, or jacks, you turn down ten cards before flipping one up and squaring off. For an ace, count out 11 face-down cards.

>> If another tie results, repeat the process until someone achieves a decisive victory.

If a player runs out of cards in the middle of a war, you have two possible solutions: You lose the war and are out of the game, or you turn your last card face up, and these count as your played card in the war.

Whoever wins the cards gathers them up and puts them at the bottom of their pile. The first person to get all the other player's cards wins.

You can play War with three players. The dealer gives out 17 cards to each player, face-down. The remaining card goes to the winner of the first war. The players simultaneously flip over one card each. The highest card of the three takes all three cards. If two players tie for the high card, they each place three cards face-down and then place one face-up, and the highest card collects all the cards in the pile. If you have another draw at this point, you fight another war. If all three players turn over the same card, a double war takes place; each player turns down six cards and flips one up, and the winner takes all.

Fish and Friends

The Fish family features two games: Go Fish and Authors. Both games have the same aim: Each player tries to make as many complete *sets* of four of a kind as possible.

Go Fish

Get out yer fishin' pole and head to the waterin' hole — you're about to go fishin' fer sets (four cards of the same kind).

BEFORE HAND

To play Go Fish, you need the following:

>> **At least three players**

>> **A standard deck of 52 cards**

Each player gets ten cards from the dealer. You pretend as you deal out the full deck that you have one more player than you really do. With four players, for example, you deal out ten cards (one by one, face-down, in a clockwise rotation) in five piles. Add the two leftover cards to the pretend pile and leave those 12 cards as the *stock* in the middle of the table. With three players, you have three hands of 13 cards and a stock of the remaining 13.

Starting with the player to the left of the dealer, each player has the opportunity of asking any other player at the table a question. This must be in the form of "Do you have any Xs?" (X is the rank of card; 4s or queens, for example.) The player asking the question must have at least one X to pose the question.

If the person asked has an X or two, they must hand them over, and the questioner's turn continues. The questioner can then ask the same player or any other player if they have a card in a particular set. As soon as the questioner completes a set of four cards, they put the set down on the table in front of them and continue their turn.

VARIATION

The game becomes more difficult if the responder only has to provide one card from the relevant set, even if they have more than one queen, for example. The questioner has to ask again and risks wasting a turn.

If the person asked has no cards of the rank specified in the question, they reply "Go Fish," and the questioner takes a card from the stock. The questioner's go ends, whether they pick up the card they were looking for or not. If the card that they draw from the stock completes a set, they must wait until their next turn to put the set down on the table. The turn passes to the player who sends their rival fishing.

VARIATION

Some play that if the card you draw from the stock completes any set in your hand, or if you pick up the card you were unsuccessfully asking for, your turn continues.

At the end of the game — which almost always occurs when all the cards are in everybody's hands and the stock has been used up — you count the sets. The player who collects the most sets wins. However, if one player puts all their cards into sets before the stock gets used up, they win.

Authors

Authors resembles Go Fish in many ways, with a few interesting exceptions that make it a far more subtle game.

TIP

At one time, people played Authors with special decks of cards bearing the pictures of famous authors. These decks are coming back into fashion; try www.unclesgames.com.

The big difference between Authors and Go Fish is that the questions you ask other players must relate to specific cards rather than to a type of card. For example, you ask, "Do you have the ♠7?" instead of asking for 7s in general.

The other rules on asking questions are also quite specific:

>> You can't ask for a card if you already have that card in your hand.

>> You can't ask for a card unless you have at least one card of that set in your hand.

TIP

If you have two cards of a set in your hand, hearing someone else ask for a third card in the set may pinpoint who has the cards you need. If player A successfully asks player B for the ♦Q, for example, they now have two queens, so you can collect them from that player at your next turn if you get the chance.

An unsuccessful question means that the turn passes to the left rather than to the player who unsuccessfully asked for a card. Just as in Go Fish, when you complete a set, you place it on the table.

WARNING

If you ask for a card when you have nothing in that set, if you fail to provide a card when you're asked for it, or if you fail to put down a set as soon as you can, you must give one set to the player to your left — a pretty severe charge!

When you run out of cards — because other players picked your hand clean or because you've made your hand into sets — you're out, and the game continues without you until all the sets have been completed and no one has any cards left. Whoever has the most sets at the end wins.

Cheat

Children love Cheat (which is also called I Doubt It) because it gives them the opportunity to develop their deceptive powers in a way that their parents approve of. Most children master the art of lying convincingly and looking guilty when telling the truth very early on.

BEFORE HAND

You need the following to play Cheat:

>> **Three or more players:** You can play with up to 12.

>> **A standard deck of 52 cards:** You normally play Cheat with a single deck of cards for up to five players. With 6 to 12 players, use two decks.

The object of Cheat is to get rid of all your cards as quickly as possible. To do that, you play your cards face-down, announcing what you put down — but you don't have to tell the truth.

The dealer deals out all the cards one at a time, face-down and clockwise, and the players pick up and look at their cards. The player to the left of the dealer is first to play.

The first player puts down cards onto a central pile on the table, squaring the cards up so that other players can't see precisely how many cards they have put down. They then make an announcement about their play, along the line of "three 6s" or whatever they consider appropriate. The statement can be false in more than one way. They may put down more or fewer cards than they claim, or they may put down cards unrelated to what they claim. The players who follow put their cards on top of theirs.

Some people require that the play must consist of the correct *number* of cards, whether or not they are what you claim them to be.

If no player challenges the claim (and anyone can do so), the turn moves clockwise to the next player. The next player also makes a play face-down, and they have three choices:

To make a challenge, someone calls out "Cheat," and the player accused has two options:

>> They can concede (gracefully or otherwise) by picking up the entire pile.

>> They can turn over the cards they just put down to demonstrate that they were telling the truth, in which case the challenger must pick up the whole pile.

The player who picks up the pile from the center gets to start the next round with whatever number they want.

If you have a dispute over who called out "Cheat" first, the player nearest to the left of the accused has priority.

If no one has called "Cheat," then the next player has to pick up from the last set put down. They have three choices as to what to play.

>> **They can claim to be playing the same rank as the previous player:** If the first player claims to lay three 6s, the next player can take this choice by putting down a number of 6s.

>> **They can claim to be playing cards of one rank higher:** If the first player claims to put down 6s, "cards of one rank higher" means as many 7s as they want.

>> **They can claim to be playing cards of one rank lower than the previous move:** If the first player claims 6s, any number of 5s works for the next player.

The second player can't pass. They put their cards face-down on the table, on top of the previous play. Of course, they may be lying!

The next player has exactly the same set of options (play the same rank as the previous player or one higher or one lower), and play continues until someone makes a challenge.

The winner of the game is the person who succeeds in playing all their cards first. A player can go out by withstanding a challenge on their final turn or by going unchallenged before the next player makes a play. In practice, someone always challenges a player going out, but if you can conceal that you have no cards left on your last play (not easy to do!), you may avoid a challenge.

VARIATION Some people play that the second player's turn is far less flexible. If the first player plays 6s, the next player must play 7s, and the one after that must play 8s. This variation takes away some of the flexibility in the play, but it makes it much easier for younger children to determine what they should do. Because only one play is possible, everyone knows what comes next.

Old Maid

Old Maid allows you to keep card strategy and psychology simple, making it an ideal game for younger children.

BEFORE HAND All you need to play Old Maid is the following:

>> **At least three players:** There is no real upper limit, if you have enough decks of cards.

>> **One or more standard decks of 52 cards, with three queens removed:** Use a single deck of cards for up to six players. For seven or more players, use two decks, but take care that the decks have the same markings. You can play the game with special commercial decks, too, with animal faces on the cards and just one Donkey in the deck. You can also play with a special Old Maid deck, with one ugly Old Maid card.

The object of Old Maid is to get rid of all the cards in your hand without being left with the one unmatched card, the solitary queen, or *Old Maid*.

The dealer deals out all the cards, one by one and face-down, in a clockwise rotation. You start by removing every pair of cards that you have (a pair can be two 5s or two kings, for example). You set these cards aside face-up on the table so that everyone can see how many pairs you have.

WARNING Take care not to remove any three of a kind — only remove pairs from your hand.

After the removal of pairs, the player to the left of the dealer fans out their cards face-down on the table, and the player to their left takes one card. The player who's offered the cards must take one of them, and then they look at it to see whether it forms a pair with another card in their hand. If it does, they discard the pair onto the tabletop.

Whether the card they draw forms a pair or not, the second player spreads their cards face-down and offers their hand to the player on their left, who must then choose a card.

The game continues, with players dropping out as they get rid of all their cards. Eventually, one player gets left with the lone queen, and other players torment that player with taunts of "Old Maid!" until a new hand starts.

VARIATION

Both France and Germany feature special versions of Old Maid. In France, they take out three jacks from the deck, leaving only the ♠J: the *vieux garçon* or "Old Boy." The Germans have special decks with a *Black Peter* card, often showing a cat in military attire. In each game, the loser is the player left with the odd card.

TIP

You can use a certain element of psychology or reverse psychology to persuade people to take the lone queen away from you. If you arrange your cards with some paired up and more prominently positioned than others, the next player may think that you want to pass off the prominent cards. Make sure that the prominent cards are "safe" ones, so you increase the chance that the player takes one of the other cards — perhaps the queen.

Spit (or Speed)

As its alternative name suggests, Spit is a game where fast reactions are critical. In fact, Spit is rare in that the players don't take turns in sedate fashion to follow suit in turn. Instead, each player makes the effort to play as quickly as possible, not waiting for their opponent.

BEFORE HAND

To play Spit, you need:

>> **Two players**

>> **One deck of cards**

I suggest you keep a special deck for this game; after one session your cards may never be the same again.

The object of the game is to get rid of all your cards as quickly as possible. The dealer shuffles the cards and deals each player 26 cards.

Each player then deals out 15 of their 26 cards into a triangle — one pile with five cards, one with four, one with three, one with two, and one with a single card. The piles that form the triangle are called the *stock piles*. On each of the piles, you turn the top card over. That leaves you a pile of 11 cards, which you leave face-down and don't look at. This is your draw pile, or *spit cards*.

VARIATION

Some people play with only four stock piles that fill with four cards, three cards, two cards, and one card.

After each player sets up the spit cards and stocks, all players call out "Spit!" and turn over the top cards of their piles of 11, putting them in the middle of the table. These two cards make up the two *spit piles*. The slugfest is about to begin. Using only one hand (playing cards with both hands is forbidden), you attempt to get rid of the cards from your stock piles onto the spit piles before your opponent can do so.

Legal moves involve playing a face-up card from your stock piles on to the spit piles. You can play a card if it's one rank higher or one rank lower than the card on the top of the spit piles, and aces count as high or low, so you can put them on a king or a 2. Suits are irrelevant for the purposes of this game.

VARIATION

Some people play that the cards you play on the spit piles must alternate in color (you must play a red king on a black queen or ace, for example).

REMEMBER

When you exhaust a pile, you can move a face-up card from any pile to fill the gap. You can never have more than five piles, come what may.

VARIATION

Some people play that if you have two cards of the same rank on the top of different stock piles, you can move one of them on top of the other, thereby creating an additional option and making a blank space to allow you to bring another card down.

When neither player can make a legal move, the first phase of the game has ended, and you're ready for the second phase, which essentially repeats phase one.

In phase two, each player simultaneously calls out "Spit!" again, turning over the top cards from their spit cards face-up onto the already existing spit piles. The game continues, with both players trying to get rid of their stock piles as quickly as possible. Eventually, one of three situations occurs:

» You get rid of all your stock cards; let's call this event the end of a round. When this happens, you have your choice of spit piles, and you'll naturally take the smaller one. The second player takes the other pile, and you both collect your unplayed cards, shuffle them all together, and lay them out in the traditional format.

VARIATION

An alternative is that when a player gets rid of all their cards, both players can reach for the spit piles, and whoever has the fastest reflexes gets the choice. I prefer the standard rule, however; it seems right to reward the player who plays better in the first stage.

>> Both players get rid of all their spit cards, and neither player can play a card. In this case, whoever has fewer stock cards left gathers up all their cards and adds the smaller spit pile to them, leaving their rival to add the other pile.

>> After the first round, the player who has the larger spit-card pile may have spit cards left to turn over, but their opponent doesn't have any. In the case, the player must select a pile on which to put their spit cards, and they must go with that pile to put *all* their remaining spit cards on for the rest of this run. Of course, that may bring the other player back to life, because as new cards appear on the pile, they may find a way to get rid of some stock cards as a result.

Whenever one player has fewer than 15 spit cards left in their hand at the start of a new round, they deal out the cards into the five stock piles as best they can, starting with the single card and working up to the five-card pile, and then they turn over the top cards as before. But only one communal spit pile exists now because one player has no spit cards with which to make a pile. At this point, whoever gets rid of all the cards from their stock piles gets no additional cards at the end of the round. If that player is the one with no spit cards, they win the game. If the player with the spit cards wins the round, the other player picks up the central pile and their unused stock cards, and the hand continues.

Spit is a game of skill as well as speed. You have to manage about four or five tasks simultaneously with only one hand. You have to play your cards as quickly as possible, turn over new ones, create new piles, and prevent your opponent from playing. In addition, if you have time to plan, you must make your choice of actions that help you and not your rival. All this requires practice and excellent peripheral vision.

2

Getting Rid of Cards

The first two games I discuss in Part II (Rummy and Canasta) all involve improving your hand by picking up cards (usually from a stock pile) and discarding those you don't want. You, in effect, exchange your cards (or hope to) in order to get the best hand possible.

In games such as Eights and Fan Tan, you strive to go out as quickly as possible by matching cards. Each game has its own definition of what it means to *match a card,* and I explain the rules of each game in depth.

Chapter **4**

Rummy

Althought the word *Rummy* may conjure up some beverage-related memories — some of them possibly involving headaches — I can assure you that in this book, Rummy refers to a variety of fun games that you don't have to be over 21 to play.

In this chapter, I show you how to play Rummy and two popular Rummy variations, Gin Rummy and 500 Rummy. After you get the basics under your belt, feel free to call up some friends, throw a party, play some Rummy, and drink the beverage of your choice (gin or not). And before the party, pick up a few rum-based beverage recipes in *Bartending For Dummies* by Ray Foley (Wiley). Enough with the shameless promotion. Time to play some cards.

Rummy: Throw a Combo and Go

In this section, you master the basics of Rummy and discover some playing tactics, including how to go for your opponent's jugular, when to minimize the risk of getting caught with a number of cards left in your hand, and how to take advantage of other players' strategies.

**BEFORE
HAND**

To play Rummy, you need the following:

» **Two or more players:** For six or more players, you need a second deck of cards. You can play with up to 12 players with a second deck.

>> **A standard deck of 52 cards:** Jokers are optional, depending on whether you want to play with wild cards (see the section "Rummying with wild cards" later in this chapter for information).

>> **Paper and pencil for scoring:** You can use a pen or computer, too. I'm not picky.

Setting up and laying out the objective

Rummy is a card game in which you try to improve the hand that you're originally dealt. You can do this whenever it's your turn to play, either by drawing cards from the undealt pile (or *stock*) or by picking up the card thrown away by your opponent and then throwing away (or *discarding*) a card from your hand. Your aim is to put (or *meld*) your cards into two types of combinations:

>> **Runs:** Consecutive sequences of three or more cards of the same suit.

>> **Sets:** Three or four cards of the same rank (also known as a *group* or *book* in North America). If you are using two decks, a set may include two identical cards of the same rank and suit.

Figure 4-1 shows some legitimate Rummy combinations.

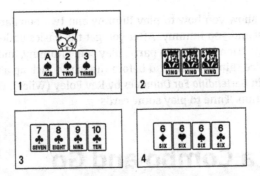

FIGURE 4-1:
Legal runs follow the same suit; legal sets consist of the same rank.

Figure 4-2 shows an unacceptable combination. This run is illegal because all cards in a run must be of the same suit.

FIGURE 4-2:
An illegal run.

REMEMBER

In most Rummy games, unlike the majority of other card games, aces can be high or low, but not both. So runs involving the ace must take the form A-2-3 or A-K-Q but not K-A-2. For example, you can't put down ♣2-♣A-♣K. You have to wait until you pick up the ♣Q in order to combine the ♣A and ♣K in a legitimate run.

The first person who manages to make their whole hand into combinations — also called *melds* — one way or another, with one card remaining to discard, wins the game.

Dealing the cards and starting the Rummy

When playing Rummy with two, three, or four players, each player gets ten cards; when playing with five players, each player gets six cards. With more than five players, you must use two decks of cards and a hand of seven cards. Yes, I promised you no high-level mathematics, but you can cope with a few numbers here and there.

VARIATION

The two-player game can also be played with seven cards each.

Designate a scorer and a dealer at the start of the game. To determine who should be the scorer, just volunteer the person closest to the pencil and scorecard. Always try to be on the other side of the room when someone asks, "Have you got a pencil on you?"

To decide who should be the dealer, each player takes a card, and the person who draws the lowest card is the dealer for the first hand. The deal rotates clockwise for each following hand.

Deal each player a card, starting with the player on the dealer's left and moving clockwise. When each hand is complete, put the undealt cards face-down on the center of the table as the stock and place the top card, turned upward, beside the stock as the first card of the discard pile.

TIP

Pick up your cards slowly; you don't need to play Rummy with excessive haste, so give yourself time to think about all your possible card combinations before starting play.

Misdeals — accidents during the deal, such as a card getting turned face-up or too many or too few cards dealt out — generally result in another deal, with no penalties attached.

The player to the left of the dealer plays first. That player can do one of two things: They can either pick up the card on the discard pile or the top card from the stock. If they can put some or all of their hand into combinations, they may do so (see the following section, "Putting down and adding to combinations"). If not, they discard one card from their hand, face-up onto the discard pile, and the turn of play moves to the next player.

The next player can either pick up the last card the previous player discarded or the top card from the stock. They can then meld some or all of their cards down in combinations, if they want to. The play continues clockwise around the table. When the stock runs out, shuffle the discard pile and set it up again.

REMEMBER

You cannot pick up the top discard and then throw the card back onto the pile.

WARNING

If you pick up two cards from the stock by accident and see either of them, you must put the bottom card back, which gives the next player an additional option. They can look at the returned card and take it if they want it. If they don't want it, they put it back into the middle of the stock and continue with their turn by taking the next card from the stock.

TIP

When you pick up a card from the stock that you don't want, don't throw it away immediately. Put the card into your hand and then extract it. No player, regardless of skill level, needs to give gratuitous information away.

During the play, you work your way through the stock, taking one card from it (or the discard pile) and discarding a card from your hand. If you completely use up the stock, the dealer reshuffles the discard pile and turns over a new upcard, and play continues.

Putting down and adding to combinations

You can only put down a combination during your turn. The correct timing is to pick up a card from the stock or discard pile, put down your meld, and then make your discard. The advantage of putting down a combination before you're ready to go out completely is that you reduce your exposure if you lose the game (for the details on scoring, see the section "Going out and tallying your score" later in this chapter). However, you do run a few risks by putting down a run or meld.

The disadvantage of putting your cards on the table is that any player can now add to your meld of three of a kind (by adding the fourth card) or extend your runs. Although adding to your combinations proves very beneficial to your opponents, the longer the game goes on, the more wary you should be of keeping melds in your hand.

Conversely, you can add to your opponents' combinations — or, if you draw the right card, you can add an additional card to your own melds. If you want to add a card to an existing combination, put down any combinations you have, add to the existing set or run, and then make a discard. Your turn finishes with the discard, so make sure that you don't mix up the order of events. If you do, you can't put down any combinations you may have until your next turn.

WARNING

If you put down an imperfect run, you simply pick up the cards and put them back in your hand. But by revealing the cards in your hand to everyone else at the table, your chances of getting anything useful from the other players decrease. Better put on your glasses and double-check before laying any cards on the table.

When you have a set of four of a kind, no card can add to the combination, if you are playing with a single deck of cards, so you're safe to put these sets down immediately. The only reason to hold them is if you're close to going out and you want to play for the extra score (see the section "Going out and tallying your score" later in this chapter for more information). Additionally, if you can possibly use a card in the set for a run, you may want to retain the combination in your hand until you know how you want to use the cards. For example, you may want to hold some of the cards in Figure 4-3 until you get some more information.

FIGURE 4-3:
Waiting for the right cards.

In Figure 4-3, you could use the ♥9 both in the set and in a run with the ♥10 and ♥J. Holding the cards for a turn gives you a chance to pick up the ♥Q or ♥8, which would improve the run.

Rummying with wild cards

VARIATION

You can also play Rummy with wild cards, or cards that can represent any card you like. You can add the jokers that come with the cards to the deck, treating them as wild cards, or you can make the 2s wild, for example.

You can substitute the card represented by a wild card when it is your turn to play. So if a combination including a joker, standing in for the ♥4 is put on the table, the next player can put in the ♥4 and pick up the joker for use elsewhere.

If you put down two eights and a joker, you do not have to announce which eight the joker represents, but with a run such as 5-6-joker, the assumption is that the joker represents the 7.

TIP

When playing with wild cards, you may not want to put combinations containing wild cards down immediately; you don't want to give another player the use of a wild card by way of the substitution. Of course, if you feel obliged to put down the set or run, try to ensure that the card your wild card replaces has already been played in some other set or run.

Going out and tallying your score

The first player to be able to put seven of the eight cards in their hand into combinations (including the card that they pick up in their current turn), or ten of their 11 cards, as the case may be, *goes out* (places all their cards on the table) and wins. You discard your remaining card as you go out, usually having made the others into one combination of four and one combination of three. You do not have to make the plays at one turn; you may have put down some cards into sets already, of course. If your last two cards are two 7s, and you pick up a third 7, most people play that you can go out by making a set, without needing a final discard.

The winner collects points from all the other players. They base their point total on the remaining cards in the other players' hands, regardless of whether the cards make up completed combinations or not — which is a good reason to put down melds as soon as you get them.

The players put their cards face-up on the table and call out how many points they have left for the winner. You score the cards according to the following scale:

>> **2s through 10s** get their face value, meaning, for example, that a 5 is worth 5 points.

>> **Jacks, queens, and kings** receive 10 points apiece.

>> **Wild cards** cost you 15 points each, if you are playing with them.

>> **Aces,** in keeping with their lowly status during the game, charge you 1 point only.

For example, if you're left holding ♠K, ♦K, ♦Q, and ♣A at the end of the game, the winner of the game scores 31 points. With more than two players, the winner cumulates the points from all the other players.

REMEMBER

Laying all your cards down in one turn is called *going Rummy*, which doubles your score; obviously, the availability of this bonus affects your decision to put down combinations earlier rather than later. If you think that you can claim this bonus, you may want to delay putting down your combinations.

The first player to score 100 points is the winner. For a longer game, you can play to 250 points.

Simple Rummy strategy

When you first start playing Rummy, you may find that putting your cards into combinations is quite challenging. The best strategy is to aim for melds that have the best chance for completion.

The cards in your hand and on the table give you information about your chances for completing certain combinations. For example, if you can keep only two cards from the ♠7, ♠8, and ♣8, and you've already used the ♦8 in another run, you should keep the spades because you have two chances for success this way — the ♠6 or the ♠9. Keeping the two 8s gives you only one possible draw, the ♥8.

Another typical problem is knowing when to break up a pair in order to increase your chances elsewhere. For example, imagine that you have to discard from a collection such as the one shown in Figure 4-4.

FIGURE 4-4:
Time to choose or lose.

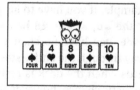

The solution to this problem is to throw the ♥10 away. Keeping your two pairs gives you a reasonable chance to make three of a kind, and the ♥10 gives you only a single chance of making a combination — by drawing the ♥9.

In general, you don't want to split up your pairs. But life (or at least Rummy) isn't always so simple. Suppose that you have the cards shown in Figure 4-5.

FIGURE 4-5:
Dismantle a pair
and perhaps
draw a building
card.

If you need to throw out one card, throw a 4 away. The ♠7 is a useful *building card*, meaning that it fits well with the ♠8; mathematics says that the nest of 7s and 8s gives you four possible cards with which to make a combination (the ♠9, ♠6, ♣8, and ♥8). You have the same number of options if you throw the ♠7 away and keep the two pairs. But the real merit in throwing away one of the 4s is the degree of freedom you attain for a future discard. By throwing one 4 away, you allow yourself to pick up another potentially useful building card (such as the ♦7) at your next turn, and then you can throw away the other 4. By contrast, throwing away the ♠7 *fixes* your hand and gives you no flexibility.

TIP

The odds favor your draw to the run rather than your hopes for a set. When you make a run, you can build on it at either end. A set, on the other hand, has only one possible draw. For this reason, be careful about which cards you discard. If you must give your opponent a useful card, try to let them have the sets of three or four of a kind instead of helping them build their runs.

Keeping your eye on the discard pile

You can't go through a game of Rummy thinking only about the cards in your hand — you also need to watch the cards thrown into the discard pile. Monitoring the discard pile helps you keep track of whether the cards you're hoping to pick up have already been thrown away. For example, if you have to keep two cards from the ♠7, ♠8, and ♣8, consider whether the ♠6, ♠9, or ♥8 has already been discarded. If both spades have already gone, you have no chance of picking them up — at least not until you work your way through the entire stock, at which point you may get a second chance at the cards when the deck is reshuffled. In such a stuck position, you should settle for a realistic chance, however slim, of picking up the last 8 by discarding the ♠7.

TIP

Try to avoid *drawing to an inside run* — keeping, for example, a 3 and a 5 in the hopes of drawing the 4. Holding onto *builders* (cards that may be helpful elsewhere) is better than relying on a single card.

You can't review the discard pile for clues. You have to remember which cards were thrown away — or be very adept at taking stealthy peeks at the discarded evidence!

Thinking about your opponents' hands

Contemplating what your opponent has in their hand helps you make smarter choices about what cards you should discard. After all, you don't want to throw away that ♥K if your opponent can use it to complete a run with the ♥Q and ♥J.

You compile a picture of your opponent's hand by reading the negative and positive messages you get from their plays. For example, if you see your opponent throw away the ♥Q, you can be sure that they aren't collecting queens. That information in itself doesn't make discarding any queen safe, however, because they may be collecting high diamonds. But if do you subsequently throw down the ♦Q, and they pick it up, their action provides you with an informative message; you can safely infer that they are collecting high diamonds.

Making a good discard

Early in the game, try to avoid discarding exactly the same rank of card as your opponent; they may be trapping you. For example, if you hold the ♣J, ♦Q and ♦10, you may be able to persuade your opponent to let their jacks go by tossing your ♣J at the first opportunity. This trick is good strategy — so try it yourself, but be aware that your opponents may be on the ball, too.

Kings are the most attractive discard, followed by queens, because fewer runs involve kings and queens than involve jacks or 10s. (Kings can only appear in K-Q-J runs, but jacks can appear in runs of K-Q-J, Q-J-10, and J-10-9.) Of course, discarding court cards reduces your potential exposure if you lose the game. The higher the card, the more points you may present to the player going out.

Picking up cards from the discard pile

Another critical strategy dilemma in Rummy is whether to pick up *builder cards* — cards that lend themselves well to combinations — from the discard pile. Say, for example, that you start the hand with the ♠Q and ♦J, and early in the game an opponent throws away the ♦Q. Should you pick it up?

You would automatically keep the ♦Q if you picked it up from the stock, of course — doing so doesn't give your opponent any clues as to which cards you may find helpful. But if you take a card from the discard pile, you tip off your opponent to part of your hand. If you're playing against a good player who carefully watches cards, you probably shouldn't take the builder card. On the other hand, picking up a card that multiplies your options, such as the ♥7 with the ♠7, ♠8, and ♥8 in your hand, is definitely a good idea because the ♥7 gives you some flexibility in two directions.

TIP

Along with your opponents, you should watch the discard pile like a hawk. Technically, the cards should be arranged one on top of another, but in reality, you can generally see many cards below the top card. Crafty opponents keep a sharp eye on the pile; so should you.

Try to remember the cards that haven't been discarded as well as the ones that do appear on the discard pile. If you've almost worked your way through the entire deck and you see your first 5, assume that your opponent is collecting them — if your opponent isn't interested in collecting 5s, you probably would have seen a 5 before reaching the end of the deck.

Assume that your opponents are honest until they prove you wrong. If they hesitate on your discard, assume that they want to pick it up; their possible need for that card may affect your future discards. If you subsequently discover that they simply paused for effect, say nothing, but remember that they may do the same thing next time. You should be able to draw the right inferences after observing the first performance!

Gin Rummy: Knocking Your Foe Down

Gin Rummy is very similar in aim to regular Rummy (see the previous section), but Gin has some additional wrinkles that make it a more interesting and challenging game.

BEFORE HAND

To play Gin Rummy, you need the following:

>> Two players: If more than two people want to play, you may want to send the extras out for ice cream or a walk.

>> A standard deck of 52 cards: No jokers allowed in the Gin house.

>> Paper and pencil for scoring: For more on scoring, head to the section "Boxing up the scoring system" later in this chapter.

Getting a fair deal

Both players get ten cards. The dealer turns the rest of the cards into the stock by placing them in the center of the table and turning over the first card. The upcard is offered to the nondealer first. If they don't want the upcard, the dealer may take it, and then play continues. Gin Rummy play resembles regular Rummy, except for how you go out, and the fact that you do not put down combinations mid-hand. (For more information on how to play Rummy, see the section "Rummy: Throw a Combo and Go" earlier in this chapter.)

TIP

The first upcard is a free card; be prepared to take it, even if it has no relevance to your hand because the option reverts to your opponent if you don't take advantage of it. If nothing else, taking the card misleads your opponent about the combinations in your hand. You cannot take up the discard and then immediately put it down — just as at Rummy.

Going Gin and tallying your score

The most difficult (and therefore rewarding) way to go out and win the game is to put all your cards into melds, which is called *going Gin*. If you go Gin, you score 25 points, plus the sum of whatever your opponent fails to make into complete combinations — their unconnected cards, or *deadwood*.

REMEMBER

You must pick up a card, either from the stock or the discard pile, before you go Gin.

To better understand how to score points after you win (and I do assume that you'll win because you're reading this great book), take a look at the cards in Figure 4-6.

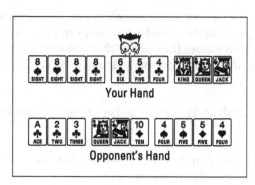

FIGURE 4-6:
The winner collects points from the deadwood in the loser's hand.

The example opponent has 18 points left: two 4s and two 5s add up to 18 points; no calculators allowed! Together with the 25 points you get for going Gin, you score 43 points.

You can play to 100 or 250 points, depending on how long you want the contest to last. (For more on scoring, see the section "Boxing up the scoring system" later in this chapter.)

Knock, knock! Another way to go out

The most intriguing facet of the rules of Gin Rummy, compared to the standard Rummy rules, is that you have more than one way to go out. Instead of forming all your cards into combinations, you have the option to *knock* (which involves literally tapping the table).

You knock when

>> You've put almost all your cards into combinations.

>> The cards that don't make melds total less than or equal to 10 points.

If you meet these criteria, you can knock (just once will do — no matter how happy it makes you feel) and then put your cards down on the table.

After you knock, play stops, and the tallying begins. Your score comes from the deadwood — the cards that aren't part of combinations. If your opponent's deadwood exceeds yours, you pick up the difference between your total and theirs. If your opponent's deadwood doesn't exceed yours, you must face the consequences.

WARNING

Sometimes your opponent can outdo you when you knock because they have an additional way to get rid of their deadwood. They can put down their melds, and those cards don't count toward their score. They can also add their loose cards to your combinations. After your opponent adds any loose cards, only their remaining cards count.

Take a look at the cards in Figure 4-7 to get an idea of how to score after you knock.

If you count up all the cards in Figure 4-7, you see that your 5 points against your opponent's 28 leaves you with 23 points.

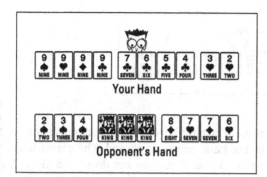

Your Hand

Opponent's Hand

REMEMBER

If you knock, you don't get 25 points for going out.

Glance at the cards in Figure 4-8 for another example of how scoring can work after a player knocks. Your opponent knocks with 6 points, and you appear to have 11. But you can add your ♦J to their run, reducing your total to 1. You now *undercut* your opponent by 5. You score 25 points plus the difference (5), so you get 30 points.

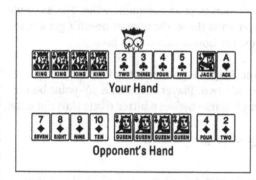

Your Hand

Opponent's Hand

VARIATION

In Oklahoma Gin, which is the most common form of competitive Gin Rummy, the number of the upcard further restricts your ability to knock. You can knock only if your deadwood total is less than or equal to the initial upcard. And if the upcard is an ace, you can go out only by going Gin.

TIP

Always knock if you can do so early in the game, unless your hand is highly suitable for going Gin. For example, if you can knock early in the game with the cards shown in Figure 4-9, go ahead and knock away; only three cards allow you to go Gin, so your chances are below the average expectation. If five or more cards allow you to go Gin, play for Gin instead. The longer the game goes on, the more wary you should be of knocking because your opponent likely has less deadwood and will be able to undercut you.

FIGURE 4-9:
Go ahead and
knock with this
hand.

REMEMBER

In Gin Rummy, the hand doesn't have to be played to conclusion. If the stock gets down to two cards, the hand comes to an end. The player who draws the third-last card can knock or go Gin. If they do not do so and discard, the other player can pick up that discard and go out as well. If not, the game is over. Just throw in the cards and start all over again.

Boxing up the scoring system

When you reach your game-winning target, you get 100 points simply for winning. In addition, you're awarded bonuses based on the number of hands that you win compared to the number of hands your opponent wins. The bonus comes in the form of a *box*, which is 25 points added to your score for each hand you win minus the number of hands your opponent wins. For example, if you play six hands and each player wins three, the winner doesn't get a bonus. But if the winner wins more hands, the bonus comes into play.

Say that Player A and Player B go through six hands in a game. If Player A wins four hands to Player B's two, Player A scores a 50-point bonus. Table 4-1 shows the scoring of a sample game between bitter rivals Harry and Sandy.

Table 4-2 shows the after-game totals.

TABLE 4-1   **Hand-by-Hand Score of a Sample Gin Rummy Game**

Harry's Score	Sandy's Score	Notes
52	—	-Harry went Gin, and Sandy had 27 points in her hand.
—	26	-Harry knocked with 6, but Sandy undercut with only 5 points.
11	—	-Harry knocked with 3 and, Sandy had 14 points.
28	—	-Harry went Gin and caught Sandy with 3 points.
—	27	-Sandy knocked with 6 and caught Harry with 33 points.
41	—	-Harry went Gin, and Sandy had 16 points.

TABLE 4-2

Harry and Sandy's Final Scores

Harry's Score	Sandy's Score	Notes
124	53	Total scores
–53	—	Harry subtracts Sandy's score
71	—	Harry's margin of victory
+100	—	Harry's bonus for winning
+50	—	Harry's box bonus
221	—	Harry's total winning score

If you're fortunate enough to reach the winning post — be it 100 or 250 points — without allowing your opponent to win a single hand, you *blitz*, *schneider*, or *skunk* them, and your final winning score is doubled.

VARIATION In the Oklahoma variation of the game, you get an additional feature to boost the scoring: If the initial card turned over is a spade, all scoring elements are doubled for that one hand, including the box awards. However, the spade upcard has no impact on the strategy of the game.

VARIATION Hollywood Gin Rummy produces a much more complex and potentially expensive scoring system. Instead of keeping a single column of scoring for each player, Hollywood Gin requires three columns for each player.

Each of the three columns records different combinations of scores. You record the first and all subsequent scores for each player in Column 1; the second and all subsequent scores for each player is recorded in both Column 1 and Column 2; and the third and all subsequent scores for each player is recorded in all three columns.

The first player to reach 100 points in a column wins that column; you then score the column as I describe earlier in this section.

Taking Harry and Sandy's game from Tables 4-1 and 4-2, the following table shows how the Hollywood scoring system would compare:

Column 1		Column 2		Column 3
A	B	A	B	A
52		11	27	28
	26	28		41
11		41		
28				

Column 1	Column 2	Column 3
	27	
41		
Column 1 Total		
132	53	
−53		
Victory Margin and Bonus		
79		
+50		
Final Score		
129		

The Hollywood scoring method increases the chances of a blitz, because each player needs to win three hands before registering a score in Column 3. Hollywood Gin Rummy just provides a way to increase the stakes of Gin Rummy.

500 Rummy: Moving the Pile

500 Rummy, like all siblings, shares certain traits with the entire Rummy family. Like an older brother with a car, however, it offers additional attractive features. You can play it with more than four players, the game offers a premium for quick reactions, and you have the opportunity to score plenty of points very quickly.

BEFORE HAND

To play 500 Rummy, you need the following:

>> Three or more players, but five or so players are perfect. (Gin Rummy is a better game for two players; see the previous section.)

>> At least one deck of 52 cards, preferably with two jokers. If you intend to play 500 Rummy with five or more players, a second deck of 54 cards is necessary.

>> Paper and pencil for scoring, unless you have a laptop handy.

VARIATION

You can play 500 Rummy in its original form: without jokers.

Winning at 500 Rummy

The objective of 500 Rummy is to score points by making runs or sets, or adding to your opponents' melds, in order to be the first to get to 500. Unlike in regular

Rummy, where you have to wait until your turn to lay down combinations, you occasionally get the opportunity to preempt other players in 500 Rummy — particularly if they overlook a chance to make a meld or add a card to anyone else's meld.

In contrast to Rummy and Gin Rummy, you aren't restricted to take only the top card of the discard pile. You can take more than one card in order to reach a card lower down, which you can then use in a meld. The other feature of the game is that you score positively for melds you put down, as well as negatively for cards you fail to play. As a consequence, high cards are sought after, rather than shunned, particularly at the start of the game.

Making a square deal

The dealer gives out the cards one at a time, clockwise, starting with the person to the left, until each player has seven cards. The remaining cards form the stock and are placed face-down in a position accessible to every player. The dealer flips over the top card of the stock and places it face-up. This is the first card of the discard pile. Make sure you spread out the discard pile so that all cards are visible. Don't neatly stack it so that only the top card is visible.

Understanding the rules of combination combat

As in basic Rummy, you place combinations of cards from your hand face-up on the table until the end of a hand. There are two types of melds:

>> A **set** consists of three or more cards of the same rank.

>> A **run** consists of three or more consecutive cards of the same suit.

Just as in regular Rummy, you can put down your own melds or extend melds that already sit on the table, which is called *laying off*. You can add the fourth card of the same rank to a group of three. If you are playing with a double deck, a set must consist of cards of the same rank, but of different suits. Alternatively, you can add extra consecutive cards of the same suit to a run at either end. You can add to your combinations or those of other players, but you can't change your mind as to which set you want to add that extra card to later on.

An ace can be counted as high or low at 500 Rummy.

REMEMBER

Because every card you play scores points for you, you keep the cards you add to other players' combinations in front of you. You do not add your cards on to their sequences — they would end up scoring points for your play! You keep the cards face-up in front of you.

All joking apart

Jokers are wild and can stand for any card in a meld. A player putting down a run that includes a joker must identify which card it represents, and this designation can't change. For example, if you put down J-Q-W, the joker (W) represents the king, whereas W-J-Q identifies the joker as a 10.

If you want to make a combination of three cards that includes two jokers (which you normally don't do unless you wanted to pick up a large number of cards from the discard pile), you have to state whether your meld is a set or a run.

Imagine your three cards are the ♠A and two jokers; you have to choose whether the combination represents A-K-Q or A-A-A (you would never choose A-2-3, because that would make your ace into a one-pointer rather than a 15-pointer; see the section "Scoring the numbers game" later in this chapter for scoring info).

If you opt for the set, you don't need to specify which suits the jokers represent. Any player can subsequently lay off a different ace to complete a group of four aces. You can't add a fifth ace, even to a set with jokers in it.

Mastering the game play

The player on the dealer's left begins play. The turn to play passes clockwise. A single turn consists of three parts, performed in sequential order:

1. Drawing.

You must either draw the top card from the stock and put it in your hand without showing it to the other players, or draw one or more cards from the discard pile. You can always draw the top card from the stock or the top card from the discard pile. If you take the top card from the discard pile, you don't have to use it immediately in a meld, but you can't discard that card on this turn.

Some sticklers play that if you take the top card from the discard pile, you must make it into a meld during that turn.

The big difference 500 Rummy offers is that you aren't restricted to take the top card in the discard pile. You may take any card in the discard pile — as long as you immediately combine the card into a new legal combination or lay it off on an existing meld. If you do that, you must also take all the cards above your selected card you melded into your hand.

2. **Combining.**

When your turn arrives, you may, if you want, lay down any valid combinations in your hand by placing them face-up in front of you. You may also lay off cards on existing melds.

3. **Discarding.**

Unless you manage to use up all the cards in your hand (in which case the hand is over), you must make a discard of one card from your hand; put it face-up on top of the discard pile. If you draw more than one card from the discard pile, you may let go of the card that was previously on top of the pile after melding.

Announcing "Game over!"

Play continues until a player makes all their cards into melds or when a player combines all but one of their cards, in which case they can discard the last card.

Alternatively, if no cards are left in the stock and the person to play doesn't want to draw from the discard pile, the hand ends and is scored up. Play comes to a complete stop; no additional sets or runs can be put down.

TIP

At the beginning of a round, the prime object is to acquire as many additional cards as possible. But be careful about picking up a heap of cards from the discard pile if you can see that one or more players are close to going out.

Scoring the numbers game

When the hand is over, you score points for all the sets and runs you have made, using the scoring system below. Any player with cards left loses points, using the following scoring system:

>> **2s through 9s** receive their face value, so for example, an 8 is worth 8 points.

>> **10 through king** are worth 10 points each.

>> **Jokers and aces** score 15 points each — unless the ace is part of an A-2-3 sequence; then it only scores 1 point.

You can have a negative total for a hand — or the whole game — if your laid-down point totals don't exceed the point totals from the cards still in your hand. (Of course, you won't after reading this book, I'm sure!)

Some players count 2s through 9s as 5 points each. The 10s and court cards still count as 10, and jokers count as 15. The ace counts as 5 points rather than 15 if you use it as a low card in a sequence such as A-2-3.

Drawing from the discard pile

Great Rummy players consider it a significant early game advantage to take as many cards from the discard pile as they can. You may change your mind about this strategy, however, if another player looks to be on the verge of going out.

Imagine that at an early point in the game, the discard pile looks like this from bottom up: ♦Q, ♣7, ♠6, ♥9, ♦10, and ♠A.

Assume your hand consists of the following seven cards: ♠K, ♠9, ♥7, ♥4, ♦J, ♣9, and a joker.

If you pick up all the cards from the discard pile, you're obligated to make a combination using the ♦Q (the bottom card). No problem! You put down the ♦Q-♦J-♦10 and the ♠9-♥9-♣9, leaving you with the ♠A, ♠K, ♥7, ♣7, ♠6, ♥4, and a joker.

You could have put down the joker into a run of spades or a set of 7s, but that move would have been premature. Instead, you stay patient and wait for a 7 or the ♠Q to appear on the discard pile. You may also get lucky and pick up one of those cards from the stock on your next turn.

Early in a game, if the discard pile grows large, your hand may have no safe discard. In such an instance, try to match a card near the top of the pile rather than one far down. That way, anyone who you help to complete a meld only gets to pick up part of the pile, not the whole thing.

Calling "Rummy!"

Unlike almost every other game of Rummy, 500 allows you to preempt other players and take their turn, if you're fast enough to spot an error in discarding.

If a player lets go of a card that they could add to another meld or if they discard and leave a complete set in the pile, you can shout "Rummy!" and pick up the relevant section of the discard pile that includes the set. After your bounty, you continue as if it was your normal turn. When you discard, the player to your left is next to play, as usual.

For example, say that you have already put down ♣9-♣10-♣J, and the discard pile looks like this: ♦8, ♠6, ♥5, ♠Q, ♦9, and ♣4.

If another player throws away the ♣8, you can shout "Rummy," retrieve that card, and add it to your run (keeping the card in front of you). Equally, anyone who pitches the ♦7 will hear the same shout and see someone pick up the whole pile and put down the ♦7-♦8-♦9.

This gives rise to a general point of strategy: If you pick up the ♥8 from the stock pile to add to the ♥7 and ♥6 in your hand, don't put them down on this turn. Wait until your next turn, and pick up the discard pile from the ♥5 upward. If you put the run down on this turn, someone else may preempt you to the punch.

Note: You can't call out "Rummy!" after your own discard. In fact, some people play that you can only call out Rummy to take the top discard, not for cards deeper in the discard pile. I call those people spoilsports.

VARIATION

Many games require a player who goes out to keep one card for a discard at the end of the turn. In this version, you can't make combinations out of all your cards, leaving yourself nothing to discard. This variant is called *floating*. If you have no discard, play continues around the table while you float. When the turn comes back to you (if no one else can go out), you can draw a card from the stock and discard it, which ends the game. (You can also take several cards from the discard pile and make combinations out of all but one of them, giving you a discard to end the game.)

If you meld the card you draw from the stock or all the cards you draw from the discard pile, you get to float again for another round. If you draw cards from the discard pile, meld some, discard one, and still have at least one card in your hand, the game continues in its normal fashion.

WARNING

If you play with the floating variation, some people require that your final discard not be a card that can be melded. If you use this rule and err by trying to go out with a playable card, someone can yell "Rummy!" and meld your card, leaving you a floater again.

Chapter **5**

Canasta

One reason for Canasta's widespread popularity is its use of wild cards, which make the game high scoring and unpredictable. Canasta is also one of the few partnership games (other than Euchre and Bridge; see chapters 10 and 12, respectively) where the players can work in unison, although it also functions perfectly well as a two- or three-handed game.

The rules to Canasta may seem a little cockeyed, but bear with me. After you acquaint yourself with a couple of unique ideas, you'll have smooth sailing and a great way to pass the time with a few competitive friends. Additionally, the game has spawned two very popular variations, Hand and Foot, and Modern American Canasta, both of which I discuss later.

BEFORE HAND

To play Canasta, you need the following:

» **Four players:** You can also play Canasta with five players (two against three, with one player sitting out each hand) or with six players (three against three, with one of each trio sitting out in rotation).

» **Two decks of 52 cards, including the jokers in each deck (108 cards total):** The backs of the cards don't have to be the same, but identical backs do look better.

» **Paper and pencil for scoring:** Unless you have a math whiz in the bunch. But is the math whiz prone to tell little fibs?

Accepting Your Canasta Mission

The object of Canasta is to pick up cards and fit them into groupings. You score points for the groupings, or melds, so the more melds, the merrier. The first team to score 5,000 points wins, and if both teams hit five grand on the same hand, the team with the higher score wins.

Making melds

You score points by making *melds*, which are combinations of three to seven or more cards of the same rank. For a meld to be valid, all the cards in it must have the same rank, such as a meld of queens, but they don't have to be of the same suit.

A meld of seven cards, such as seven 9s or seven kings, is called a *Canasta*. Making a Canasta is especially valuable for a number of reasons: You need to make a Canasta to go out, and it also helps your score mount quickly.

Getting wild and forsaking suits

The 2s and jokers in the deck are *wild cards,* meaning that they can represent any value you want them to. Each meld can include one wild card, but a meld must have at least two non-wild cards in it and no more than three wild cards. For example, a meld of three can contain one wild card, and a meld of four can have two wild cards. A meld that includes no wild cards is known as a *natural* or *clean* meld. A meld with one or more wild cards in it is a *mixed* or *dirty* meld.

Suits don't play a role in Canasta (except when it comes to choosing partners; see the section "Picking partners" later in this chapter); a meld of three queens can consist of the ♣Q, ♦Q, and a wild card. The only real significance to the suits lies in the distinction between red and black 3s, which I explained in the sections "Laying down the red 3s" and "Separating the black 3s," later in this chapter.

Looking at some legal melds

Melds can take on many different guises, including the ones shown in Figure 5-1.

FIGURE 5-1:
Legal melds follow the wild card and ranking rules.

If you try to put down a meld like the ♠7-♣2-♦2, you won't get too far; this meld is illegal, because it contains too few natural cards; at least two natural cards are the minimum requirement. Similarly, ♠7-♠8-♠9 isn't a legal meld. The only legal melds are groups of the same rank, not runs of the same suit.

Calculating the value of your cards and melds

Each card has a scoring value, and these values are important, especially when it comes to laying down the first meld for a partnership. (I discuss the minimum value required to lay down the first meld in the section "Making the first meld for your partnership," later in this chapter.) Fortunately, the card values aren't too complicated:

» **Jokers:** 50 points each

» **2s and aces:** 20 points each

>> **Kings through 8s:** 10 points each

>> **7s through the ♠3 and ♣3:** 5 points each

REMEMBER

You can't use red 3s in melds. See the section "Laying down the red 3s," later in this chapter, for more information.

Picking partners

Canasta game play focuses on making melds, scoring points, and eventually going out as a partnership, so the first thing to do is determine the lineups.

You can pick partners based on your company, such as girls against guys or couple against couple, or you can draw cards, with the two highest cards playing together against the two lowest cards. If two players draw cards of the same rank (two kings, for example), the rank of the suits decides which card is higher — the spade is the highest-ranking suit, followed by hearts, diamonds, and clubs. Partners sit opposite each other.

Dealing and creating a discard pile

After forming your partnerships, each player draws a card randomly from the deck. The person who draws the highest card plays first, and the dealer is the player to that person's right.

The dealer shuffles the deck, and after an opponent cuts it, the dealer doles out 11 cards to each player, one by one, in a clockwise rotation. At the end of each hand, the deal moves clockwise one place.

After each player receives 11 cards, the dealer turns up one card to the side of the *stock* (the remaining cards) to start the *discard pile*. If the card the dealer turns is a red 3 or a wild card (a joker or a 2), they turn up another card, placing the card on top of the discard pile, until they come to one that is neither a red 3 nor a wild card.

Laying down the red 3s

The red 3s are like bonus cards — they play no major part in the strategy of the game, but they can score your side some extra points if you're lucky enough to draw them. You can find out how much they earn you by checking out the section "Tallying Your Scores," later in this chapter.

As soon as you pick up a red 3, you must put it face-up in front of you and pick up another card from the stock. If you pick up the discard pile and it includes either the ♥3 or ♦3, you still put the card down in front of you, but you don't need to take a replacement card from the stock.

If you pick up a red 3 and forget to put the card down at that time, you can do it during a later turn without penalty. If the game ends, however, and you have a red 3 in your hand, you incur a 500-point penalty.

Moving around the table

After the deal, the game starts. The player to the dealer's left (the person who drew the highest card at the start) picks up a card from the stock or the whole of the discard pile (see the following section, "Picking up the discard pile," for more information; you can't pick up from the discard pile at all until the move on which you make your first meld). That player can either put down a meld or hold on to their cards. They finish their turn by placing a card face-up on the discard pile, covering all the other cards so that their discard is the only card visible.

The play moves in a clockwise rotation, with each player picking up a card, making a meld or holding on to their cards, and then discarding, until a player goes out by getting rid of all their cards but one, and then discarding the last card, which finishes the hand.

Drawing more than one card from the stock carries no penalty. However, you must show the card to all other players, and the next player has the option of taking the returned card or shuffling it into the stock.

Discarding is a critical part of Canasta; if the discard pile grows to a significant size, one false discard can be disastrous. Err on the side of caution by throwing out what you're sure your opponents don't want. And make the dangerous discards early — the cost of an error is much cheaper then. How do you know what discards are dangerous? You can discover what your opponents don't want by what they throw away and by what they don't pick up from the discard pile.

Picking up the discard pile

You can pick up the top card from the discard pile to create or improve a meld. However, if you choose to take the top card, you must put down a meld immediately, using the discard in that meld.

After you put down your meld, you take the entire discard pile and add it to your hand. You immediately grow a huge hand — if there were plenty of cards in the discard pile when you picked it up, of course. You also have the ability to make many melds and score points.

REMEMBER

You can't take that top discard unless you can make a meld with it or add it to an existing meld or Canasta — and sometimes not even then! I get to the restrictions in the section "Freezing the discard pile," later in this chapter.

After you pick up the discard pile, you can make any further melds you want. When you discard, your turn ends.

After you or your partner make the initial meld for the partnership, you can pick up the top card from the discard pile (and thus the whole pile) on your turn and put it down in a meld of three that includes a joker. Or you can pick up the pile if the top card matches one of your melds. But this only applies so long as the pile isn't *frozen* (no wild cards are in the pile — see the following section for more details).

WARNING

If you pick up the discard pile in error, either as a result of a miscalculation (the meld you envisioned isn't high-scoring enough; see the following section, "Making the first meld for your partnership") or because you can't make a legal meld with the card, you incur a 100-point penalty.

Making the first meld for your partnership

The first meld for each partnership must be worth a certain number of points before you can put it down. Here's the bad news first: Not only does this requirement apply for the first hand, but also for all subsequent hands, and the task gets more arduous as the game goes on. The good news: When you make the first meld, you lift the load from your partner's back simultaneously.

You must meet the following requirements to put down your first meld of the hand:

>> You must use the top card from the discard pile in your initial meld. If you make your first meld entirely from your hand, you do not get to pick up the discard pile.

>> The first meld can contain only the top card from the discard pile. After you meet that initial requirement, however, you can pick up the discard pile and add to the meld or make new melds by using cards from the discard pile.

>> You must make the initial meld on your own — your partner can't help you out.

>> You can put down more than one meld to make up the required numeric total (see Table 5-1), but all the cards that make up the additional melds must be from holdings already in your hand (not from the discard pile).

>> The first meld must be worth a certain number of points, and the point totals increase as the game progresses. The value of the melds you put down depends on your team's cumulative total at the start of the hand, as you see in Table 5-1. Refer to the section "Calculating the value of your cards and melds" earlier in this chapter for more information on assigning points to cards.

TABLE 5-1   ## Initial Meld Point Requirements

Your Side's Total Score	Points to Put Down a Meld
Negative	0 (any meld will do)
0 to 1,495	50
1,500 to 2,995	90
3,000 or more	120

WARNING

If you put down an initial meld that doesn't meet the minimum point requirement, you can put down additional melds on that same turn to make up the required total without penalty. You can also take back your attempt, but the minimum total you have to meet the next time you try goes up by 10 points — quite a severe penalty.

TIP

Bear in mind that you can pick up the top card from the discard pile in the process of making your first meld of the hand. It's better to make your first meld by using that card rather than to make melds purely from cards already in your hand. Even if you can make the initial meld by using only cards from your original 11 cards, doing so is poor strategy; wait to put down melds until you can pick up the discard pile in doing so.

If you put down three queens and three kings from your own hand, for example, you know that the player who discards before you won't throw a king or queen to enable you to pick up the pile, but they may do so if you haven't shown them the melds in your hand. Don't let your opponents know what you're collecting — until it's too late!

REMEMBER

Also, the bonus for a Canasta, ♦3, or ♥3 can't be taken into account in the initial meld. That comes at the end of the game, not when you put the meld down.

One additional exception: If after having drawn from the stock you can meld your entire hand (including a Canasta) with or without a final discard, then you may go out at once, even if the values of the cards you put down are less than your side's current, initial, minimum point requirements.

TIP

When the initial meld requirement is 50, do not waste wild cards to make your initial set. If you do, you often find picking up the discard pile very hard. If you wait a go or two, you may be able to use your wild card more effectively. With a high, initial meld requirement, make your first set as fast as possible (using the smallest number of cards to do so).

Unfreezing the deck with the initial meld

The discard pile is automatically frozen for your side at the start of the game until your team makes its initial meld. However, that does not mean you can't use it — but you can only use it under specific circumstances, as I explain in the following section, "Freezing the discard pile." Until the first meld comes, each player on the team can only take cards from the stock.

Because the discard pile is frozen, you can't use the top discard (and thus pick up the pile) unless you can use it on that turn in a meld with two cards of the same rank — in making that meld, no wild cards are allowed unless your combination already includes three natural cards.

REMEMBER

Bear in mind that after you or your partner make the initial meld for your side, this restriction is lifted — but as I explain in the following section, when either side discards a wild card, the pile freezes again for both sides.

Freezing the discard pile

You can use wild cards (2s and jokers) for whatever card you want them to be. Wild cards are also *stoppers* — which means that you won't normally be able to pick up a discarded wild card (and thus the pile as a whole) if the previous player lets go of one of them as a discard.

If you throw a wild card away (normally an act of desperation), it *freezes* the discard pile — which makes it more difficult for subsequent players, including yourself and your partner, to pick up the discard pile. Freezing doesn't make taking the discard pile impossible — just harder. If the pile is frozen, any subsequent player can only pick up the top card from the discard pile if that player can use it to form a natural meld, using two cards of the same rank from their hand.

When you throw away a card that freezes the deck, be it permanently or temporarily, you place the card sideways to the rest of the deck.

The first player to make a natural meld (a meld with no wild cards) with a set that utilizes the top card of the discard pile "unfreezes" the discard pile, allowing that player to pick up the discard pile.

TIP

When trying to prevent your opponents from taking the discard pile, throwing a black 3 is always safe. Wild cards are safe, but they come at a cost. Throw the cards that your opponent has not picked up before, or cards that you can see a lot of — either in your own melds or in your opponents'.

Separating the black 3s

The black 3s require some special consideration. You have to keep the following things in mind when you come across one of the black 3s in play:

>> Like wild cards, the black 3s block the discard pile, but only for one turn. Do not put them down sideways onto the discard pile — as soon as they are covered the pile is no longer frozen.

>> You can only make black 3s into melds on the turn when you go out.

>> You can't meld black 3s with wild cards.

The ♠3 and the ♣3 really play no helpful part in the game for the player who picks them up, other than their tactical value to prevent the next player from having a chance to take the discard pile. The black 3s can be a bit of a drag, because they're so tough to make into melds.

TIP

Don't discard the black 3s prematurely. Save them for the last possible moment, when you think that the next player may take a large discard pile if you put down a helpful discard. As guaranteed stoppers, black 3s have significant strategic value.

Building a Canasta

A *Canasta* is a meld of seven or more cards. Your partnership must make a Canasta before either of you can go out; only one Canasta per team is necessary. A Canasta can start as a meld of three cards that either you or your partner can build up to the required seven.

A Canasta can include wild cards. A natural or clean Canasta has no wild cards, and is worth more than a mixed or dirty Canasta, which includes wild cards. See the section "Tallying Your Scores," later in this chapter.

When you make a Canasta, square up the pile so that only the top card is visible — a red card if it's a natural Canasta, a black card if it's mixed. Set the pile off to the side. You can still add more cards to it, of course, but it helps your team's strategy to know whether the Canasta is already mixed.

TIP

When you start a meld with natural cards only, try not to let it get dirty by adding wild cards, even if so doing can make a Canasta. You have two reasons for doing this: It scores more points, and it prevents your opponents from discarding this card — for fear of letting you make a clean Canasta.

On your turn, you can add cards at any point to your team's melds, but not to your opponents' melds, after drawing your card, but before discarding.

The partnership's assets are joint; you add to your partner's meld. The player who makes the first meld gets to herd the partnership's stable of melds.

Going out

You can't get rid of all your cards and go out until your team makes a Canasta (see the previous section, "Building a Canasta," for details). To go out, you can either make your whole hand into melds, or you can make a discard as you go out — the choice is up to you. The hand stops as soon as one player goes out.

Going out without first making a Canasta carries a penalty of 100 points. After picking up your card from the stock, and before you put down your hand to go out, you can, if you want, ask your partner, "May I go out?" You have to abide by your partner's decision, but you don't have to ask the question at all. If you don't abide by the decision, or you ask the question after putting down your cards, you're fined 100 points, and your opponents can stop you from going out if they want. Similarly, if your partner gives you permission to go out and you can't, that costs you 100 points.

TIP

Asking your partner if you can go out gives them the chance to tell you "No" and then put down the melds in their hand on their next turn so they won't be caught with too many unnecessary points when you go out on your next turn. During play, you can ask the other players how many cards they have left. The answer can help you decide whether to go for a big pick-up of the discard pile; you may not want to be left holding a massive hand if a player from the other team is about to go out.

End-game strategy

In Canasta, you try to kick your opponents when they're down; go for the biggest possible hand when you've made melds and they haven't. Conversely, cut your losses if it seems that your opponents have all the cards by terminating the game as quickly as possible.

If you use up the whole stock, the game essentially comes to a stop. But it may continue for a short while longer, because the player who takes the last card of the stock throws away a card, and if the next player can take this card and add it to one of their existing melds, they must do so — and take the discard pile, too. They then discard a card, and the same rule applies to the next player. As soon as the next player can't use the discard, the game ends, and the usual scoring takes place. If the last card of the stock is a red 3, the game ends at that point.

You make a *force-play* by forcing the next player to take the pile of cards by discarding something they *must* pick up. Create a force-play when you want to land the next player with a big pile of cards that they can't get rid of. The play has an element of danger to it, but if the player has only a few cards left in their hand, you can be relatively confident that this strategy can succeed.

Conversely, if you think that the next player wants to pick up the pile, prevent them from doing so by discarding a black 3 or a wild card, which, as you know, they can't pick up.

TIP

Do not always put down your melds as soon as you form them in your hand. You make put-down melds easier for your opponents, maybe using up wild cards, if they can see you are close to going out. They may hold sets in their hands, trying to complete clean Canastas but put them down if they can see you are close to going out. Try to surprise them by going out when they are left holding melds in their hands.

Tallying Your Scores

At the end of the hand, as soon as one player goes out, the scoring starts. Add up the points for the bonuses and melds and subtract the negative points from that score.

The bonuses you may be eligible for are as follows:

>> You get a 100-point bonus for going out.

>> You get a 200-point bonus for going out *concealed*, which means going out without first putting down any melds. If you can go out with a concealed hand after your opponents pick up a large pile, you can reduce the damage caused by the points left in your partner's hand.

>> Every Canasta is worth 500 points if it has no wild cards, or 300 points if it is a mixed Canasta, with wild cards. A Canasta of wild cards is worth 1,000 points.

>> Every red 3 your team has is worth 100 points. If you have both pairs of red 3s, you get a 400-point bonus for 800 points in all. If your side hasn't made a meld, you subtract the bonus values of the red 3s from your score.

Then you add up the score for your melds (refer to the earlier section, "Calculating the value of your cards and melds," for more info). And subtract from that the total negative points that go against you, for the cards left in your hand.

TIP

Consider going out if you can to leave yourself just below one of the critical points of moving into a new zone for the initial meld requirement. You are better off having a total score of 1,495 rather than 1,525, because you need fewer points to get started on the next hand.

VARIATION

Modern American Canasta is a younger cousin of the game of Canasta I explain here. The game is played to a score of 8,500 and has many variations. For the full story, visit https://www.pagat.com/, but following are some of the main differences:

>> Melds of 7s and aces are subject to special rules. You cannot use wild cards to make a meld of 7s at all. Additionally, if you start a meld but do not complete the Canasta, you are subject to penalty. A meld of aces cannot contain wild cards unless it is the initial meld. Again, if you start a meld and do not complete the Canasta, you are subject to penalties.

>> Initial point requirements exist for your first play, but you can get around them by making your first play a natural Canasta or a Canasta of wild cards.

>> Certain special hands allow you to go out after drawing, without discarding.

  • A *Straight* contains one card of every rank from ace to king plus a joker.

  • *Pairs* has seven pairs of cards; no jokers or 3s allowed. Also the hand must either have no wild cards or include a pair of 2s, 7s, and aces.

  • *Garbage* consists of two sets of four of a kind and two sets of three of a kind.

Making Do with Two (or Three): Short-Handed Canasta

VARIATION

Canasta works perfectly well as a two-handed game, and the rules are almost identical to the four-handed variety (refer to the section "Accepting Your Canasta Mission," earlier in this chapter) — except, of course, that all partnership elements don't come into play. The major differences when playing with two players include the following:

>> Each player gets 15 cards rather than 11.

>> When your turn comes, you can either take the top discard or draw from the stock. But if you draw from the stock, you take *two* cards and discard only one. Your hand grows fast, effectively speeding up the game.

>> You need two Canastas (any variety counts) to go out.

Most of the penalties are eliminated in this version of the game because you don't have a partner who can benefit from any unauthorized information.

VARIATION

The three-handed game, which is often called Cut-Throat Canasta, is very similar to the two-handed variety, except for the following differences:

>> Each player gets 13 cards.

>> The first player to pick up the discard pile plays against the other two in tandem for the rest of the hand. At the end of the hand, the lone player gets a score based on their hand only; the partnership gets a collective score in every respect but one — the red 3s.

>> The red 3s only count for the person who turns them up, not for the tandem; in all other respects, the team's scores are identical.

>> You traditionally play to 7,500 points.

Hand and Foot

Hand and Foot is a homegrown American variety of the South American game Canasta. After you read the previous sections and familiarize yourself with Canasta, figuring out Hand and Foot is like counting fingers and toes!

The game is best played by four players in two partnerships or by six players in two teams of three. But you can play the game with any number of individuals (up to eight), so no, you don't have any excuse to keep away the annoying neighbors.

For the four-handed game, you need the following items:

>> **Five complete decks of cards,** including two jokers for each deck — 270 cards in all. Add a deck for every additional player you use.

>> **Paper and pencil,** and a scoremaster to keep track of the tally.

Getting started

After you find your lucky seat and ready the refreshment tray, follow these steps to get the game going:

>> Choose your partners, or give each player one card face-up. Lowest card is the dealer, and the partners are selected on the same basis as in Canasta. Partners sit opposite each other.

>> The dealer takes part of the deck and deals out four stacks of 11 cards face-down, one for each player — what's known as the *hand.*

>> The dealer gives out four more stacks of 11 cards face-down — what's known as the *foot* — you don't look at the foot until your hand is used up. The hand will come to an end when a player uses up both their hand and their foot.

>> The remainder of the cards is the stock (you can split the cards into two or more piles to stop them from falling over!).

>> Turn the top card of the stock up to form the discard pile. The player to the left of the dealer plays, and play progresses clockwise.

You can also deal out 13 cards to everyone in both the hand and foot. In fact a bunch of other variations exist. Check out rogerdem.tripod.com/variations.htm for other possible ways to play.

Knowing your objective

Over the course of four deals, which make up a complete game, the object is for each partnership to score more points than their opponents by making melds, just as in standard Canasta. The deal passes clockwise for each hand.

The winner of the game is the partnership with the most points after four deals. Unlike Canasta, Hand and Foot is not played to a specific target score.

VARIATION

The first to 10,000 points wins. This variation obviously leads to a much longer game.

Putting down melds

Melds are combinations of at least three cards of the same rank. As in Canasta, no runs are allowed, and a minimum point score is required before you can put down your first meld. See the following section, "Laying your initial meld," for details.

You may add to your partner's melds at your turn to play, but not to your opponent's. A partnership can't have two incomplete melds of the same card. For example, if you have a meld of 8s, your partner must add to your meld instead of starting their own until your meld has seven cards and is therefore complete.

Laying your initial meld

If you make your first meld with cards from the discard pile, you must include at least two natural cards from your hand; you can add more cards, including wild cards, to the meld to meet the minimum-points requirement. If you pick up from the discard pile, you must use the top card for the meld. To achieve the minimum requirement, you can't use other cards from the discard pile, but you can use a complete meld from your hand, with or without wild cards. The points requirements for the initial meld are

>> **1st hand:** 50 points

>> **2nd hand:** 90 points

>> **3rd hand:** 120 points

>> **4th hand:** 150 points

Red 3s and the Canasta bonus don't count toward the starting requirement.

TIP

Try to keep your melds clean for as long as you can. This allows you to keep wild cards in your hand — which gives you more options with the discard pile — and also makes for potentially high-scoring melds.

Playing your hand (and foot)

At each turn, the player either picks up two cards from the stock and discards one card or picks up the top discard from the stock — just the top card — so long as it can form into a meld, using two or more natural cards. If so, the player gets to take the next six cards from the top of the discard pile as well, making seven cards in all. The player then discards and ends the turn.

REMEMBER

To take from the discard pile at any point in the game, you must use at least two natural cards from your hand to match the discard — not one natural card and a wild card, for example.

VARIATION

Some people play a variation that states after you successfully take the top discard, you pick up the whole pile, not just the top seven cards. Some play a variation where you take five cards total.

TIP

Try to remember the last few discards so you have some idea of what you're picking up — this may influence whether you want to pick up the top discard later in the game.

Wild cards

Not all cards are normal. Twos and jokers are wild, just as in standard Canasta. You can use wild cards to make melds, but if you're making a meld of normal (non-wild) cards, more than half of any meld must be natural. You can, however, make a meld entirely of wild cards. Jokers and 2s can be discarded — not that you would normally do this. If you do, you temporarily block the discard pile. The next player can only pick the top card from the discard pile if they can make a set of 2s or of jokers. In that case, they can take the top seven cards, as before.

Threes

Threes cannot be melded. The only way to get rid of black 3s is to discard them, one at a time. Black 3s temporarily block the deck — the next player may not pick them up. You can put a red 3 down in front of you as part of your turn, as if it were a meld, in which case you score points for each one (see the section "Assessing card values," later in this chapter) and you then take a new card from the stock.

VARIATION

Some people play that you can only get rid of red 3s in the discard pile — in which case, they freeze the discard pile forever. You cannot pick up any card below a red 3 until the entire stock is used up.

Clearing your hand and starting the foot

If you combine all but one card from your hand, you discard to clear out your hand altogether, and that ends your turn. You pick up your foot, and start playing it at your next turn in the normal fashion. If, however, you put all your cards into melds, without a card left over, then your turn does not end. Instead, you can continue your turn by picking up your foot and playing on.

TIP

If you begin your foot before your partner, don't complete your team's melds because it may restrict your partner's ability to get rid of their remaining cards from the hand.

Going out

The game ends when you use up your foot, with or without a discard, and you make the required number of clean, dirty, and wild sets. Your side must have one clean Canasta, one dirty Canasta, and one consisting exclusively of wild cards. If you play with a partner, they must have a foot started before you can go out. Going out earns you a bonus as well.

After one team goes out, all the cards left in the other players' hands count against them. If a player hasn't started getting rid of the foot, the points in the foot still count against them. As in standard Canasta, you must (or, according to some people, *may*) ask your partner's permission before going out, and you must abide by their decision.

VARIATION

You can play a variation where two clean and two dirty Canastas are necessary. Some people play that a wild Canasta isn't necessary.

WARNING

As soon as your opponents start using up their foot piles, be careful about taking from the discard pile unless you can be sure that the benefit outweighs the potential cost. When the end of the hand is near, make sure you get rid of your hand to get to your foot as soon as possible.

Assessing card values

When you finish the hand, add up the points for your side's melds and Canastas, the bonuses for going out, or for red 3s, and then take off for any cards left in your side's hand and foot. This is the scoring table:

» The bonus for going out is 100 points.

» Each red 3 is worth 100 points.

- » 4s through 7s are worth 5 points.

- » 8s through kings are worth 10 points.

- » Aces and 2s are worth 20 points.

- » Jokers are worth 50 points.

- » Any red 3 left in your hand at the end of the game costs you 500 points, and black 3s in your hand are worth –5 points. (**Note:** If you do not get around to looking at your foot, any red 3 still costs you 500 points.)

- » A completed meld of seven cards (also known as a *pile,* or clean Canasta) is worth 500 points. A clean Canasta has a maximum of seven cards.

- » A dirty Canasta is worth 300 points and can have no more than three wild cards in it.

- » A wild Canasta, consisting entirely of wild cards, is worth 1,500 points — and worth trying to complete as soon as possible because of the high score associated with it.

VARIATION

You can play so that both clean and dirty Canastas can be extended beyond seven cards, but remember: A dirty Canasta must always have more natural cards than wild cards.

TIP

At the start of the game, go for the high-value cards and let the low-value cards go. As the game goes on and players get closer to going out, you should revise this strategy. If you say no when your partner asks if they can go out, make sure to unload everything you can on your next turn. You should only say no if you have a meld or two in your hand you want to get rid of at once.

Chapter **6**

Eights

Until I started writing this chapter, I had no idea that so many varieties of games come from such a simple start. This chapter takes you on a tour of several games in the Eights family. Eights appeals to everyone because while an element of strategy exists in the game, you can play it at the simple level of getting rid of one of your cards at every turn, without any pre-planning, and still win if the cards cooperate.

BEFORE
HAND

To play Eights, you need the following:

» **Two or more players:** There is no upper limit for players, so long as you have more than one deck of cards. If you only have the one deck, six is about the upper limit of players.

» **At least one standard 52-card deck of cards:** No jokers appear in most versions of Eights, but you may need at least one more deck of cards because the game can allow for large numbers of players.

» **Paper and pencil for scoring:** Whatever the size of the group, someone needs to be fast with the pencil and paper to keep score.

Eights: Simple Is as Simple Does

Eights, also known as Crazy Eights, is an ideal game for younger children because no game is easier. The basic rules are very simple; after you know them, you can play with friends and family of any age or experience level.

The object of the game is to be the first to dispose of all your cards. Everyone plays individually, no matter how many players participate. The first player to go out scores points according to the cards left in their opponents' hands (see the later section "Paying the price when your opponent goes out"). The first player to reach 250 points wins.

Dealing the cards

The players cut for the deal, with the person drawing the lowest card awarded the task. You deal the cards one card at a time, clockwise and face-down. Each deal progresses one place to the first dealer's left.

Each player starts with the same number of cards. With two to four players, each player gets seven cards. With more than four players, each player gets five cards. When the number of players climbs above six, add a second deck.

Playing 8s and suits

After all the cards go out to the players, the dealer puts the remainder of the deck, or the *stock*, face-down in the middle of the table and turns over the top card to start the discard pile. The player to the dealer's left is the first to act, and they have three distinct choices about which card to play:

>> They may play a card that coincides with the suit (clubs, spades, diamonds, or hearts) or the rank (2s, jacks, and so on) of the top card.

>> They may play an 8. All 8s are *wild*, meaning that you can play an 8 at any time, no matter what the previously played card was. Moreover, when you play an 8, you can nominate any suit (but not a rank), and the next player must play a card of the nominated suit or put down another 8 and earn the right to name a new (or the same) suit.

If they can do neither, they must pick up a card from the stock. (If the first card the dealer turns over is an 8, the first player can play whatever they want.)

>> They may pick also up the top card from the stock and add it to their hand if they are unwilling or unable to play a card. After a player takes a card from the stock, the play passes clockwise to the next player. You may not pass, then play a card that you pick up from the stock. Your turn is over after you pass.

Some people say you must play if you can. Some say that you can put down the card that you pick up from the stock. Still others insist on your continuing to pick up cards from the stock until you get to a card that you can legally play.

It isn't necessarily *right* to play a card just because you *can*. For example, you may not want to let go of an 8 early in the game so you can dictate what suit is played at the end of the hand. Also, building up a supply of cards in one suit (or *cornering a suit*) early in the game can be an advantage because it allows you to make a series of moves at the end of the game when no one else can play, forcing them to pick up cards.

Some people require that you must play a card if you can, preventing you from adding to your hand whenever you like.

If the first player elects to play a card, they place their card on top of the discard pile. Their card now dictates what the next player to their left can do. That player has the same three choices: They can follow suit or match the rank of the card just played, play an 8, or pick up a card from the stock.

And so the play goes on until someone goes out. For example, if the first card turned over is the ♠7, the first player can play the ♦7. That card allows the second player to play the ♦Q. The third player must play a diamond, a queen, or an 8, or they can pick up.

When you reduce your hand to one card, you must announce "one card" immediately as you play your next-to-last card.

If you forget to say "one card" and other players notice (they will!), you must pick up two cards from the stock.

Paying the price when your opponent goes out

The game concludes when one player goes out. At that point, the winner assesses the damage they have caused the other players:

>> Each *court card* (aces, kings, queens, and jacks) is worth 10 points.

>> All other cards, except the 8s, are charged at face value.

>> The 8s come in at a painful 50 points each.

The winner collects the points that remain in their opponents' hands. Folks usually play that the first player to 250 points wins.

When the game seems to be reaching its finale, make sure to unload your 8s as fast as you can, because the penalty for holding an 8 at the end of the game outweighs the tactical advantage in keeping an 8 to play later.

Mau Mau: Staking Out a Stock Pile

Mau Mau is the German version of Eights, and its pronunciation rhymes with *pow pow*. It offers the simplicity of Eights but with a few twists thrown in.

To play Mau Mau, you need the following:

>> **Three to five players,** with each player battling individually.

>> **A standard deck of 52 cards,** with the 2s through 6s removed.

>> **Pencil and paper for scoring,** with one eager scorekeeper.

After you select a dealer for the first hand by cutting the deck and nominating the person who draws the lowest card, each player receives five cards. The dealer stacks the rest of the cards face-down in the middle of the table as the *stock.*

The dealer turns up the top card of the stock to start a separate pile, and the first player must play a card that matches the turned-up card either in rank or suit. Alternatively, they may play a jack, which acts as a wild card, allowing them to name the suit that the next player must follow. The suit that they choose doesn't need to be the suit of the jack that they play. (If the first card the dealer turns over is a jack, the first player can play any card they want.)

The play then moves clockwise to the next player, who must play a card that matches, either in rank or suit, the card that the first player put down, or they must play a card in the suit announced after the laying of a jack.

A player who can't *follow suit* (play a card in the correct suit) or *rank* (play a card of the same number as the last card played) must draw one card from the stock, as long as any cards remain in the stock. If no cards remain in the stock, the turn passes to the left. After picking up from the stock, they may play that card if they can, or they may choose to keep it in their hand. Whether they play a card or not, the turn moves clockwise, and the next player has the same options.

Even if you can play one of the cards in your hand, you can choose to make a draw. The only justification for this is if you want to hold on to a jack.

VARIATION

Many players introduce special rules for cards other than the jacks. For example, on the play of a 7, the next player must pick up two cards, or on the play of an 8 the next player skips their turn. I like these variations, and you can add more if you feel like it, such as using a 10 to reverse the direction of the play.

The first person to go out says "Mau," unless the last card played is a jack, in which case they say "Mau Mau," thereby doubling the penalties to the other players. If you forget to say "Mau" or "Mau Mau," you do not win. You must pick up four cards, and the game continues.

At the point that a player goes out, all the other players are penalized by the value of their cards, according to the following scale:

>> **7s and 8s** = 0 points

>> **9s** = 9 points

>> **10s** = 10 points

>> **Jacks** = 20 points

>> **Queens** = 3 points

>> **Kings** = 4 points

>> **Aces** = 11 points

VARIATION

As an alternative scoring scale, you can make jacks worth 2 points each and 8s and 7s worth face value. I prefer this alternative, because I don't like getting rid of all my cards and catching an opponent with no points at all, even though they have cards left in their hand.

The first to accumulate 100 penalty points loses and buys the drinks. Of course, if you are not playing close to a bar, you can use this scoring system with the low score being the winner, or you can play for stakes.

Neuner: Matching and Stacking

As with the game of Eights (see the first section of this chapter), Neuner, which sounds like *noyner* and is German for *"nines,"* involves matching cards to achieve the ultimate goal of going out. The danger that comes with Neuner, however, is that your hand can grow to unspeakable proportions as you wait for luck to come your way.

To play Neuner, you need the following:

>> **Three to five players**

>> **A standard deck of 52 cards**

Remove the 2s through 6s and add a joker, making a total of 33 cards in play (use the ♠2 if your deck doesn't have a joker).

>> **Paper and pencil for scoring**

After you select a dealer for the first hand by cutting the deck and nominating the person who draws the lowest card, the dealer gives five cards to each player and places the rest of the deck in the middle of the table, to create the *stock* (discard pile), turning over the top card to start the discard pile. The player to the dealer's left starts, with play progressing in the clockwise direction.

The first player must play a card that matches the turned-up card in rank or suit. Alternatively, they may play either a joker or a 9, which act as a wild card, allowing them to name the suit that the next player must follow. If the following player also lays a wild card, they name the suit to be played next.

If the first upcard is a joker, the player to the dealer's left can play any card first. If the upcard is a 9, they must follow the suit of the 9 or play a wild card.

If a player is unable to play any of the cards in their hand (or if they want to horde the cards they do have), they draw cards one at a time from the stock until they get a legal card that they can (or want to) play. They must play that card on that turn instead of waiting until their next turn.

TIP

You can draw cards even when you have a legal card to play. You build up a supply of cards, which reduces your opponents' options by leaving them with cards that they can't play as you tackle other suits. This tactic may allow you to go out more quickly in the long run. But beware: This strategy may backfire catastrophically if your opponent goes out when you have a big hand.

When the stock is exhausted and a player has no legal move, the turn passes to the player's left. If no player has a legal card to play, the player who put down the last card can play whatever they want.

When someone goes out, play stops, and the winner scores the total of the points left in all the players' hands, according to the following scale:

>> **7s and 8s =** face value

>> **9s =** 15 points

- » **10s =** 10 points

- » **Jacks =** 2 points

- » **Queens =** 3 points

- » **Kings =** 4 points

- » **Aces =** 11 points

- » **Jokers =** 20 points

The first player to reach 150 points wins the game.

Switch: Avoiding the Double Agents

Switch is also known as "Two Four Jack" or "Black Jack" (not to be confused with Blackjack; see Chapter 18). The game resembles "Uno," a popular commercial version of the game played with a special deck of cards. It is the British version of Eights.

The object is to be the first to get rid of all your cards. However, a series of obstacles can make that simple endeavor slightly complicated.

BEFORE HAND

To play Switch, you need the following:

- » **At least two players:** You can play Switch with any number of players, but a group of five to eight is ideal.

- » **A standard deck of 52 cards:** With four or more players, add a second deck, and with eight players, bring in a third deck.

- » **Pencil and paper for scoring:** Along with a second deck, have a second scorer on hand in case the first gets tired!

Preparing for a Switch

The player who draws the lowest card during the initial cut does the dealing. The dealer doles out the cards one by one, face-down, in a clockwise direction. With two players, the dealer gives out 12 cards; otherwise, each player gets ten cards. After dealing the cards, the dealer turns over the top card of the deck to form the discard pile next to the remaining cards.

The player to the dealer's left starts the game by playing a card of the same suit or rank as the upcard, unless the upcard is a jack, which forces the dealer to start (see the following section for further wacky Switch details).

However, as the name of the game suggests, a number of cards change their identities in Switch. Instead of being "extras," they become stars, with minds — and roles — of their own.

Play goes clockwise around the table initially, but that order can change, depending on which cards are played.

Identifying some key cards

In Switch, some cards can influence the play in special ways:

>> **Aces:** Aces are wild and can be played at any time. You nominate the suit to be played thereafter.

>> **2s:** In Switch, 2s are your basic bad guys. When you play a 2 on a card of the appropriate suit, you offer the next player a choice of alternatives: If they have no 2 (or if they have one but choose not to play it), they must draw two cards from the stock and miss their turn. If they have a 2, they can play it and avoid picking up additional cards.

If the second player puts a 2 on the first 2, the next player has even more unpalatable alternatives: They must play a third 2 or draw four cards. And the fourth player must play a 2 or pick up *six* cards. As soon as a player must draw, the spell is broken, and the count goes back to zero.

After a player draws, the next player to go must follow the suit of the last 2 played.

>> **4s:** After a 4 is played, the next player must play a 4 or pick up four cards from the stock and lose their turn, the second player has the choice of playing a 4 or picking up eight cards, and so on. After a player draws cards and loses a turn, the next player follows the suit of the last 4 played.

>> **8s:** If you play an 8, the next player misses their turn, and play continues with that player being skipped.

>> **Jacks:** Jacks reverse, or *switch,* the direction of play. After someone plays a jack, the next turn goes to the player to their right.

REMEMBER

An almost unlimited number of variations along the themes I outline above exist. However, it's generally true to say that whichever variation you turn into, there is a card (maybe a different one from the ones I mention) that performs the action skipping, reversing, penalizing, or acting as a wild card.

Going out and scoring

When you reduce your hand to one card, you must announce "one card" as you play your next-to-last card.

WARNING

If you forget to say "one card" and someone else notices, you lose your turn and are forced to pick up at least one card from the stock — local rules vary on the penalty.

The first player to run out of cards wins. The winner scores the value of the cards left in their opponents' hands. Most cards are scored at face value, with the following exceptions:

>> **Aces** = 20 points

>> **2s, 4s, 8s, and jacks** = 15 points

>> **Kings and queens** = 10 points

The first player to reach 150 points wins the game.

Chapter **7**

Fan Tan

You can get along just fine playing Fan Tan with remarkably little grasp of the underlying strategy. However, to be really good at Fan Tan, you can't rely solely on the luck of the hand you're originally dealt. To play well requires a fair degree of skill and an understanding of the mechanics of the game; so, here I am to the rescue! In this chapter I tell you everything you need to know about this exciting game.

And for those of you who require a little money action with your card games, Fan Tan works very well as a gambling game, and I fill you in on how to bring the monetary element into the game in this chapter, too.

BEFORE HAND

To play Fan Tan, you need the following:

» **Four players:** Three, five, or six players work, but four are ideal.

» **A standard deck of 52 cards:** No jokers required.

» **A pencil and paper:** Use these for keeping score.

A typical contest at Fan Tan consists of playing to a set score, the objective being to avoid scoring points by leaving your opponents with cards in their hands. When you win a hand of Fan Tan, you score zero, but each opponent scores the number of points equal to the number of cards left in their hand at the end of the game. Playing to 11 or 15 points means a game is likely to last half an hour or so.

Accepting Your Fan Tan Mission

The objective of Fan Tan is relatively uncomplicated. You deal out the entire deck of cards among the players, and you spend the game trying to get rid of all your cards before the other players can manage the feat.

You get rid of cards by adding them to an already existing *run*, or sequence of cards in a suit, which builds up during the play. You can play a single card whenever it's your turn. You have to build the cards up and down in consecutive order, starting from the 7 in each suit. After someone plays the 7 of a suit, the next player can legally put on the 6 or 8 of the suit. If the 6 hits the table, the next player has the choice of adding the 5 or 8. If they play the 8 on the 7, the next player can put down the 6 or the 9, and so on.

After the first 7 is played, if the next player has no 7 or can't add to the cards on the table, they pass. You must play if you can.

Wheeling and dealing

To determine who gets to deal first, pick someone to deal a card face-up to each player until someone receives a jack; the lucky prince gets to deal the first hand. For subsequent hands, the deal passes one place clockwise.

If you play the game for money, everyone puts in an initial *ante* — a fixed unit — before the start of the hand. (You can make the stakes whatever you like; it only takes a small stake to get the blood racing. Because additional bets can be made, a nickel may be quite enough for the ante!)

After shuffling and offering a cut to the player on their right, the dealer gives out all the cards, face-down and clockwise. If you're playing with four people, everyone gets the same number of cards. If you're playing with three, five, or six players, some people get more cards than others (you just can't divide 52 evenly by 3, 5, or 6). This imbalance gets corrected over the course of a round of Fan Tan because everyone deals a hand and gets extra cards on some hands during play.

If you play the game for stakes, you can make it that the players with fewer cards put in an extra unit to compensate for starting the game with such an advantage.

Letting the cards hit the fan

The player to the left of the dealer has the first opportunity to play. If they have a 7 in any suit, they must play it by placing it face-up in the center of the table. If they don't have a 7, they pass.

TIP

If you have more than one 7, do not automatically put down the one in the suit in which you have more cards. Put down the 7 where you have more awkward end cards such as aces and kings, or 2s and queens.

If you're playing for money, any player who passes must put an additional unit into the pot. Fan Tan's original name, Play or Pay, was very much to the point.

After someone starts the game with a 7, the next player can make one of the following plays:

>> You can play a 7 in another suit if you have one. If you want to play another 7, you place it directly above or below the other 7.

  You don't have to play another 7 if you have a different legal move that you would prefer to make.

>> You can build up or down on any 7. If you have an 8 or a 6 in the appropriate suit, you put it down to the right or left of the 7.

>> If you can't make any other move, you pass.

Similarly, the next player can either build up or down from the existing structures or pass.

In Fan Tan, aces can only be low, so you can only play an ace after a 2, not after a king.

If you can play, you must do so, however tactically unwelcome it may be to release a card that you'd rather keep in your hand. Often, you find that you don't want to play a card that simply makes other people's lives easier — but that's Fan Tan life, I'm afraid. A player who's caught holding back in a stakes game can't win the hand on which the offense occurs.

After a few turns around the table, the cards form into piles on both sides of the 7s that may look like the ones shown in Figure 7-1. In the spade suit, for example, the ♠8, ♠9, and ♠10 are nestled beneath the ♠J, and the ♠6 and ♠5 are invisible below the ♠4.

In Figure 7-1, the next legal cards to play would be the ♠Q or ♠3, the ♥9 or ♥2, the ♦10 or ♦4, and the ♣9 or ♣6. The player with the action can play any one of these cards or pass if they can't.

When a pile comes to the end of its natural life (when an ace or king stops the sequence from advancing any further), turn over the pile to indicate that fact.

The first person to get rid of all their cards wins, and play immediately stops. They take the pot (which consists of the antes plus any additional contributions made during the hand) if you're playing the game with stakes, but before they do that, all the other players put in one unit for every card left in their hands.

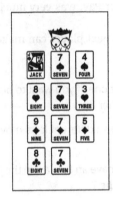

FIGURE 7-1:
Running high
and low in
all the suits.

Expanding your Fan Tan smarts

To play Fan Tan well, you need to familiarize yourself with a few essential elements of strategy. First and foremost, if you only have one card that you can play, you don't have much choice but to play it. Your Fan Tan strategy starts when you have more than one card you can play.

Assuming you have more than one playable card, look first at the suits in which you hold *end cards* — the aces and kings in each suit. End cards pose all kinds of problems because you can't get rid of them until every other card in the suit has been played, usually close to the end of the game. Your strategy should revolve around persuading people to play cards in the suit in which you hold end cards. You give persuasion by playing cards in that suit, and if you have the choice of leading or playing different 7s, look at the suits with the end cards.

Choosing between 7s

Starting at the beginning of a hand, your first idea is to play as quickly as possible any 7 in a suit in which you have an end card. Similarly, if you have 2s or queens, think about playing the 7s in those suits right away. If you're playing in a four-player game and you hold back a 7 in a suit filled with end cards, you may increase your chances of not finishing last, but you reduce your chances of winning.

For example, let's say you get the cards shown in Figure 7-2.

FIGURE 7-2:
Letting go of the
hot potato loaded
with end cards.

You want to play the ♠7 as soon as possible to encourage others to play on the suit. You have both a high (♠K) and a low (♠3) card in spades — time to get cracking on the suit at once!

With your mid-range cards in hearts, you may keep the ♥7 back for as long as possible, because it's to your advantage to keep players from being able to play hearts for the time being. If hearts are the last suit played, you're more likely to win the game.

Given the choice, you should start with suits in which you have end cards (aces, 2s, kings, and queens) rather than suits in which you're comfortably placed with middle cards (between the 3 and the jack).

Playing your end cards through sequences

In general, you want to minimize your opponents' opportunities to play — and thus to restrict their freedom of action so that they have to release cards they want to retain in their hands. Following that logic, playing an end card (an ace or a king) whenever it is legal to do so is generally a good idea. The end card gives no new opportunity for play. Make the other players release cards they're reluctant to let go, which in turn allows you to play your other cards.

For the same reason that end cards are potentially attractive plays, you often find that you can use a run in your hand to force others to play. A run occurs when you hold something like the ♠Q-♠J-♠10-♠9; playing the 9, 10, or jack gives no other player an additional opportunity and thus forces your opponents to make moves that they would rather not do. With any luck, those moves will help you get your end cards out.

Think carefully about whether you want to release a card in a suit to give other players opportunities to play, rather than play an end card or work on a sequence. The answer depends on whether you want your opponents to play on the suit in which you have that card in the middle of a suit, or whether you want to hold that card back to inconvenience them and make their lives more difficult. If you hold, say, a 9 and also the Q of a suit, you may want to put the 9 down quickly to encourage play on that suit. With a 9 and no card higher than it, keep the 9 for as long as you can. Why help others to play their end cards if you do not have to?

Break out your sequences only after you've made all your plays in the suits where you have end cards.

Double-Deck Fan Tan

All your friends will want to join in when you play Fan Tan, which is where Double-Deck Fan Tan comes in — it's a great game for large groups, when a single deck leaves you with too small a hand to start with.

To play Double-Deck Fan Tan, you need the following:

>> **Seven or more players**

>> **Two standard decks of 52 cards without jokers**

>> **A pencil and paper for scoring**

>> **A big table and plenty of chairs**

You play Double-Deck Fan Tan just as you play Fan Tan — see the section "Accepting Your Fan Tan Mission" earlier in this chapter for the details. The biggest difference is that you have eight rows of cards in Double-Deck Fan Tan rather than the four rows in traditional Fan Tan (eight 7s compared to four).

With two of each card circulating in the double-deck, you have no assurance that you'll be able to put down a card when a space arises, because someone may fill in the vacancy first. More 7s are around, but you still don't know exactly when you can get your cards out. When the player on your left puts down the ♦J, will you be able to get your ♦Q out, or will someone with the other ♦Q beat you to it?

Double-Deck Fan Tan is more random than standard Fan Tan, and thus less strategic, which you may view as a disadvantage. At the same time, Double-Deck Fan Tan equals out skill levels, so it's appropriate for adults and children playing together, and the longer game fits well in social atmospheres.

The scoring works as in regular Fan Tan, with players playing to a specific target, or for stakes.

Trump Fan Tan

Are you getting bored with regular Fan Tan? Well, try spicing it up with the introduction of a *trump suit* (a wild or boss suit). Yes, I agree, this is not a conventional trump suit, but that is what the game is normally called. Sue me.

You play Trump Fan Tan exactly as you play traditional Fan Tan — see the section "Accepting Your Fan Tan Mission" earlier in this chapter for the details — with one important difference. In Trump Fan Tan, the spade suit is wild, meaning that you can play every spade as the equivalent rank from any other suit. Take the cards in Figure 7-3 as an example.

FIGURE 7-3: In Trump Fan Tan, spades can have multiple identities.

You can use the ♠10 as the ♥10, ♦10, or ♣10 to get you out of a jam.

What happens to the ♦10 if you displace it with the ♠10? Logically enough, cards displaced from their suits by spades go into the spade suit and can only be played there.

The rules of the trump suit don't apply to the ♠7, which retains its identity as a spade. You can't put down the ♠7 to represent any other 7, but all other spade cards can be the equivalent rank in any other suit.

Play your spades as early as you can in the place of cards in other suits, unless you have good reasons to keep your wild cards — for suits in which you have end cards, perhaps. But all things being equal, you want to mess up other people's strategies by playing your spades as soon as possible.

Getting stuck with a usurped king or ace is bad news, because the spade suit always seems to get built at the very end. Because players put their spades down as quickly as possible for wild cards, you have to wait for some time before the spades are advanced with all the leftover cards.

At the end of the game, spades and regular cards score the same: 1 point for each card left.

Crazy Tan

Folks with a tenuous grasp on reality really seem to enjoy Crazy Tan. Proceed at your own mental risk.

The basic idea is similar to Fan Tan (see the first section in this chapter), in that the object of the game is simply to get rid of all your cards. You need all the same equipment for Crazy Tan, too.

However, you give only seven cards to each player, which leaves a stock of undealt cards. The player to the dealer's left leads, if they have a 7. If they can't play a 7, they pick up a card from the stock. If they pick up a 7, they must immediately play it.

If the first player can't put a card down and picks up a card that isn't a 7, the next player is under slightly greater pressure. If they can't play, they must pick up *two* cards. And if the third player can't put a card down, they pick up *three* cards. As soon as anyone picks up a playable card, the count goes back to zero. Of course, the more cards you pick up, the more likely it is that you'll get something that you can play.

VARIATION

As you might guess, variations for Crazy Fan Tan abound. The following are some of the more popular:

» To speed up the game, you can introduce *runs*. Instead of playing only one card at a time, whenever you have a run in the same suit, such as the ♥9-♥10-♥J, you can put them all down at the same time. You do not have to, but you can. In some positions you might prefer to play the cards singly, so as not to let other players get their end cards down quickly.

» In the same ilk as playing runs, playing multiples allows you to play two or more of the same card at the same time. In other words, when you have two 10s (from different suits) that you can legally play at the same moment, you may put them down on the same turn.

» If multiples and runs aren't enough for you, you can go to the well again. How about *multiple parallel runs*? If you have two runs of 4-3-2, you can try to put them down in two suits at the same time! A multiple parallel run may not happen very often, but you can look back on it with great pleasure when it does.

FAN TANNING ONLINE

You can play Fan Tan online by going to www.evolution.com/our-games/fan-tan. You can also play a computer opponent (known as Sevens in this incarnation) at www.classicgamesandpuzzles.com/Sevens.html. Beware, however; this game features some variations from the rules I present in this chapter. Be sure to read up on the site's rules before you jump in.

3

Taking Tricks

The title of this part contains a card-playing word that may be new to you on days other than Halloween: *trick*. Don't worry if you don't know what a trick is on the card table — I explain the concept to you at the start of each of the games I cover in this part.

Besides picking up some new vocabulary words (I promise, I don't use too many fancy-schmancy words), you come to this part of the book to get the lowdown on games such as Whist, Oh Hell!, Euchre, Spades, and Bridge — all of which revolve around taking tricks to score points.

Chapter **8**

Whist

This chapter should come with a warning label: Whist is a highly addictive game. After you figure out the fundamentals, you may find yourself spending more time at the Whist table than the dinner table. If your non-Whisting friends complain that they never see you anymore, you may want to consider taking up another hobby (or be an enabler and get them addicted, too!).

What makes Whist attractive is that it is a trick-taking game, which is an important stepping stone on the way to games such as Spades (see Chapter 11) and Bridge (see Chapter 12). Mastering the elements of this game can make you a better all-around card player.

BEFORE HAND

To play Whist, you need only basic equipment:

>> **Four players:** Two players for two teams.

>> **One standard deck of 52 cards (no jokers):** You may prefer to have a shuffled second deck on hand to speed up the dealing a bit. One player can shuffle one deck while another player deals the other deck.

>> **Pencil and paper for scoring:** Or make one of your complaining friends all-time scorer!

What's the Whist All About?

The object of Whist is to score points by winning *tricks*. During the game play, each player at the table lays down a card. One player *leads*, or plays first, a card; the rest of the players are honor-bound to play a card of the same suit (or *follow suit*) if they can. The player who puts down the highest card in the suit wins the trick and collects all four cards.

Each team scores points for the tricks it wins. The first team to score 7 points wins (see the later section "Tallying your score" for more information on winning the game).

Winning tricks with the trump suit

Whist cards rank from the ace (highest) to the 2 (lowest). However, one type of card, a *trump card*, can beat any other card from any other suit.

The *trump suit* acts as the master suit. If you play a card in the trump suit on a card from another suit, the trump card wins the trick (unless another player plays a higher card in the trump suit). You determine the trump suit in one of three ways (agreed on in advance):

>> **Cut the second deck, if you have one, and make the suit of that card the trump suit.**

>> **Cut your only deck before the deal starts and make the suit of that card the trump suit.**

>> **Turn the dealer's last card face-up and make the suit of that card the trump suit.**

REMEMBER

The last method gives the dealer the advantage of possessing a trump card, but the disadvantage for the dealer is that everyone knows one of the cards in their hand.

VARIATION

In Britain, the trump suit typically rotates. The first deal is played with hearts, then clubs, diamonds, spades, and back to hearts again. Some people insert a no-trump round after spades.

WARNING

You can't play a trump card whenever you feel like it — the rules of Whist require you to follow suit at all times if you can, meaning that you must play a card in the suit that another player leads if you have one.

If you have no cards in the appropriate suit, you have the option of playing a trump card or *discarding* (throwing away) any card that you want to get rid of. You don't want to play a trump card when your partner leads an ace or follows suit with an ace because you're playing as a partnership, and your partner has already made a pretty fair stab at taking the trick. Save your trump cards for a more valuable moment; however, you do want to take a trick if you can, and sometimes playing a trump card is the only way to win the trick.

REMEMBER

Be careful about following suit; the penalty for *revoking*, or failing to follow suit, is three tricks. You lose the tricks, and the other side gains them. For example, if you revoke and end up winning all 13 tricks, your opponents score 3 tricks, and your side only scores 10 tricks.

Dealing and playing the cards

You have the option to play in arranged partnerships or to cut the deck for partners. If you cut the deck, the players who turn up the two highest cards play against the players with the two lowest cards. After you determine partnerships, the partners sit opposite each other.

After all players are seated, you cut for the deal, and the lowest card (with aces low) deals the first hand. The deal passes clockwise around the table.

The dealer passes out all 52 cards — face-down, one by one, and clockwise — starting with the player on their left.

The player to the left of the dealer plays the first card of the trick. Play proceeds clockwise around the table, with each player contributing a card. Whoever wins the first trick (by playing the highest card in the suit led or by playing the highest trump card) leads the next card, and play continues until all the cards have been played.

REMEMBER

You must play a card in the led suit if you have one. If you don't, you can play a trump card or simply discard a card in another suit.

One player in each partnership (it doesn't matter which) takes care of the tricks for their side; they stack the four cards that make up the trick neatly in front of them so that at the end of the hand each side can see how many tricks each team has won. At the end of the hand, unless something goes horribly wrong, the two sides have 13 tricks between them.

After you score the hand (see the next section for details), you move on to the next hand.

Tallying your score

After the last trick hits the table, each team counts its tricks. The time of reckoning is upon you.

Scoring trick points

The first six tricks you win count for nothing. After the sixth trick, each additional trick scores your team 1 point. For example, if your side wins 11 tricks, you score 5 points.

Your goal is to score 7 points before your opponents do. If you make that magic 7, you score a *game*. Scoring two out of three games wins you the contest, also known as a *rubber*.

VARIATION

In Britain, one of the most common variations occurs when you play in a Whist Drive — a tournament of 24 deals of Whist. You score 1 point per trick (not only for tricks beyond the 6th) and play a fixed number of deals. The winners are the players with the most points at the end.

Scoring honor cards in the trump suit

If neither partnership scores a game (7 points) after counting the tricks won by each side, you have another chance to register points: You look at the trump-suit honor cards (ace, king, queen, jack) originally held in your hand. This variation is rarely used in modern Whist varieties, though.

The side with the most trump-suit honor cards gets 1 point apiece for however many of those cards they have than their opponents. For example, if your side has all four honor cards, you get 4 points; if your side has three honor cards, you score 2 points (because you have two more honor cards than the other team); and if each side has two honor cards, no points are scored. (FYI: Whist is where the phrase "honors are even" comes from.)

If you can score your trump-suit honor cards, you first record the trick score, and then you add on the honor points and move on to the next hand.

REMEMBER

You can't win the game with honor points if you need just 1 point to win. If you have 6 points at the start of the hand, you can only *reach game* by scoring trick points. Simply ignore the honor points in that case. You can win with honor points if you have 5 points at the start, however.

If trick points get one team to score a game, the other side doesn't get to count its honor-card points. For example, say that your side has 5 points and your opponents have 4 points. You win 8 tricks (worth 2 points), but your opponents have 4 points for honor cards. Who wins? You do, of course — you don't think that I'd let you lose!

Scoring the rubber

You carry forward your point total from the previous hands until one side reaches the winning figure of 7, in which case both sides start again from zero. Whichever side wins two games first wins the rubber, whereupon you have the *final reckoning*, or scoring, when you calculate the precise margins of victory and defeat.

The winners subtract the losers' score from their own at the end of the rubber, and the difference is the margin of victory. Note that you can win two rubbers, lose one, and still be outscored — if you lose big and win small.

Incorporating Basic Whist Strategy

You can play Whist as a social game, without putting any special work into the play of the cards. You don't have to try to remember the cards your partner plays or what suit they lead initially. If you play Whist in this manner, you're sure to find the game an enjoyable pastime — even if you find that you don't do especially well!

However, if you're more the competitive type who bets with friends on everything from sports to eating contests, check out the following sections that detail the strategies of the game.

Remembering the cards

One vital aspect to a winning strategy is remembering the high honor cards for each hand. You can easily recall what cards you started the hand with, but also try to recall the salient high cards as they appear during the hand. Remembering which high cards have been played tells you which ones are still lurking out there, waiting to take your tricks.

Also make note of the suit your partner leads. They may have good cards in that suit, and they probably want you to lead that suit if you get the lead.

Landing the leading role

The first card played to every trick is the *lead*. Of all the leads in a hand, the lead to the first trick (the *opening lead*) is the most important because it dictates the way that the play advances. The opening lead affects all subsequent leads, so the question is: What suit should you lead, and which card in the suit should you play?

If the dealer gives you a sequence of honor cards, lead the top card from that sequence. For example, from K-Q-J, you lead the king, and from Q-J-10, you lead the queen. However, if the sequence starts with the ace, lead the lowest card; for example, from an A-K combination, lead the king, and lead the jack from A-K-Q-J.

If you have to make a lead early in the hand, and you don't have a comfortable suit from which to lead, such as one that includes a sequence of honor cards at its head, think about using one of the following reasonable alternatives:

>> **Lead a small card from a long suit of four or more cards, particularly one in which you have high cards, such as the king, queen, or jack.** By leading a *long* suit, or a suit in which you have many cards, sometimes you can force your opponents to use up their trump cards prematurely to take the trick — cards with which they may win a trick anyway.

    If you lead from a suit in which you have length, lead your fourth-highest card, which gives your partner some general perspective on your hand. For example, if you have the ♠Q, ♠9, ♠7, ♠5, and ♠2, lead the ♠5. Leading low from a suit in which you hold a few fairly high cards creates the chance that the other players will play all the other high cards in the suit at once (because everyone must follow suit). If this happens, your fairly high cards become the new highest cards left in that suit. Your partner doesn't know exactly what you have in the suit, but they may be able to guess that your lead of a small card suggests that you have some length in the suit.

    If you have K-9-5-2 of hearts, lead the 2. Your partner can work out that you have only four hearts. Why? Because if you had five hearts, your fourth-highest heart couldn't be the 2, could it?

>> **Lead a *singleton* (a holding of just one card) in a suit that isn't the trump suit.** The next time someone attacks that suit, you won't have any cards left in

it, so you can play a trump card and win the trick. This move tends to be one that you only follow with bad hands — it may cross partner up, or it may set up your opponent's long suit.

TIP

Don't consider this lead if you have a lot of trump cards, because you may win tricks with those trump cards anyway. A better move may be to lead your long suit or even to lead a trump card.

>> **Lead a trump card.** Seriously consider this lead if you have five or more trump cards. If your highest trump cards come in a sequence, lead the highest card in the sequence; otherwise, lead your smallest trump card.

You should also lead trump cards early if you have plenty of high cards but only two or three small trump cards — cards that you won't win a trick with if someone leads the trump suit. By leading trump cards, you reduce the number of your opponents' trump cards, which prevents your side's high cards from being trumped.

You may find that some of my advice contradicts itself. You can't make the right lead on every hand by applying formulas to it. No hand fits one pattern, and hands come in many different shapes. These leads are only suggestions, not a guaranteed route to success. What makes Whist such fun is that you need to apply your brain and take chances.

TIP

Although this section is all about opening leads, let me throw in a piece of advice that applies to subsequent leads. When in doubt, play a card in the suit that your partner leads at their first opportunity. Your partner may play a card from a strong suit for their opening lead, so playing a card in that suit gives them a chance to play a card from their strong suit. This move has the great advantage of retaining partnership harmony. After all, your partner can hardly blame you for following their subtle advice!

Playing second to a trick

REMEMBER

If you're the second person to play to a trick, play a low card (preferably your lowest card) in the led suit. The logic is to save your firepower for later. Because your partner still has to play on the trick, you hope that they can take care of things for your side.

However, you may have some good reasons not to play your lowest card:

>> **You have a sequence of honor cards in the suit led.** If you have such a sequence, play the lowest card in the sequence. Thus, if you have the Q-J-10-9-4, play the 9, the lowest card in the sequence.

>> **You have the ace in the led suit.** One very awkward decision you must make as second hand is whether to play the ace in a suit other than the trump suit if you have it. You should play the ace if you have five or more cards in the suit or if the card led is an honor card — the king, queen, or jack.

The strategy of playing the second hand low is to let your partner, who plays last to the trick, have the chance to play a significant card on the trick. If you play low, the third hand still needs to put out a high card to give their side a chance to win the trick. But when you have the ace in the suit led, you may not want to risk losing the trick, because one opponent may be able to trump the next round of the suit. When an honor card leads the trick, and you know that you can capture a high card in the process of playing the ace, it's very tempting — and probably right — to do so. It is also often right to cover an honor card (such as a queen or jack) with the next highest honor, even in second seat.

Playing third to a trick

When you play third to a trick, or *third hand*, you have the benefit of seeing which card your partner leads to the trick. You have valuable information about how to play your hand.

When you play third hand, you usually play the highest card in the suit your partner leads. You don't want your opponents to win a trick with a lower card than is necessary, so force them to win the trick with a high card.

When you have a sequence of honor cards, follow suit with the lowest card in your sequence, which can help give your partner a clearer picture of your hand. When your partner sees you play a 9 and the fourth hand captures your 9 with an ace, they have a fairly good idea that you have a number of cards in the middle, because the fourth hand would've won the trick with the 10 or jack if they could, instead of wasting their ace unnecessarily.

Playing fourth to a trick

When you play fourth to a trick, you're entirely on your own. Try to win any trick that your partner hasn't already won for your side.

WARNING

If you have an ace in your hand, and you don't play it at the first opportunity to take the trick, who knows what fate your ace will suffer? Maybe the rats will get it; one opponent may trump your ace on the next round.

If you can't win the trick, play your lowest card.

Showing some finesse

In the real world, *finesse* refers to tact, diplomacy, and the ability to behave properly at cocktail parties. In the world of cardplaying, a *finesse* is an attempt to win a trick without using the highest possible card in your hand. A finesse saves your highest card for later.

When you play your medium-sized card, you hope that the opponent who plays after you can't beat your card. If they can, your finesse fails.

Figure 8-1 shows you a finesse in action. The figure looks only at the clubs in each player's hands; they have other cards, too.

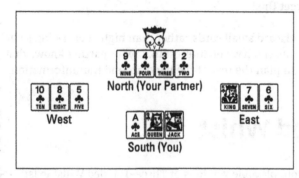

FIGURE 8-1:
Play a finesse to
save your high
cards for later
tricks.

Your partner leads the ♣2. When East plays the six (second hand low, remember), if you play the ♣A, you win the trick. You can play the ♣Q now, but the opponent on your right plays the ♣K, winning the trick.

But notice the difference if you play the ♣J initially. If you play the ♣J at your first turn, it wins the trick. Now if you tackle another suit, you hope to let your partner lead the club suit when they get the lead again. You can put in the ♣Q when your turn comes. With the ♣A still to come, you collect three tricks without losing one. You exploited the good fortune that East, not West, has the ♣K. Playing the ♣J (or ♣Q) as a finesse allows you to win a club trick with a lower card than your top one (the ♣A).

REMEMBER

If your highest and second-highest cards in the suit led are separated by one card, consider not playing the very highest card you have if you play second or third to a trick. For example, consider playing the jack from a holding such as K-J or the queen from a holding such as A-Q. Playing your second-highest card may give you the chance of exploiting the favorable distribution of your opponents' cards to win the trick and save your highest card for later.

Making discards

When a player leads a suit in which you have no cards left, you have two options:

>> Try to win the trick by playing a trump card.

>> Throw away a card that you feel no need to keep.

Throwing away a card is called *discarding*; if someone leads a trump card and you have none (bad luck!), you have no choice but to discard.

REMEMBER

When you make a discard, you want to throw away losers and keep winners — it may sound obvious, but you may be surprised at how often experienced players seem to forget this!

In general, discard small cards rather than high ones. Doing so helps your partner see which suits you have no interest in. If your partner knows that you discard this way, they can plan the rest of the hand around that information.

Three-Handed Whist

VARIATION

Two common, playable versions of Three-Handed Whist exist: One involves three players and a *dummy* hand (a hand that all players can see), and one involves three players and an optional fourth hand.

Playing with a dummy (hand, that is)

You begin by dealing 13 cards to all three players and the dummy hand, which you situate opposite the dealer. You determine the trump suit in the standard fashion (by cutting a separate deck or the deck you're using to reveal a suit), and the player to the left of the dealer plays the first card. At that point, one player (it doesn't matter who) turns over the dummy hand and exposes it to the light of day. Make sure to sort the dummy hand and lay it out on the table.

From this point on, the dealer chooses the plays of both their hand and the dummy hand. Play progresses in the standard clockwise fashion. The two other players team up together — one plays before the dummy hand and one after it. At the end of the hand, the deal moves clockwise, and the new dealer takes on the other two players, again with the aid of the dummy.

You score the game the same as traditional Whist (refer to the section "Tallying your score," earlier in this chapter). Both players record the score for the partnership as their own scores; the players compete against each other in the scoring regardless of what they score as a team. The first player to score 7 points wins.

Dealing an optional fourth hand

This variation may involve less skill, but it creates more excitement.

Deal the four hands and then determine the trump suit for the hand by the traditional cut. The dealer and the other players look at their hands. If the dealer dislikes their hand, they have the option of exchanging with the fourth hand — an irreversible decision.

TIP

If you deal and decide to exchange your hand with the fourth hand, take care to memorize the hand before switching.

If the dealer doesn't want to make the switch, the option goes to the player to the dealer's left and then to the third hand. If the dealer does switch their hand, the player to the dealer's left can exchange their hand with the discarded hand. If they choose to stick with their hand, the option goes to the third player.

WARNING

Swapping your cards for the dealer's discarded hand is truly an act of desperation, but sometimes the only way is up! If you do exchange your cards, the dealer knows your hand precisely, which should prove to be a big advantage to them. If your cards truly reek, however, you may need to take the risk.

TIP

If you're the dealer and have two or fewer aces and kings and fewer than four trump cards, you should definitely exchange hands, because the bonus for knowing the placement of an extra 13 cards proves very valuable. Even if your hand is good in terms of aces, kings, and queens (you can expect to have about one of each, on average), the tactical merits of exchanging hands may be worthwhile.

When the swapping is complete, you play the game three-handed. The discarded hand takes no part in the play, and everyone plays individual hands against the other two players (see the section "Dealing and playing the cards" earlier in this chapter for more information on game play). You score by the amount of tricks you manage to take, converted into points. For example, if you win 6 tricks, you score 6 points.

You can play to a finite number of hands, or you can state that the first to 50 points wins. You don't score honor cards at all.

German (Two-Handed) Whist

VARIATION

German Whist is a game for two players, which may explain why the game is also referred to as Honeymoon Whist. If you decide to play this game on your honeymoon, you must be very devoted card players.

The dealer deals 13 cards to each player and turns over the top card of the remaining 26, or the *stock*. This card defines the trump suit for the whole hand (refer to the section "Winning tricks with the trump suit" earlier in this chapter for more information).

The game progresses in two stages: the preparation stage and the actual play of the hand, although the nature of the two stages may seem pretty similar.

Improving your holding cards

During the preparation stage, you attempt to improve your hand by playing out cards and receiving cards in return. Both players fight for the right to pick up either the face-up card or the face-down top card of the stock. Depending on whether the face-up card is a good or bad card, you try to win the trick or lose it.

The nondealer may lead any card in their hand, and the dealer must follow suit. The winner of the trick takes the face-up card on the discard pile; the loser takes the face-down card from the top of the stock. You turn up a new card and repeat the process. The winner of the previous trick leads, and you repeat this process 13 times.

REMEMBER

This procedure is all preparation, because these 13 tricks don't count for anything toward the scoring of the hand. They just set you up for the finale.

VARIATION

Not that I'm encouraging you to cheat, but one of the problems with the traditional game I describe is that it's frequently impossible to detect a revoke. Say you lead the ace of trumps early on in the hand and instead of dropping my singleton king, I throw a card from another suit. How will you know? The only way around this is to be very trusting, or ethical, or to vary the basic rules of the game to score for all 26 tricks, but not to require suit to be followed until the last 13.

Playing the hand

Now the serious part of the game begins. During this final stage, you want to win as many of the 13 tricks you play as possible. You keep the same trump suit you had for the first 13 tricks, and you play out the cards one at a time. The player who wins the last trick of the preparation phase leads first, and the other player responds by playing a card, following suit if they can. The winner of the trick leads to the next trick, and play continues this way for all 13 tricks.

TIP

German Whist offers a great test of memory as you try to keep track of what happened in the initial phase of the game and who ended up with which cards. Try to keep track of all the aces, kings, and queens at the very least, so that as the preparation stage comes to an end, you can lead middle cards out and force a high card from your opponent's hand.

For example, say that the top card you're playing for is the ♣7, and clubs are the trump suit. If you have the ♥10 and the ♥9, and the ♥K and ♥Q have already been played, leading the ♥10 may force your opponent to relinquish their ♥A if they want the trump card (♣7). Of course, they may have the ♥J.

Don't try to win tricks during the preparation phase of the game unless you want the top card. Try to weigh how good the card you led is against the top card. Don't, for example, lead an ace just to get a king of the same suit, because you simply exchange a good card for another one. This move also gives your opponent a chance to throw a card of their choice in the suit led — and what if they pick up something good in exchange?

TIP

You may want to lead trump cards in the early stage to *kill*, or reduce the effectiveness of, your opponent's hand. This tactic may prove particularly relevant if you believe that your enemy has trump-card control as the preparation stage of the game runs down. You may also want to get rid of a particular suit (other than trump) in the early part of the game so you can trump when your opponent leads that suit to win a key card.

Bid Whist

Bid Whist is a partnership trick-taking game, played with a deck of 52 cards plus two jokers, which should be clearly distinguishable from one another. The object of the game is to score 7 or more points, or to drive your opponents negative by more than 7 points.

You deal out the cards clockwise, one at a time, 12 to each player. You also deal out the remaining six cards during the deal, face-down to a kitty in the center of the table. (The timing of dealing to the kitty is up to the dealer.)

The bidding

Bid Whist has five possible trump suits; the regular four suits and no-trumps. Each suit can also be defined as *uptown* or *downtown*. At uptown trumps, the order of the cards goes from ace to 2 with the big joker and little joker the boss two trumps. At downtown trumps, the jokers retain their pole position, but the other cards rank from ace to king — so the king is the least important card. At no-trump both uptown and downtown, the order is identical to the order trumps, but both jokers are irrelevant.

Starting with the player to the left of the dealer, each play gets one chance to bid the number of tricks (or *books*) more than 6, which they intend to take. For example, a bid of 3 (the smallest legal bid) represents the intention to take 9 tricks total. To make a bid, you have to outbid the previous call.

The order of bids is 3 (uptown or downtown), 3 no-trump, 4 (uptown or downtown), 4 no-trump, and so on, all the way up through 7 no-trump.

If none of the first three players bids, the dealer must act. Because no bonus exists for bidding exactly to your contract, the dealer always opts for the minimum, namely 3, be it uptown, downtown, or no-trumps.

Note also that some element of every call is left to the imagination. If you specify you are going uptown or downtown, you do not name the trump suit yet. If playing at no-trump, you do not specify whether you are going uptown or downtown. The catch is that you have to do so immediately after winning the auction.

How can anyone bid for 7 tricks, or 13 in all, when everyone only has 12 cards? Well, whoever wins the auction gets to take up the kitty, add those cards to their hand, and throw away any six cards. Those discards now represent their first trick — so they are already well on their way to their contract.

The scoring

If you successfully achieve your contract by making more tricks than you bid for, you score as many points as you took tricks over six. So if you bid 3 uptown and made ten tricks, you score 4 points. If you go down in your contract by failing to make what you contracted for, you lose the number of points equivalent to your bid and may go negative. Your opponents get nothing. No-trump bids are scored double.

Dealing with jokers

At no-trump, the jokers are a mere cipher. You can only play them when you are out of a suit, at which point you can discard them. If a joker is led to a suit, the next player can play anything they like — and that card serves as the lead for the trick.

VARIATION

Some people play that the joker can be played at any point in the hand, not just as a discard, in which case they become far more useful by allowing you to preserve your honors, instead of having to sacrifice them under a high card.

Chapter 9

Oh Hell! and Other Exact Bidding Games

Oh Hell! (the exclamation point always accompanies the title) is ideal both for children and adults, in that it requires sufficient skill to make it an enjoyable challenge and involves just enough luck that everyone has a reasonable chance to win — or at least a chance to not lose by too much. (If you lose to your children, you can emphasize the luck factor; if you win, you can console them with the thought that when they get older, they may finally beat you.)

Oh Hell! goes by a wide variety of other names. You may know the game as Pshaw, Blackout, Up the Creek without a Paddle, and the rather boring Nomination Whist.

BEFORE HAND

To play Oh Hell!, you don't need to bring any satanic paraphernalia with you. Just have the following on hand:

» **At least three players:** Oh Hell! is best played with four players, but you can play it with up to eight players.

» **One standard deck of 52 cards:** No jokers allowed.

» **Paper and pencil for scoring:** You may want to construct a score sheet set out in columns, with a column designated for each player.

Oh Hell!

Oh Hell! is based on taking *tricks*. During game play, players take turns putting a card face-up on the table. The person who plays the highest card wins and collects all the played cards — one trick. The winner of the trick plays the first card to start the next trick. The process continues until all the cards play out.

Like in most games that involve taking tricks, the players in Oh Hell! score points for winning tricks. However, winning is more than just a matter of taking tricks. Before the actual play of the hand, you must estimate *precisely* how many tricks you think you'll win in the hand (see the section "Placing your bid" later in this chapter).

The importance of accurately predicting your trick total far outweighs the reward for actually winning tricks, so picking up a bad hand isn't necessarily a problem. Indeed, a terrible hand may be easier to judge than a great one. Making accurate estimates about your hand determines your success at the game, which is a very satisfying ingredient for a card game.

Dealing the cards

You give a card to each player to determine the dealer. The player who draws the lowest card deals the first hand.

The dealer deals out every card in the deck, starting with the player on their left, as long as everyone gets the same number of cards. You deal the cards face-down. You put down the remaining cards and turn over the top card to determine the trump suit (see the next section for more information) for that hand; the other undealt cards play no further part in the game. For a four-player game, in which all the cards go out, cut the deck to determine the trump suit before you deal out the first hand.

After a hand ends and you tally the scores, the deal passes clockwise for the next hand, and that player deals out the cards. For the subsequent deal, however, you deal one fewer card to every player, and the reduction continues for each subsequent hand until each player receives only one card. Following the single-card hand, the number of cards goes *up* by one each hand. The sequence progresses until you reach the maximum again. The game ends after the second maximum hand, and the winner is the player who finishes with the highest total.

You can also start with one card, work your way up to the maximum, and then come back down to one card. Either way works, and the variation you choose really doesn't matter.

If two players tie for the lead at the end of the game, the deal passes on, and everybody plays one more hand with the maximum number of cards. Additional deals with the maximum number of cards continue until you determine a winner.

Taking tricks with the trump suit

You must play a card in the suit led, or *follow suit*, if you can. If you don't have a card in the suit led, you can play a card from the *trump suit*, which automatically wins the trick — unless an opponent plays a higher trump card. You can also let go (or *discard*) a card from any other suit — in which case you can't win the trick. The smallest trump card beats even the ace of a *side-suit* (any non-trump suit).

Placing your bid

After you look at your hand, you swallow your pride and place a realistic bid. Your bid represents the number of tricks you intend to take during the course of the hand. The *bidding* starts with the player to the left of the dealer, who can bid any number of tricks that they like up to the maximum, which is the number of cards received by each player.

How much you bid depends on your high cards, your trump cards, and what the other players bid around you. The more the players around you seem to be bidding, the less you should rate your hand to be worth — and vice versa. Additionally, if you can gauge that the players with good hands are to your immediate right (so that you play after them and capture their honors), you may again up your bid by a trick.

The bidding continues clockwise until it comes back to the dealer, who has the final bid. Nothing stops the players from bidding, as a group, for too many tricks or too few tricks, and any player can try for no tricks at all.

Everyone but the dealer can bid for as many tricks as they think they can take, up to the number of cards dealt to each player. One of the little peculiarities of Oh Hell! that can lead to pleasurable aggravation (if you aren't the unfortunate dealer) is that the total number of tricks the players are going to go for can't equal the number of tricks available. For example, if five cards go to each person, the total number of tricks bid can't be five; therefore, if the first three players bid one, two, and one, respectively, the dealer can't contract for one trick because doing so makes the total five.

Why this stipulation, you ask? Allowing the number of tricks contracted for equal the number of tricks available presents the possibility that everyone could nail their bids — a situation that's inherently unsatisfying, I suppose. And the smaller the number of cards you deal, the more potentially arduous this rule can be, and on the round when only one card is dealt, it can produce particularly irritating results for the dealer, who bids last.

Note: It isn't universal to play the rule that dealer is restricted by the number of tricks available. I think it spices up the game, but not everybody sees it the same way.

The designated scorer writes down the bids on the score sheet as players call them out so that they can check the accuracy of the bids afterward and tell the dealer what bid (or *call*) is forbidden.

If you make a bid out of turn, the bid stands, and the other players can take advantage of it by having more information. However, if the dealer makes a bid out of turn, it doesn't stand because the disadvantage of bidding last must go to the dealer.

Don't bid too high; when in doubt, remember that playing to lose a trick is generally much easier than playing to win it. Look at the hand in Figure 9-1 to see what I mean.

FIGURE 9-1:
A hand with plenty of potential — but no guarantees!

Suppose that four people are playing, and you hold this hand as first to bid. Because hearts is the trump suit, you may, on a very good day, win all four tricks — you're virtually certain to win at least one, if not two. The odds are in your favor; however, it may be smarter to bid two rather than three and then listen carefully to the rest of the bidding to determine your play strategy.

Playing for your bids

The player on the dealer's left leads to the first trick, and play continues clockwise. Cards rank in the standard order, with aces high, and you have to follow suit (play a card in the suit led) if you can. If you can't follow suit, you have the choice of discarding (playing a card in a non-trump suit) or trumping with the trump suit.

In the early phases of the game, when you have plenty of cards, leading a suit in which you have only one card (a *singleton*) can be a good idea. Depending on whether you win or lose that trick, you can be more flexible in your strategy with other suits. If you win a trick unexpectedly, you go out of your way to lose another trick that you may have won (by undertrumping, say). If you lose a trick that you expected to win, you know to go all out to make up for it elsewhere.

When leading, if you do not have any singletons, consider leading a high honor such as a queen or a king. That way you find out early whether the card is destined to win a trick, which may affect your strategy for the play of other suits. When in doubt, get the middle cards out of your hand. Leave yourself with high cards or low cards, allowing yourself maximum flexibility to win a trick or not.

Always trump other people's aces if you can. If an opponent leads an ace, they surely want to win the trick — why help them out by letting them do so? Similarly, if you're going to lead from an ace-king, play the king first. Other players won't be quite so sure that you really want to win the trick.

At the end of a hand, all players announce how many tricks they took, and the scorer writes down the scores for each player. For every trick that you get on each hand, you score 1 point. If you make your bid, you get an additional 10 points. The player with the highest total after the second maximum-card hand wins the game (see the section "Dealing the cards" earlier in this chapter for more dealing information).

If you expose a card by playing it out of turn or by dropping it, it becomes a *penalty card*, and you must play it at the first legal opportunity. If you err by failing to follow suit, you may correct your mistake before the next trick starts. Your *revoke card* (the card that you played by mistake) becomes a penalty card to be played on your next turn, and all the other players who played after you on the previous trick can change their cards if they want. If they don't spot the revoke in time, the deal is canceled, and the revoker suffers a 10-point penalty.

CATCHING (OH) HELL! ON THE WEB

You can play Oh Hell! online at sites such as https://cardgames.io/ohhell/ and https://dkmgames.com/CardSharp/OhHell/.

Romanian Whist

One of the main variations on Oh Hell! is called Romanian Whist, for the surprisingly good reason that it comes from Romania. In fact, the game is called plain old Whist in that country.

BEFORE HAND

To play Romanian Whist, you need the following:

>> **At least three players:** You can play with up to eight players.

>> **One standard deck of 52 cards:** At the start of the game, pare down the deck so you have eight cards per player in the deck, using only the highest-ranking cards. For three players, prepare the deck so that it has only the aces through 9s in it; in other words, a 24-card deck. If you have six players, use a 48-card deck. With seven or eight players, you play a six-card game.

>> **Paper and pencil for scoring:** You may want to construct a score sheet set out in columns, with a column for each player.

Dealing the cards

You cut the deck to determine the dealer. The dealer gives each player the appropriate number of cards, dealing clockwise. The appropriate number depends on what stage of the game you're currently in (see the section "Dealing the cards" earlier in this chapter).

Romanian Whist differs from Oh Hell! in that you start with one card for the first trick, work your way up to eight cards, and then work your way down again. But the differences don't end there. The progression of Romanian Whist is a rather labored one because instead of going up one card at a time, every player takes a turn to deal a hand with one card each (thereby eliminating the dealer disadvantage I discuss earlier). After each one-card trick, the deal progresses normally until you get to the round of eight cards. At that point, everyone takes a turn at dealing eight cards, and then the progression retreats back down to one again for another complete round.

Choosing your trump suit, making your bids, and playing your tricks

Determine the trump suit by turning over the top card of the undealt-card pile. When you play the eight-card round, you play the hands with no trump suit at all (refer to the section "Taking tricks with the trump suit" earlier in this chapter for the details on trump suits).

All the normal Oh Hell! rules apply to the bidding (see the section "Placing your bid" earlier in this chapter) and to the playing of the tricks (refer to the section "Playing for your bids") — with one exception.

The exception is that in Romanian Whist you are forced to play a card from the trump suit if you have no cards in the suit led. In Oh Hell!, you can discard anything you like; if you have no trumps, you can throw anything you like.

Scoring the tricks

If you make your contract, you score 5 points, plus 1 point for each of the tricks you take. If you take fewer tricks than you contract for, you lose the value of your bid. If you take more tricks than you bid for, you lose the value equivalent to the tricks you took.

The scoring routine sounds complicated, but it really isn't. Look at how the scoring may apply to the four-handed game shown in Figure 9-2. Each player has three cards, and clubs are trump. North player deals.

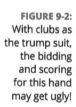

FIGURE 9-2:
With clubs as the trump suit, the bidding and scoring for this hand may get ugly!

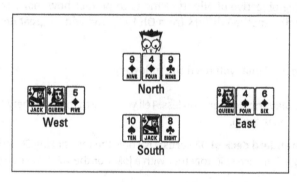

East bids zero, South bids one, West bids one, and North bids zero — rather unhappily. A bid of two by the dealer is a valid option here, but the diamond suit just seems too unlikely to generate two tricks (hey, you can see the other players' cards — North can't!).

East leads the ♠4, and South plays the ♠10. West wins the trick with the ♠J, and North discards the ♦9.

For the second trick, West leads the ♦5, North plays the ♦4, and East plays the ♦6, which creates a problem for South. If South trumps this trick and leads the ♥J, the lead may well win the last trick. Because discarding brings the bonus of defeating East's contract, South throws away the ♥J, giving East an unwanted trick. North wins the last trick with the ♣9, the highest trump card left.

The scoring goes like this:

>> **West** nails the bid of 1 and scores 6 points.

>> **East** underbids and loses the single trick, or 1 point.

>> **South** overbids by one trick and loses 1 point.

>> **North** underbids and loses 1 point.

One highly entertaining variation to the last one-card hand is to hold your card on your forehead so that everyone but you can see your card. You have to make your bid in the usual fashion, without knowing your card, based on the bids that everyone else makes and the cards you can see.

Ninety-Nine

Ninety-Nine combines the skill of Oh Hell! with some unique twists and attractive features. The objective of Ninety-Nine is to predict how many tricks you'll take, but the bidding method differs from Oh Hell! and adds a great deal of spice to the game.

To play Ninety-Nine, you need the following:

>> **Three players:** No more, no less. Tell your fourth to play Ninety-Nine bottles of beer on the wall.

>> **One standard deck of 52 cards:** Use only the top-ranking 36 cards (ace through 6 in each suit) together with a joker or the ♣2 if you don't have a joker.

>> **Paper and pencil for scoring:** Keep the score in three columns — as I explain later, you do not have to write down the bids in this game.

Dealing the dozen and determining the trump suit

Deal your trio a dozen cards each and turn over the last card in the deck to establish the trump suit for the hand (refer to the section "Taking tricks with the trump suit" earlier in this chapter for more information on trump suits). If the card you turn over is the joker or a 9, you play the hand with no trump suit.

NINETY-NINE: THE NEW KID ON THE BLOCK

Most of the card games I cover in this book have an established pedigree. Ninety-Nine, however, is a relatively modern game, and unlike most card games, which evolve over the passage of time, David Parlett invented Ninety-Nine in 1968 and laid out all its ground rules. He gave us all an outstanding game, and one of my absolute personal favorites. Check out his website at www.parlettgames.uk/ for lots of great insider advice.

Another approach to selecting the trump suit is to play the first hand with no trump suit. You play each subsequent hand with the trump suit determined by the number of players who successfully predicted their previous contracts. The trump suit is clubs if all three players succeeded, hearts for two, spades for one, and diamonds if everyone strikes out.

The game consists of exactly nine hands, called the *rubber*, with the deal passing clockwise at the end of each hand. The winner is the player who scores the most points overall.

Discarding your bids

Bidding, which is determining how many tricks you'll take, presents the most interesting part of Ninety-Nine. Although you get 12 cards, you use only 9 during game play; you discard the others before the hand starts, and what you discard determines your bid with the remaining 9 cards.

The suits of the three cards you discard signal your bid. It works like this:

>> **For every club you discard,** you contract to win three tricks.

>> **For every heart you discard,** you contract to win two tricks.

>> **For every spade you discard,** you contract to win one trick.

>> **For every diamond you discard,** you contract to win no tricks.

>> **If you discard the joker,** it takes on the value of the face-up card that determines the trump suit. The joker represents the number associated with the turned-up card. If the turned-up card is the ♠7, for example, discarding the joker represents a bid of one trick (for the spade).

The cumulative total of your discards represents your bid. For example, discarding a club, a heart, and a diamond gives you a bid of five tricks, as does a discard of a club and two spades or two hearts and a spade.

You discard your three cards face-down so the other players don't know what you're aiming for.

Selecting the proper discards

Say that you get the cards in Figure 9-3 and that spades are trump.

FIGURE 9-3:
Aces and trump
cards make
for a strong
Ninety-Nine
combination.

The realistic way to look at your hand is to concede that taking more than five tricks is unlikely; the other players have too many aces and trump cards. Can you discard, say, a club, heart, and diamond to leave you with a realistic chance of five tricks? Probably not. The other players won't bid that low because not so many diamonds are out, so they may stop you from winning five tricks. So how about going for four, discarding two hearts and a diamond? Not a bad idea. Three tricks seem too low as a possible target, because you have too many aces and kings, so go for four.

After you decide to discard two hearts and a diamond, you must decide which hearts and diamond to throw. I suggest discarding your middle cards for flexibility. Getting rid of the ♥Q, the ♥10, and a high diamond (the ♦K, for example, to reduce the overall trick-taking potential of the hand) is probably the right move here. You want to get the lead early and find out whether your *side-suits* (suits other than the trump suit) will win tricks. If so, lead low trump cards at each opportunity. If not, lead high trump cards.

You often find that the trump suit gets in your way when it comes to bidding what you want, even if you have cards in all the suits. For example, look at the hand in Figure 9-4; clubs are trump.

FIGURE 9-4:
You may have
plenty of trump
clubs, but you
have no
convenient
discard.

You have the potential to win seven tricks out of nine, but to bid seven tricks requires that you discard two clubs (you can't discard two hearts and a club, because you have only one heart). If you discard two clubs, you won't have enough winners left. It looks like your best bet, therefore, is to discard a club, a heart, and the ♠Q to go for six tricks.

When diamonds are the trump suit, players often discard most of the diamonds because that tactic allows for a low number and reduces the hand's strength simultaneously. Bear in mind that when diamonds are the trump suit, if you leave yourself a single middle diamond, you're much more likely to win a trick than with, say, a middle club.

However, a bad hand without diamonds can cause you severe problems. Imagine that you're dealt the hand in Figure 9-5 with spades as trump.

If you have to let go any of your trumps, this hand surely can't win more than a trick — if that — because other people's aces are sure to capture your middle honors (or they'll trump any club winners you establish). But the minimum bid you can make is for two tricks (by discarding two spades and a diamond). Do so, and hope for the best.

One other strategy is possible, although it reeks of desperation. If you accept that you have no chance to win two tricks with this hand, perhaps your optimum strategy is to mess up the other players' chances. Discard your high cards and try to make the other two players overbid. With the hand in Figure 9-5, you can discard the ♦J, the ♥Q, and the ♥8 and try to lose every trick to make the others go too high. I prefer this approach — anything that can irritate the other players has to be a good policy.

Discarding middle cards if you can is nearly always a good strategy because you leave yourself with (relatively) sure winners and sure losers. Under normal circumstances, if you have the ace, jack, and 7 in a suit, discard the jack — unless you want to avoid winners at all costs, in which case you throw the ace.

Making premium bids

Occasionally, you're dealt a hand that's so clear-cut you can afford to play for higher stakes and *declare* your bid by showing it to the other players.

If you declare your bid and succeed, you get a 30-point bonus on top of your normal score (see the section "Tallying the scores" later in this chapter), but if you fail, you must give an extra 30 points to each opponent. You need to be quite confident to try it out — or quite desperate toward the end of the game.

The truly bold and desperate have a second, more extreme alternative. If you're convinced you have a sure thing, you can declare your bid *and* reveal your hand to your opponents by turning it face-up. If you succeed, you get 60 points on top of your normal score; if you fail, you give 60 points to each of the other players. This tactic is known as *revealing*, although in practice, you reveal your hand *and* declare your bid.

(Incidentally, if you reveal your hand and go for all the tricks by discarding three clubs and are the only person to make your bid, you score 9 for the tricks, 60 for the bonus, and 30 for being the sole person to make your contract. That is worth 99 points — hence, the name of the game.)

Both tactics are called *premium bids.* If you fail in a premium bid, you still get your trick score, which is not much consolation, I grant you!

Only one player can make a premium bid on each hand. The player to the left of the dealer gets the first chance to declare their bid or reveal their hand. If they opt to reveal, they win the right to a premium bid; if they opt to declare, the player to their left or the dealer can outbid them by revealing. If the first player opts to pass, the second player gets the same options, and finally the choice is up to the dealer.

Don't automatically assume that trying to defeat a premium contract is in your best interests. Say that the player on your left declares their bid when they are 60 points behind you. The player on your right is 12 points ahead of you. Even if the premium bid goes through, you'll still be comfortably in front of the bidder, as long you make your contract. Concentrate on beating your real opponent by making your contract, and let the player who declares succeed if they can.

Well, I declare!

Take a look at a hand that lends itself to a declaration in Figure 9-6 — spades are the trump suit.

FIGURE 9-6:
Low cards and aces are a potent combination for a declaration.

The decision to declare on this hand is by no means cast in stone, but think about how likely you are to make exactly one trick if you discard the ♠Q, the ♦K, and the ♦Q. This discard represents a bid of one trick, and you hope to win with the ♥A, lose the lead with the ♠7, and find a way to avoid winning a trick in any of the other suits. This strategy isn't a lock to succeed, but you do stand a pretty good chance.

Another example is shown in Figure 9-7. Hearts are trump.

Again, nothing is certain in life except death and taxes, but discarding the ♠A, the ♠9, and the ♦10 and going for two tricks seem reasonable. I advise leading the ♦A and hoping that it wins a trick. If it does, take the ♣A, and then get off lead with the ♣6.

The ♦A in the preceding example is by no means sure to win — someone may have discarded all their diamonds. But discarding all diamonds means that the player intends to bid low, so they may not want to trump your trick. In abstract, the other aces are more likely to get trumped because by discarding cards in another suit, you are committing yourself to take tricks, unlike those cases when you discard a diamond.

Revealing your choices

Hands that tempt you to reveal have to be fairly cut and dried. Again, of course, circumstances alter cases; if you're not playing for stakes, you often see desperate measures toward the end of a rubber. Keep in mind that you play nine hands in a contest, which makes up one rubber. And nobody remembers who finishes second.

Under any circumstances, the hand in Figure 9-8 qualifies. Suppose that hearts are trump in this case, and you're the first player to bid.

FIGURE 9-8:
Nearly a
sure thing.

You have a virtual lock on zero tricks if you discard your three diamonds and lead the ♥7. Unless a player starts the hand with, and keeps, all four outstanding spades (keep in mind that each suit has only nine cards), you're safe because your low spades ensure that you can avoid taking a trick in the suit.

One variation of the revealing tactic is to allow the player who reveals or declares to choose the trump suit — although it may make the bids a little too easy to attain. Limiting this option to reveals may be less disruptive. In this variation, a player who reveals can also choose 9s as the trump suit. You create a separate trump suit of the 9s, ranking in descending order: clubs, hearts, spades, and diamonds.

Playing the hand

Unless a player makes a premium bid (see the section "Making premium bids" earlier in this chapter), you leave your bids face-down on the table, and the player to the left of the dealer leads to the first trick. The normal Oh Hell! rules apply: You must follow suit if you can, or play whatever you want if you can't. (See the section "Playing for your bids" earlier in this chapter for basic game play information.)

At the end of the hand, all players announce their tricks taken and whether they met their contracts. If they made their bids, they turn over their bids to confirm it.

Tallying the scores

After you play the hand, you score it up. Each player scores the number of tricks taken with 1 point each, and you add a bonus if you make your contracts. The bonus varies depending on how many players meet their contracts:

>> **If only one player succeeds,** add a 30-point bonus.

>> **If two players make their contracts,** they each get 20 points (bad luck for player three!).

>> **If everyone succeeds,** you all get an additional 10 points — rather like kissing your sister.

You can consult your bid during the course of play to remind yourself of your bid and which cards you discarded. Make sure that you don't mix your bid cards with your tricks taken or switch a trick with your bid cards!

Instead of playing exactly nine hands and determining the winner by the highest score at the end, you can also score by reference to games. A game is 100 points, and the first player to reach two games wins. As soon as a player reaches 100 points, they get a bonus of 100 points, and a new game starts again. A *rubber* is the best of three games, and a player's scores from the three games are cumulative.

This form of scoring doesn't lend itself to scrambles at the end to overtake the hand in the lead by desperate declarations or revelations. I prefer the simple scoring, because everyone has a chance to win to the end.

Chapter **10**

Euchre

E uchre is an excellent social card game, simple in concept but with a high degree of subtlety in the play. The game offers myriad variations, because you can play it with any number of players and as a long or short game.

BEFORE HAND

To play Euchre, you need the following:

» **Four players:** Two teams, two players to a team.

» **A standard deck of 52 cards:** Take out the ace through the 9 in each suit, making a deck of 24 cards for the game.

» **Paper and pencil for scoring:** You can also keep score with some of the remaining playing cards. See the section "Tallying Your Score" at the end of this chapter for more information.

Acquainting Yourself with Euchre

Euchre is a trick-taking game at heart. Each player receives five cards, and you play one card at a time; the player who lays the highest card in the suit of the first card played — unless someone contributes a trump, in which case it is whoever lays the highest trump card (see the section "Determining the Trump Suit" later in this chapter) — collects all four cards together and stacks them in front of them, thus taking the *trick*.

In Euchre, you win a hand and score points for taking the majority of the tricks in a hand, which means winning three or more of the five tricks available. You get more points if you take all five tricks (see the section "Tallying Your Score" at the end of this chapter). But to summarize: You score points for bidding and making a contract or defeating the opponents when they are trying to make their contracts. The first to a specified total of points, generally 10, wins the match.

You play the game with partners, but under special circumstances, one member of a partnership can elect to go solo — if they think that going alone is worthwhile. See the section "Playing for Bigger Stakes Alone" later in this chapter for the details.

PLAYING EUCHRE ON THE INTERNET

If you yearn for a Euchre game day and night, visit the home of WebEuchre at www. pogo.com; the site lets you download WebEuchre, a program written by Michael Riccio, for all types of computers. Just follow the WebEuchre Wizard's instructions at the site, and you join other Euchre fans online for live games.

Programs like MeggieSoft, MVP Software, and DreamQuest allow you to play Euchre online or against your computer. You can pick your preferred game of Euchre on the Net or program with which to play Euchre if you visit John McLeod's site at www.pagat. com/euchre/euchre.html.

Picking Partners

You play Euchre with two teams of two players, either with prearranged partnerships or with partners selected by cutting the deck. If you cut the deck for partners, the two highest cards take on the two lowest cards.

Make sure the partners sit opposite each other. In partnership games, you almost always sit across from your partner, probably to keep you off each other's throats.

Striking a Fair Deal

You can select the dealer at random, or you can deal out the cards until a jack appears. Whoever gets the jack becomes the dealer.

The dealer shuffles the cards and offers them to the player on their left to cut. That player can cut the deck or tap (*bump*) the cards to indicate that no cut is necessary.

You deal the cards clockwise. Just to make the game interesting, the dealer deals out five cards, face-down, in packets of two to each player and then three to each player (or three then two if you absolutely insist). Go figure. After dealing the cards, you turn over one card and place it in the middle of the table on top of the other three unused cards. These three cards, or the *kitty*, play no further part in the hand. The upturned card represents the trump suit (see the following section, "Determining the Trump Suit").

At the end of each hand, the deal rotates clockwise.

WARNING

A *misdeal* can occur in several ways, but for the most part, no serious consequences arise from a misdeal. If the deal is flawed for whatever reason — because a card turns over on the table, the deck has a face-up card in it, or the deck contains the wrong number of cards — you cancel the deal and redeal the hand.

REMEMBER

If a player deals out of turn and someone notices before they turn the top card over, you cancel the deal. However, if the player turns the top card up before anyone notices, the deal stands, and whoever misses their deal simply loses out. (As you see in the following section, "Determining the Trump Suit," dealing carries an advantage, so you don't want to skip your deal.)

If a player receives the wrong number of cards and discovers it before the first trick starts, a redeal takes place with no penalties. If the error isn't corrected in time, however, play continues, and whichever team has the player with the wrong number of cards can't score on that hand. The moral of the story is: Count your cards!

Determining the Trump Suit

After the deal is complete, the dealer turns over the top card of the four remaining cards. This is called the *upcard*, and it determines what the trump suit is for the current hand. The remaining three cards play no part in the current hand.

REMEMBER

The trump suit represents the boss suit, meaning that a trump card beats any card in any other suit. In Euchre, you have to *follow* the suit that the first player leads (play a card in the same suit), but if you can't follow suit, you can play a trump card and win the trick (unless someone plays a higher trump card).

The dealer can add the turned-up card to their hand and discard an unwanted card of their choice — under certain circumstances (I explain those circumstances in the later section, "Bidding for Tricks").

Jacking Up the Card Rankings

When you pick up your hand, you can sort it into suits. The standard ranking order applies — within each suit, the ace is high, and the values descend to the lowly 9.

The only exception to the normal ranking rules lies in the trump suit, which ranks as follows:

>> The highest trump card is the jack of the trump suit, often referred to as the *right bower* (rhyming with "flower" and deriving from the German word *bauer*, which means "jack" — surprise, surprise!).

VARIATION

In England, you play the game with a joker, which ranks as the master trump. The joker is known as the *Benny,* or the Best Bower.

>> The second-highest trump card is the other jack of the same-color suit, often called the *left bower*. The jack deserts its own suit and becomes a trump card for the hand; for example, the ♠J ceases to be a spade when clubs are the trump suit — it becomes a club.

>> The remaining five cards in the trump suit are the ace, king, queen, 10, and 9, ranking from highest to lowest in that order.

For example, if clubs are the trump suit, the cards rank in the order shown in Figure 10-1. Diamonds and hearts rank from the ace through 9 in the normal fashion.

FIGURE 10-1: Card ranks when clubs are the trump suit.

Bidding for Tricks

After you pick and sort your cards, you get a chance to make your bid. Everyone sees what card gets turned over for the trump suit; the question is whether anyone wants to bid to take three or more tricks with that suit as the trump suit. Each player gets the chance to take on that assignment or refuse the invitation. If all players refuse, the bidding goes into its second phase. To make your decision, you need to value your hand for play in the trump suit.

Because the second phase of the game involves playing with the trump suit of your choice, you also have to look at your hand and value it for play in a different trump suit.

Starting the bidding

Each player in turn, starting with the player on the dealer's left, can agree to play the suit of the upcard in the middle of the table as trump on behalf of their partnership, or each player can pass. If any player accepts the suit of the upcard as the trump suit, the dealer adds the upcard to their hand and throws one card away face-down.

The partnership that makes the decision to take three or more tricks (as opposed to passing) are called the *makers*, and the other players are the *defenders*. You follow these protocols during the first round of bidding:

1. The first player either plays with the predetermined trump suit, called *ordering it up* (meaning that they ask the dealer to pick up the upcard), or they pass by saying "I pass."

2. The second player, the dealer's partner, can pass, or they can accept the current trump suit by saying "Partner, I assist," "I'll help you," or "Pick it up."

3. The third player follows the pattern for the first hand by ordering the trump up or passing.

4. The dealer accepts the choice of the trump suit by saying "I pick it up" and taking up the card to add it to their hand, or they reject the card by saying "Over" or "I turn it down."

   If they reject the trump suit, they take the upcard and put it face-up at a right angle to the deck below the other three cards to indicate what suit isn't acceptable as the trump suit for the second round of bidding (see the later section "Entering the second phase of bidding" for more information).

Knowing what to bid

The most delicate strategy in the game hinges on your decision to accept the trump suit and make a bid or not. As a general rule, you should expect your partner to help you get one trick. If you look at the tricks you think you can take from your hand and see two sure tricks, you have enough to consider bidding. If you hold three good trump cards, you definitely have enough to make a bid.

You must also consider whether a different trump suit may work better for you and your partner. If no one wants to play in the initial trump suit, each player has a chance to select a different trump suit, so evaluating your hand for both purposes is important.

TIP

The state of the score is also critical. Euchre is played to a set target; if you (or your opponent) are close to winning, consider whether your hand plays better in the specified trump suit than another suit. Picking that suit as trump may be your best chance to win — or stop your opponents from winning.

You get rewarded if you succeed in your bid and penalized if you fail, so you want to get your decision right if you can. If you fail to get the required three tricks, you get *euchred* — hence the name of the game. (See the section "Tallying Your Score" later in this chapter for all the scoring information.)

Each member of the partnership who didn't deal the hand — with the member to the dealer's left being the first to speak on both the first and second rounds of bidding — needs a relatively good hand to accept the trump suit on the first round. You shouldn't accept the trump suit without at least three probable tricks in the early phases of the game (and thus before tactical considerations of the state of the match enter into the equation). The nondealing partnership gets first crack at selecting the trump suit on the second round of bidding if everyone passes, which is an advantage. In addition, the fact that the dealer picks up a trump card tilts the odds in their favor and pushes their side toward making an aggressive bid to select the trump suit in the first round.

Keep in mind that the left bower (the second-highest jack) may be of more use to you during the second round of bidding, particularly if you aren't the dealer. If you have the left bower, consider passing the trump suit on the first round and then selecting the suit of the same color on the second round. The dealer doesn't get to take the upcard to improve their hand, and your left bower becomes the boss trump card, the right bower. Of course, you won't enjoy a second round of bidding if another player accepts the initial trump suit, but that's a risk you have to take if you don't have a good enough hand to order up the trump suit.

A variation to the bidding is played widely in Australia, England, and Canada. If the partner of the dealer accepts the trump suit, they must accept on their own (thereby playing solo; see the section "Playing for Bigger Stakes Alone" later in this chapter) instead of accepting for the partnership.

Entering the second phase of bidding

If all four players pass on the trump suit, you turn the top card down, thereby eliminating the dealer's inherent advantage. On the second round of bidding, players may again accept the responsibility of going for three tricks, naming any other suit as the trump suit. You can't bid the suit of the original upturned card during the second bidding stage. That suit is only a possible trump suit for the first round.

If a player on the second round calls the same trump suit as the upturned card, their side can't participate in the bidding.

Again, the bidding goes around the table, starting with the player on the dealer's left, who can pass or name the trump suit. If they pass, the next player has the same choices, and so on around the table. Whoever selects a trump suit wins the bidding — now all the partnership has to do is make the bid good. If all four players pass, you throw the hand in, and the next player deals a new hand.

In a variation called "stick the dealer," the dealer *must* call trump at their second turn if no one else has taken on the responsibility. The penalty for failure remains the same for them as if they had voluntarily taken on the task.

Don't forget your jacks; they become very valuable when trump is up in the air. Also remember to value the jack in the suit of the same color as the trump suit. As soon as you or someone else nominates a new trump suit, a previously irrelevant jack may suddenly become very powerful.

If the dealer doesn't accept the original trump card, it normally implies that they don't hold a bower (jack) in the trump suit or in the same color. (If they do, they may well have gone for the original suit as the trump suit.) If you don't know whether to bid and what suit to select as the trump suit, the nondealers should go for the suit of the same color as the initial trump suit, and the dealer's partner should go for a trump suit of the other color.

At the end of the bidding, both sides go for at least three tricks. If the bid comes on the first round, the dealer picks up the upcard and puts it in their hand. If you make trump on the second round, whoever chooses the trump suit announces it, and the dealer leaves the upcard alone. Is that all there is to the game? Not quite.

Tallying Your Score

The team that chooses the trump suit and then wins three or four tricks scores 1 point. If the side that makes trump gets all five tricks, it *marches* or *sweeps* the hand, and the team scores 2 points.

Three tricks are necessary to fulfill the obligations you assume when you determine the trump suit.

If the makers fail to fulfill the trick obligation, the defenders score 2 points (whether they get three, four, or five tricks) — they have *euchred* the makers. However, the biggest score comes if you go solo (see below) and make all five tricks: 4 points.

The first team to 10 points *reaches game* and wins. You can also play to 5 points for a shorter game.

KEEPING SCORE WITH CARDS

You don't need to write down the scores to keep track of the running totals. Serious Euchre players often use playing cards, placed one on top of the other, to keep their totals. Specifically, you need an extra 2 and 3 to keep score with playing cards. To indicate one point, you turn up the 3 and put the 2 face-down to cover all but one spot. Showing 2 and 3 are easy, of course. For 4, you put both cards face-up with the 3 partly over the 2. If you play to 10 points, some people use a 6 and a 4.

Playing for Bigger Stakes Alone

A player with a particularly good hand can raise the stakes by opting to play the hand *alone*. The player who selects the trump suit has this option. As soon as you indicate your intention of going alone, your partner puts their cards face-down, for this hand alone, and the game becomes three-handed.

A hand with the top three trump cards (♠J, ♣J, and ♠A, for example) is often a sure thing for going alone, especially if you have an off-suit ace. Two of the top three trumps and an ace on the side may be enough, but you may want a little more for insurance.

Why would you want to play alone? The only reason for doing so is if you have a guaranteed three tricks with a serious chance of making five tricks with your hand alone. If you make three or four tricks, you score the game the same as you do in partnership situations (see the previous section, "Tallying Your Score," for details). But if you make all five tricks, as maker, you score 4 points.

Another game version states that the penalty for getting euchred when a defender goes alone is doubled. This provides the incentive for a defender going alone.

Going alone has no real advantage unless you have a good chance to make five tricks on your own; otherwise, you simply increase the chance of a penalty without any chance of increasing the rewards. With three sure winners in your hand, you must ponder whether your remaining cards give you a chance for a clean sweep. If not, play in your partnership and hope that your partner can come through with the goods for your feeble cards.

For example, say that your partner is the dealer, the ♣9 is the upcard, and you have the hand in Figure 10-2.

FIGURE 10-2:
A promising
hand; how
many tricks can
you take?

This hand isn't assured of winning you three tricks, although it's heavily favored to do so. However, if the ♠J is in your partner's hand, is one of the three cards in the muck, or is in one of your opponents' hands without any other trump cards accompanying it (and you see three trump cards out of the seven already), you stand a fair chance of making five tricks. Still, the odds of your partner making the vital difference are almost nonexistent, because you can either win the tricks on your own or not at all. The hand in Figure 10-2 is an excellent hand to go solo on.

By contrast, consider the hand in Figure 10-3.

FIGURE 10-3:
Caution! Your
partner's help
wanted!

With clubs as trump, you're almost sure to have four clear winners in your hand, but the ♦10 isn't a favorite to win the last trick unless your opponents discard poorly; of course, their poor discarding is by no means impossible! I'd go for all the tricks with my partner's help rather than bidding alone.

TIP

Before deciding whether to go alone, here are two factors that may influence you. If the score is such that getting four points may be critical (your opponents are close to winning and you are three or four points away), that may tempt you to go for the bigger gamble. Additionally your chances of going alone and getting all five tricks are rather better on a two-suited hand than a one-suiter. With three high trumps and the A-10 in a side-suit you may well find yourself taking the last two tricks, whereas the bare 10 in a side-suit is far less likely to win the last trick.

Tricking for Points, Not Treats

After the opening lead is made (typically by the player to the dealer's left, but not always), the play goes clockwise around the table. You must *follow suit* (play a card in the suit led) if you can, but if you can't, throw off any card or play a trump card as you see fit. Whoever plays the highest card of the suit led, or the highest trump card if one or more trumps have been played on the trick, wins that trick.

When a player goes alone, the hand on their left leads to the first trick. If both a defender and a maker go alone, the defender leads.

VARIATION It is also common to play that the player to dealer's left leads as usual (or if this player has dropped out, the next active player around in clockwise order leads). This variation makes playing a loner in second or third position more difficult, where the lead comes through you, than in first position, when you have the lead, or as dealer, when the first lead comes up to you.

Failure to follow suit when you can do so is called a *revoke* or *renege*. You must correct a revoke before the winner gathers the trick. If another player identifies a revoke, the innocent side may add 2 points to its score or deduct 2 points from the guilty side. If your side is going alone and one of the opponents revokes, the penalty is 4 points.

I can offer only limited advice in the play of the cards. Part of the game lies in memorizing the cards played. You have to think about who may have what cards left to determine what to lead and what to throw away, when you have a choice. For example, the original trump card is one that you want to remember; if the dealer adds it to their hand, don't forget it.

If you have the opening lead and you have two or more trump cards, consider leading them. You should certainly lead a high trump if your partner called the trump suit because it helps your partner locate the missing cards. Otherwise, lead from a sequence if you have one. Start with high cards to help out your partner so that they don't waste their high cards unnecessarily. For example, if hearts are trump, you could lead the ♠A or ♣A to try to win a trick.

TIP Unlike some other card games, saving a winner for a rainy day in Euchre generally has no advantage. Take your tricks when you can, or you may never get them.

Chapter **11**

Spades

C ard gamers the world over are exercising great amounts of creative energy on harnessing the rules of Spades — an all-American card game created in the United States in the 1930s — which, in turn, implies that the game is likely to improve as players test these modifications and incorporate or discard them. However, because the rules are so fluid and no rules are *official*, everybody seems to have a unique version, and the scoring system is a nightmare.

So, you must bear with me. The rules that I set out in this chapter may not correspond exactly to the rules that your friends play by, but they do cover the basics of the game and allow you to play along with others or even teach your friends to play by "your" rules.

BEFORE HAND

To play Spades, you need the following:

» **Four players:** No more, no less.

» **One standard deck of 52 cards:** In some variations, you need the jokers, too.

» **An efficient scorer with pencil and paper:** Don't select the person on their cell phone in between deals.

Grasping the Basics of Spades

Spades is traditionally a game for exactly four players, played in partnership (with the partners sitting opposite each other). The players take turns playing out one card from their hands clockwise around the table. You must play a card in whichever suit is played first (or *led*) if you can, which is called *following suit*. The four cards played constitute a unit of play called a *trick*. The objective of Spades is for your partnership to accurately estimate the strength of your hands in the bidding, and then in the play to take as close to your estimate of tricks as you can.

Choosing partners

The partnerships in Spades are frequently fixed in advance, but you can alternate lineups at the end of a contest, or *rubber* (a predetermined amount of games you set; for example, a best-of-three contest constitutes a rubber; see the later section "Finishing the game" for more information about rubbers).

Reviewing the card ranks

The cards rank from ace (high) down to 2 (low). If you decide to play without adding in any wrinkles, ranking the cards is no big deal.

VARIATION

However, if you like wrinkles, you can use a number of variations when ranking the cards. One common variation is to add two jokers to the deck, making sure they have separate markings to distinguish the big and little jokers. The two jokers become additional trump cards, and big cards as that: They rank as the highest and second-highest trump cards. Because it makes the most sense to play the game with each player having 13 cards, you can either remove ♥2 and ♦2 or deal 15 cards to the dealer. The dealer then removes two cards from their hand and discards them face-down so they play no further part in the game.

Making the deal

You select the dealer at random by cutting the deck; the person who draws the highest card deals. The traditional Bridge custom of having the player on the dealer's left shuffle the cards and the player on the dealer's right cut them is as good as any.

Starting with the player to their left, the dealer distributes the deck card by card, face-down to each player, so that everyone has a 13-card hand (with two discards if you play with the joker variation; see the previous section). The deal progresses one place clockwise after each hand.

The object is to win as many tricks as possible. However, each of the four players must estimate in advance of the start of play how many tricks they will win. This estimate is called a *bid*, and your bid can include opting for no tricks or up to 13 tricks.

REMEMBER

However, the peculiarity of Spades is that, although both sides join freely in the bidding, this auction isn't competitive — both sides get to make a bid and then pursue their targets (unlike some games, in which only one side gets to make a bid, and the other side is totally occupied with stopping them).

Each player independently names a number, and then each side chases its own specific number of tricks, the total of the two players' bids. If your side succeeds, you're generously rewarded; if you fail to meet your target, you're referred to as *going set* (a phrase you will hear a lot of in this chapter) and heavily punished. But that isn't the end of the story. Spades is an *exact trick* game: If you make more tricks than you bid during the auction, you're also punished rather severely, though not as seriously as you are if you fail to meet your side's target. In fact, overtricks are known as *bags* because of the tie-in to being "sandbagged" (see the section "Getting sandbagged with overtricks" later on; bags will also crop up a fair amount in this chapter!). The trade-off between valuing your hand correctly in the bidding and making your contract exactly (rather than making too many tricks or making too few tricks) is a very fine line indeed. All these factors make Spades a fascinating game.

TIP

Your first duty for the partnership is to try to make at least as many tricks as you bid. As a secondary objective, provided you secure the first one, you try to avoid making too many overtricks. However, in most cases, you are happy to make overtricks if doing so sets your opponents.

The winner of the game is the first partnership that arrives at a set target — 500 or 250 points is a normal target — or the pair leading after a set number of deals — such as 10.

Bidding your hand accurately

In turn (around the table from the left of the dealer), each player can opt to bid any number of tricks between 0 and 13. After your opponent bids, your partner makes an estimate, and the combined total for each side is the number of tricks that the partnership needs to take to fulfill its *contract* for the hand.

REMEMBER

Bidding nil (going for no tricks at all) is different from any other bid. I discuss this bid in the later section "Bidding for nil."

VARIATION

In the constantly evolving world of Spades, even the question of who bids first generates controversy. Some people say that the dealer is the first to speak, but the standard game calls for the bidding to start with the player to the left of the dealer, or the *elder hand*.

REMEMBER

Each partnership registers its tricks as a unit — it doesn't matter whether you or your partner takes the tricks unless a bid for nil has been made by one of the players; the important thing is that your side gets them. For example, if you bid two and your partner bids three, whether you get five or your partner gets five is irrelevant; if you get five tricks between you, you make your contract.

VARIATION

A different school of bidding is much more lax about the restrictions on communications between the partners. Starting with the nondealer's side, the two players can have a brief and non-specific conversation about their trick-taking capabilities. The first player of each partnership may provide clues along the following lines: "I have a hand with three sure tricks and the possibility for up to five or even six tricks."

When you pick up a hand, consider your high cards and your trump length to try to estimate the value of the hand. There will be imponderables, of course, but the initial calculation is linked to those two factors.

MANY MISDEAL RULES

Some variations of Spades allow a player to call for a misdeal before the bidding if their hand satisfies certain conditions. For example, a player may call for a misdeal if they hold one or no spades, hold a *side-suit* (that is, not spades) of seven or more cards, or don't hold any court cards (the ace, king, queen, and jack). In these situations, the player should ask their partner if they want a misdeal before the bidding commences; however, their partner's reply isn't binding.

For example, with the hand shown in Figure 11-1, you bid two, counting one trick for the ♥A and one for the spades. Note that the ♥A is probably a trick you do not have to win; you have enough hearts to be able to refrain from playing that card on a heart lead. So you have some flexibility as to whether you want to bid one or two with the example hand. With the ♣K, you would bid three tricks. If you take this basic starting hand and change the ♣9 to the ♠K, the hand is worth four tricks: three in spades and the ♥A.

FIGURE 11-1:
Deciding what
to bid.

Basking in the dealer's choice

Being the dealer (or the fourth seat) in Spades is a significant advantage because you get to hear the other players commit themselves to a number of tricks before you have to decide on a bid.

As a player in the fourth seat, you hear the three players suggest a combined total. As a general rule, you shouldn't take the total to more than 13. At an early stage in the game, consider, for example, that your opponents have jointly contracted for six tricks, and your partner has bid for three. If you make five tricks and your partner makes their three, then you have already combined to set your opponents by stopping them from making their announced target of six. Because you have already achieved a major target on the hand, you're better off bidding four and settling for an overtrick if it accrues. Yes, your side takes a small hit, but you administer a bigger blow to the opponents in the process. Conversely, if you really need to set the opponents to have a chance to win the game, you may bid five if you're truly confident — however, the penalty of the overtrick may be too severe — see the later section "Getting sandbagged with overtricks."

TIP

As a general rule, if you have a strong hand and the player to your left bids strongly, you should go low because that player will be in a position to capture your kings and queens if they so desire. If the player to your right bids strongly, the reverse applies; you're in the catbird seat.

Figuring the value of your high cards

Your success at bidding rests largely on knowing how to value your cards:

>> You count all aces as being worth a trick to start. No surprise there.

>> Count kings as worth about two-thirds of a trick, unless you also have the ace in that suit. Obviously, you can't bid for fractions of a trick, but the point is to add on something to your sure tricks for each king. If you have the ace and king together, treat the pair as two full tricks. However, be aware that the ace-king in a *side-suit* (a suit that isn't spades) of more than five cards is potentially extremely vulnerable because the danger of your opponents trumping a high card increases. In fact, you should mentally devalue any ace or king in a side-suit.

>> Queens are difficult to value unless other court cards support them. Queens are worth something — but not much. With an ace, treat the combination as 1½ tricks; with a king, treat the combination as worth a full trick. Otherwise, treating a queen as about one-third of a trick is about right, unless it's in a side-suit of more than five cards, in which case you may discount it altogether.

WARNING

>> Valuing jacks, unless they're combined with other high court cards, is very risky business. Because a jack is unlikely to win the first or second round of a suit, and because someone may be out of the suit by then and be able to trump your winner, counting jacks at all is pretty optimistic.

>> Trump cards (any spades) are all valuable; count any trump card after your first three as worth a full trick. You should value all significant trump court cards, such as the ace, king, or queen of spades, at a full trick.

>> Whatever the suit they're in, all high court cards (A, K, Q, J) in a very short suit (meaning you don't have many in the suit) become less valuable because your flexibility is impaired. A king on its own (also called a *singleton*) and a *doubleton* queen (one in a two-card holding) can both be wiped out very easily. For example, when someone leads out an ace in that suit, you have no choice but to play your king under it if you have only one card in the suit.

>> If you have a void in spades, take off something from your hand valuation — your side-suit court cards are now more likely to be trumped.

WARNING

Hands generally fall into one of two categories: *balanced hands*, which have two to four cards in each suit, or *unbalanced* or *distributional hands*, which have some suits with plenty of cards in them (a *long suit*) and some suits where you have very few cards (a *short suit*). The more distributional your hand, the higher the danger that your high cards in the side–suits won't score tricks. For example, if you have ♥A and only one other card in the suit, everybody else is likely to have at least one heart. But, if you have five clubs, including ♣A and ♣K, counting both as sure tricks is dangerous because one of your opponents may have only one club and trump your winner by playing a spade on it.

TIP

PAINTING YOUR BIDDING PICTURE

One of the most testing areas of Spades is evaluating your hand correctly for the bid-ding. The consequences for a miscalculation in the bidding are almost equally severe whether you overestimate or underestimate your call. Having said that, the penalty for underbidding is less painful because the ax does not fall immediately. Still, getting your bid right and drawing the right inferences from other people's bids can gain you a large number of points — not to mention your partner's undying affection.

As soon as the bidding begins, each subsequent bidder can build up more and more of the picture, and using your judgment becomes easier as the bidding proceeds.

Depending on whether you believe them or not, your opponents' bids and comments should factor into your calculations. Those clues can help you work out just how good your hand really is and can help you make an accurate assessment of its worth.

Bidding for nil

You can bid for zero tricks if you think your hand really stinks. A bid of *nil* (also known as *nill*, *null*, or *nillo*) carries additional benefits and liabilities. The concept is to make no tricks at all, and you get a generous 50-point bonus for success, with an equally heavy penalty for failure.

REMEMBER

Normally, the two players on a team combine their bids to form a total contract for their side. If you bid nil, however, your success or failure depends on your own personal performance. Although your partner does their best to help you by over-taking any high cards that you play, making the contract is up to you and you alone.

It may also be worth emphasizing that when one player bids nil, their partner's bid still stands. That player must make their bid good in the usual fashion, with the standard bonuses and penalties applying.

A more unlikely option is to *blind nil*, which carries with it the same concept of not taking any tricks, but you make the bid without looking at your hand. The rewards and penalties are doubled (so the consequence is plus or minus 100 points). You can only attempt the blind nil option if your side is 100 or more points behind. Because bidding blind nil is a highly risky strategy, you should attempt it only as a last resort. It's also helpful to remember that it may be better for your side to be down 100 rather than 90 points because of this option.

In some forms of scoring, nil is worth 100, and the score for blind nil is 200, and it is only allowed if you are at least 200 points behind.

Because going blind is such a difficult feat to achieve, the player making the call can exchange two cards with their partner to improve both players' hands for their various purposes. The cards are passed face-down, and the bidder passes their two cards first, letting their partner look at the cards and select two from their own hand in exchange.

Bidding blind is a good way to randomize the proceedings if you're losing the game heavily; desperate situations demand desperate remedies. In fact, after you get 100 points down, you should seriously consider bidding blind immediately.

Bidding blind nil is a gamble, but fun. Even potentially unpromising hands apparently with too many high cards, can turn out well. Check out the potentially unpromising hand in Figure 11-2, which turns out to be quite suitable for the blind nil bid.

FIGURE 11-2:
With a hand like this, bid nil.

You can exchange the high trump cards and hope to pick up low cards in the other suits from your partner to protect you from the danger of winning a trick with your high cards in diamonds or clubs.

Turning the tables, your partner may bid blind nil when you have the hand shown in Figure 11-3.

FIGURE 11-3:
Adjust your bid if your partner bids blind nil.

You probably intended to bid for three tricks because of your aces, kings, and queens. But if your partner bids blind nil, you should increase your bid because you expect to receive at least one sure trick from your partner. Say, for example, that you bid five tricks and receive the ♣A and ♠J. Getting those cards argues for passing the ♦4 and ♥5 because you can be pretty sure that your hearts can over-take any high card that your partner has in the suit.

TIP

When your partner bids blind nil, you should protect it, even at the potential cost of not making your contract. When you lead to the first trick, start with high cards from your long suits, which lets your partner discard on later rounds of the suit. Consider not overtaking your opponent's high cards, even if you think you may need the trick to make your bid, to make sure you're left with enough high cards to protect your partner. If you lead to the first trick on your own nil, con-sider starting with a middle card in a short suit — the odds are that your partner will be able to overtake.

See the section "Going for your scores" for the details on scoring successful and unsuccessful nil bids.

Playing to the score

The scorer writes down the bids after the auction ends. A single digit for the team's score is usually sufficient, unless a nil or a blind nil bid has been made, in which case the scorer notes that element as well. When the bids hit the paper, the play starts.

TIP

Before you start, however, take time to consider whether the combined total bids for both sides mean that the players will be trying to create extra tricks or lose them. If the total is 10 or less, both sides will be trying to lose tricks, where pos-sible, to avoid overtricks, or bags. Consider overtaking your partner's winners or even trumping them if you feel confident you can make your bid even after com-bining your honors in this way. By doing so, you avoid potentially costly overtricks later on. If the total is 13 or more, the likelihood is that both sides will be risking going set, so make sure you get the most out of your cards. Don't interfere with your partner's tricks and try to win them twice! With the bid in the middle at 11 or 12, play normally, but try to preserve low cards and use up your middle cards for maximum flexibility. That way you can go high or low as the case demands.

Leading and play conventions

The play of the cards goes clockwise, starting with the player to the dealer's left. That player puts a card face-up in the middle of the table, and then all other play-ers contribute a card in turn.

If you have no cards in the suit led, you can play anything you like; if you play a spade on the lead of a heart, diamond, or club, you win the trick because spades are the master (or *trump*) suit. Even the smallest spade is higher than the ace in any other suit. The person who plays the highest card in the led suit or the highest spade collects up the four cards played and wins the trick.

At every trick, the player who won the previous trick can lead anything they like — with the exception of spades. You can't lead spades at any point in the game until the suit is *broken*. The *breaking spades* rule means that the suit is off-limits until someone trumps the lead of a side-suit or until a player on lead is down to only spades in their hand. After trump is broken, you may lead spades at any time.

Some play that the opening lead has significant restrictions; in fact, the play has no flexibility at all: Everyone must play their lowest club. If you can't follow suit, you must discard a heart or a diamond — no trumping allowed. Some authorities allow a player to trump the first trick if they have no clubs. Yet another variation is that if the ♣2 is led, all players can then play any clubs they want, not just their lowest clubs.

Most variations require you to put in some mental-homework time before you can make a successful lead.

Opening with the other players in mind

Some of the conventions more commonly used in Bridge (see Chapter 12) can also be used in Spades. To start with, when leading with an ace-king, lead the king rather than the ace in order to let your partner know you have that sequence (because your partner knows that you know an opponent would surely have taken the trick). If you follow on your partner's lead of a side-suit with a high card and then a low card, you're suggesting that you have only two cards in the suit. Conversely, playing low and then high suggests you have three or more cards.

As a general rule, early on in the play when the opponent on your right leads a suit in which you have a king, queen, or jack, together with some small cards, but no touching honor, don't put up that court card. Save it for later. Conversely, when you're in the third seat on your partner's lead, you should generally try to win the trick by putting up a high card.

When your partner shows out of a suit by trumping it, try to lead to your partner to let them do it again — unless your partner led out trumps earlier in the hand, a sure sign they didn't want you to lead a suit to force them to trump. Conversely, when your opponents start ruffing in, you should consider leading trumps — or at least not leading that suit again.

Along with your partner, you have to always keep your opponents in mind when leading. When the total of the two side's bids is 10 or less, don't allow your opponents to win easy tricks at the start. Aggressive play at the start of the hand causes your opponents to worry about making their bid, which may cause them to wind up with the overtricks themselves. In practice, weak players worry far more about bags than strong players. It may be more rewarding to look for the set, and to not worry about taking an extra bag or two, if you have any possibility of setting your opponents. Lead an ace from a long suit as soon in the play as you can. This prevents anyone discarding from the suit and trumping your ace.

Leading trump

After leading trump becomes legal, you often have a tough decision as to whether to play spades or not. Bear in mind that a long spade suit's value doesn't solely come from using a trump to capture an opponent's high card. It comes primarily from the ability to take out, or "draw," the opponents' trumps and stop them from scoring trump tricks.

Consider leading trump when you have a long spade suit, unless the lead itself is dangerous (from a holding such as ace-queen or king-jack) and your partner has bid very low. By contrast, when your partner bids high, lead trump when you can.

When you know your partner has long spades, don't weaken their trumps by forcing them to trump in on a losing card of yours.

Going for your scores

Those of you familiar with Whist (see Chapter 8) and Bridge (see Chapter 12) may think the scoring for Spades follows a predictable path — but beware the sting in the tail that comes from going set, or from underbidding, and racking up the overtricks!

Dealing with undertricks

If you fall short in your bid, no matter by how many tricks, you lose ten times the value of your bid. For example, if you bid 10 and fail, you lose 100 points.

VARIATION

A less popular version of the scoring treats the overbidding penalty as 10 points for every trick that you overbid. So calling 10 and making 8 tricks costs you 20 points, not 100.

Scoring nil bids

As I mention earlier, if you bid nil and make it, you score 50 points, but bidding nil and failing costs you 50 points. (See the earlier section "Bidding for nil" for the details.) Bidding blind nil gains you or costs you 100 points, depending on whether you succeed or not. Win or lose on a nil bid, these points do not affect your partner's bid, which is scored in the normal fashion.

If you fail in a bid of nil, the rules vary as to what happens to your tricks. Some versions play that your tricks count toward helping your partner make their bid; other variations say that you ignore your tricks for that purpose. The more standard position is to allow your tricks to count toward your partner's target.

Getting sandbagged with overtricks

If you bid and make your contract, either exactly or with *overtricks* (tricks over your bid), you multiply your bid by 10 and score that total. Any overtricks you accrue count 1 point each. For example, bidding seven and collecting nine tricks scores 72 points — not all that much different, you may think, from bidding eight and scoring nine tricks for 81 points or actually hitting the nail on the head with a bid of nine for 90 points.

You may see little reason to be cautious in the bidding — because a slight underbid hardly seems to matter — but that's before you experience the true joy of overtricks.

Here's a shock for your system: When you accumulate 10 overtricks, you automatically get 100 points deducted from your total, and the clock starts again. In the standard version of the scoring, the 10 overtrick points you gathered during the course of play are also canceled out, although some versions allow you to rack up your 10 as you lose 100. But the mainstream approach dictates that if you're at 458 points, for example, and you bid five tricks and make seven after racking up eight overtricks, your score becomes 400, not 410 (458 + 52 − 100 − the 10-point overtrick deduction = 400).

VARIATION

You can also play without the overtrick rule altogether, or you can just take off 1 point for each overtrick, but that approach defeats the main purpose of the game, in my opinion. You can achieve the same negative values for overtricks by counting each of them as −10. This accounting method simply gives you an immediate deduction for the sandbags rather than a delayed impact. (*Bags on* or *bags off* is the "in" way of referring to whether the overtrick rule applies.)

Time for some strategy. You can consider overtaking your partner's trick or even trumping it if you seem to be making your contract with ease. This may well be a sensible strategy to reduce your side's trick-taking potential, particularly when the combined number of tricks contracted for by both sides is less than 10.

If you know you can defeat, or *set*, your opponents, don't make it too obvious too soon! Otherwise, both opponents will sacrifice tricks to give you bags. Take this hypothetical situation for an example: If your opponents bid eight and you bid five, your opponents are far better off taking four tricks — giving you nine and thus four bags (which could be deemed to have a real value of −40) — than they are taking six tricks. Going set, no matter by how many tricks, still loses them the same 80 points while you collect your 50, but it only costs you two bags, and thus a notional 20 points.

TIP

When either your team or the other team is sitting at eight or nine bags, go for the set, because if you know you're to lose that 100 points, you may as well get a set out of it if you can. (Remember that if your opponents bid five and go set, it costs them 100 points, in a sense, because they lose 50 instead of gaining that number.) If your opponents are getting close to losing 100, they're more likely to overbid their hands and are more likely to overtake their winners. In turn, this makes them perfect targets for a set.

VARIATION

Some people play that you get an additional bonus for making your contract exactly by winning the last trick with a high trump card (a spade higher than the 9). In fact, if you win the last two or three tricks with high trump cards, you get a bonus of 20 or 30 points. This situation happens surprisingly often because the prohibition on playing spades before they're broken often results in the high spades remaining until the end of the game.

Scoring revokes

WARNING

The failure to follow suit (or the failure to follow with your lowest club on the first trick if playing that variation) is a serious crime. Such *revoking* or *reneging* carries varying consequences. One rather kind possibility is to award the non-offending side a 15-point bonus and abandon the hand. This approach is too lax, in my opinion. The more severe penalty is that the offenders are deemed to have failed in their contract(s), and the other side scores their contract. This may be generous to the innocent parties, but it does help to remind the guilty players of the gravity of their offense.

Finishing the game

You play until someone wins the *rubber*. Each rubber is made up of several hands, on which either side can record a positive or negative score. Usually, the first side to get to 500 points wins the rubber. If both sides go past the winning post of 500 points on the same hand, the higher score wins. You can also play the game to 250 or even to 300 or 400 points. Make sure you agree in advance!

Digging Spades for Less Than Four

Spades is primarily a four-person game, but what happens if you have less than a full quorum? Fortunately, you have a couple of variants that allow you to have an entertaining contest with either two or three players.

Spades for two

When playing Spades with two players, instead of dealing out the cards, you place the deck between both players, and you take turns drawing cards.

When you draw the top card, you decide whether you want to keep it. If you keep it, you draw the next card, look at it, and discard it face-down. If you don't keep it, you discard it face-down and then draw the next card, which you must put in your hand.

The other player repeats the process until you exhaust the stock of cards. You each have a hand of 13 cards, and you've looked at and discarded 13 cards each. Now, each player bids an appropriate number of tricks, and you play and score according to the same rules as for four players (refer to the beginning of this chapter).

Spades for three

When playing with three players, you have no partnerships; each player plays for themselves. You use one standard 52-card deck, and you deal 17 cards to each player. Toss the remaining card out of play for that particular game (face-down, of course).

VARIATION

You can play with a 54-card deck, including big and little jokers as the top two trumps (see the section "Grasping the Basics of Spades" for joker explanation). In that case, you deal 18 cards to each player.

Unlike the two-player version, playing with three requires some rule changes.

Differences in betting

Each player, starting with the player to the dealer's left, names a number (called a *bet*). Each player's object is to win that number of tricks. Some people play that the total of the three bets can't be 17 tricks so that not everyone can make their bets exactly.

Differences in play

The player who has the ♣2 must lead it to the first trick. In the rare occasion that the ♣2 is out of play, the player with the ♣3 must lead it.

As in the regular game, you can't lead spades until someone breaks trump by playing a spade on an off-suit. The exception is when a player has nothing left but spades.

Differences in scoring

Scoring is similar to the four-player game. You play to a set number, usually 300, 400, 500, or some other round number. When multiple players pass that number at the same time, the player with the highest score wins.

In the three-person game, you score the overtricks as −10 each rather than waiting to get to 10 overtricks and penalizing 100 points.

VARIATION

If you take the very last trick with a high spade (9 or above), and with that trick you make *exactly* what you bet, you gain a 10-point bonus. If you win an unbroken sequence of tricks at the end (2, 3, 4, or more tricks), all with high spades (9 or above), and you get exactly what you bet, you get a bonus of 10 points per trick (for example, if you take the last five tricks with high spades to make your bet, the bonus would be 50 points).

For successful bids of seven or more, you get an extra 10 points for each trick bid above six. For example, if you make a seven-trick bid exactly, you gain 80 points. Eight tricks exactly gains you 100 points, 9 gains you 120 points, and so on. This rewards the more daring players.

Making a bet of exactly two, one, or zero is very difficult, and is therefore rewarded as follows: Anyone who bets two and gets two wins 40 points (instead of 20). If you get three, you still get 20 points (one bag penalty). Four tricks gets you nothing, and every additional bag is −10 each (per usual). Anyone who bets one and gets exactly one wins 60 points. If you get two, you get nothing, and each additional bag counts −10 each. Anyone who bets zero and gets it gains 100 points. Otherwise, you subtract 10 for every trick taken (just like regular bags).

You may decide to not look at your cards and bet blind. This doubles your score on the hand — be it good or bad! Only attempt this if you're significantly behind in the game (although no score restrictions stop you from doing it at any time). The best time to bet blind is when you're the dealer, and thus third to speak, at which point you may have an idea of what the other players believe they can get. But it is an even bigger gamble than in the four player game — you have two enemies and no friends, and no exchange of cards to improve the odds for you.

Chapter **12**

Mini-Bridge and Contract Bridge

I n my (admittedly biased) opinion, Bridge is far and away the best card game ever invented. I love the game's constant struggle for perfection. Yet with so many unknowns, getting everything right all the time is almost impossible. This quest for perfection is what makes the game so challenging.

The other intriguing aspect, from my perspective, is that however good you are, you need to play the game as a partnership. You can't do it all alone; you must help your partner along the way, too.

TIP

Having said that, you may be surprised to discover how little of this book I devote to Bridge. I have an excellent reason for keeping my coverage of the game at a minimum: My friend and world-renowned Bridge player Eddie Kantar wrote *Bridge For Dummies, 4th Edition* (Wiley), and I can't recommend it more highly. This award-winning book provides the absolutely definitive guide to the game.

At the same time, I want to tell you a little bit about this exciting game, if only to whet your appetite. However, this chapter focuses primarily on the best way to pick up Bridge from scratch: by playing Mini-Bridge.

Mini-Bridge is a great way to introduce Bridge. The play concepts are very close to regular Bridge while enabling new players to get over the hump of finding themselves social pariahs for the first three months when they start playing actual Bridge.

Mini-Bridge

Mini-Bridge is a relatively new phenomenon, invented by the Dutch. It's perfect for children as well as adults and allows players to grasp all the basic concepts of Bridge without needing to master some of the more arcane aspects of bidding. To find out more about the history of the game, visit the English Bridge Union website at www.ebu.co.uk/.

BEFORE HAND

To play Mini-Bridge, you need:

>> **An experienced Bridge and Mini-Bridge player:** This player serves as an instructor or leader.

>> **Two to four players:** The game is best with four players, but it works with three or even two participants, although the latter is a stretch.

>> **A standard deck of 52 cards:** No jokers are necessary.

Setting up

You play Mini-Bridge as two partnerships, North and South against East and West. If you're anything like me, you may have great difficulty distinguishing East and West and left and right. The best I can do is to tell you that West and Left sound a bit alike to me.

Understanding the tricky business

Players must understand the concept of the *trick*. Each player takes a turn to lay down or *play* a card, and the highest card of the suit led wins all the cards, or the *trick*. The idea of Mini-Bridge is for each partnership to win as many tricks as possible. You must play a card of the same suit that's led whenever possible. Whoever wins the trick leads to the next trick, and the winner can lay down a card in whatever suit they like.

I discuss the idea of having a master suit, *trumps*, in the later section "Blowing your own trump-it." But if you like, you can play without a trump suit, known as "playing at no-trumps." (This option is especially appropriate for young or inexperienced players.)

Dealing the cards

Shuffle the cards and then deal 13 to each player, one at a time, starting with the player on your left.

For less experienced players, you can start by playing only with a single suit of 13 cards, with the 2 removed, so everyone gets three cards. Watch the cards carefully and try to remember what's been played. After you complete two tricks, the person holding the highest card should be able to predict that they will win the third trick. As your group gains experience, you can add a second suit (without yet introducing the concept of a trump suit) so that discarding strategy comes into the picture. Remove the 2s from both suits so that you have 24 cards in play (6 to each player). When discarding, you should remember that no matter how high the card is you throw away, it can't win the trick, because only the high card in the suit led can take the trick.

Counting the tricks

Instead of mixing the four cards played on every trick into a bundle, each player should turn over their played card and keep it in front of them so everyone can keep track of what's going on.

Turn cards in tricks won face-down and upright, and turn cards in tricks lost sideways. One way to remember the meaning of this system is by imagining that lost tricks look like a minus sign, and won tricks make a plus sign.

An important point is to count the tricks at the end of play and agree how many each side has won before collecting up the cards for the next deal. After you see how the play works, try a real hand of 13 cards.

Picking the declarer

At the start of the first hand, after the deal, count up the high card points held by each player, using the following scale:

Ace = 4 points

King = 3 points

Queen = 2 points

Jack = 1 point

When the calculations are complete, beginning with the dealer and then in clockwise order, each player announces how many points their hand contains. If the announced total of the four players' points doesn't come to 40, try again!

After the announcement, work out which partnership has the most points. The partnership with the most points becomes the *declaring side*, and the other pair is the *defending side*. You redeal if the point distribution between the partnerships is 20–20.

The stronger of the two hands in terms of total points of the two players on the declaring side becomes *declarer*. For ties, the declarer is the player who calls out their points first. The weaker of these two hands becomes *the dummy hand*. The dummy shows declarer their hand, in order for declarer to decide on the trump suit (see the next section). The dummy cards are only put face-up on the table in suits after the player to the left of the declarer makes the opening lead.

The declarer decides which cards to play on every trick from both their and the dummy's hands. Everyone can see two hands, and the declarer has to make at least seven tricks to "win" the deal — that's more than half the tricks, and it's only fair because the declaring side has more than half the points in the pack. As time goes by, you can count the tricks won and play a contest — the first to cumulate a certain number of tricks wins the game.

TIP

The most basic technique is known as *cashing winners*. For example, holding A, Q, J, 10, 4 opposite K, 2, most beginners cash the ace first, and then the king, and only then discover that they won the second trick in the wrong hand to be able to cash the remaining winners because of the rule that the lead to the next trick must come from the hand that won the last trick. However, by taking the king first and then the ace, the player would have been able to lead out the queen, jack, and 10 immediately. Equally, with A, K, 4, 3 opposite the Q, J alone, beginners may well decide to play out the ace and king, bringing the queen and jack tumbling down. The general rule is that you should cash the high cards in the shorter holding first, and don't play two high honors on a trick when one would do.

WARNING

Another common problem to be sorted out with beginners of any age is their fear of giving up a trick to the other side and thus losing the lead. Beginners usually want to play all their high cards at the first opportunity. However, it's better to establish tricks in your long suits by driving out your opponents' aces and kings before taking all your high cards in the other suits.

Blowing your own trump-it

When you're declaring, you can choose to have a *trump suit* and which one it will be. If you like, you can choose to play in *no trumps,* with no special suit designated as trumps. Any card in a trump suit — even the lowly 2 — beats any card in the other three suits — even an ace.

When you have trumps

>> You can lead a trump at any time.

>> Any trump beats any card of any other suit led.

>> If another suit is led and you can follow suit, you can't play a trump. However, if you can't follow suit, you can play a trump, or *ruff* — although you don't have to if you don't want to. (The mechanics of trump suits are further explained in Chapter 8 on Whist.)

>> If the suit led is trumped more than once, the highest trump played wins the trick.

So as declarer, when do you decide on a trump suit? The simple answer is that the declarer gets to see the dummy before the play starts, and if they have more than eight cards of any suit between their hand and the dummy, they should elect to play in a trump suit. If not, they choose no-trump.

REMEMBER

When looking to select a trump suit, the magic number is at least eight. With a total of eight cards in the declarer's and dummy's hands in any one suit, you have a satisfactory choice as trump. Any more than eight is a bonus!

And how do you decide on a trump suit? A beginner's instinct is to choose a suit in which they hold the high cards, but having more trumps than your opponents is what matters most. You want to be able to ruff your opponents' winners with your trumps, but it's no fun when they start doing the same to you.

When selecting a trump suit, quantity is better than quality. You want your partnership to have more trump cards than your opponents. Time for some mental arithmetic! Thirteen cards make up each suit, so if you have seven trump cards, your opponents have six. However, you have only a slight edge, and this isn't such good news. But if you have eight trumps, your opponents have only five, which is much better.

Drawing trump

The declarer normally should draw trumps as soon as possible. *Drawing trumps* means to play out a few rounds of trump cards in order to remove all the trump held by the defenders.

If the declaring side has at least eight trump cards, it can normally draw out the defenders' trumps in three rounds.

TIP

Drawing trumps isn't something that comes naturally for beginners, especially if the defenders hold some of the trump court cards. However, the more hands you play, the faster you will see that leaving the opponents with trumps lets them take tricks your side could have won — and that is no fun at all. You eventually encounter situations where drawing trumps is better later on in the hand, but as a general rule, drawing trumps early makes sense. However, before you get down to the nitty-gritty of beginning the play on a hand where declarer has chosen a trump suit, it is important to take time to work out how many trumps the defenders hold, how they're likely to be divided, and how many rounds of trumps you need to draw them.

WARNING

If the last trump held by your opponents is bigger than the last one you hold, you don't have to draw it. It will win a trick anyway, so you shouldn't use up two of your small trumps, which may win two tricks separately later.

Playing the numbers game

The idea of a target number of tricks is vital to scoring the game. The declaring side always has more points than the defenders, so it's only fair that the declarer should have to win more than half the tricks. In terms of scoring, the first six tricks don't count — the declarer only earns points for tricks after the first six. If the declarer makes fewer than seven tricks, the defenders earn points instead. When you fail to make your target, the defenders get *undertricks* because you went under your target.

TIP

When you start playing Mini-Bridge, you can simplify the scoring by only adding up the tricks won or lost (I explain some of the more complex scoring features in the next section). Keep a running score and note how many points the declaring side held and how many tricks were made. A pattern will soon emerge, especially if you write down how many trumps are held when the declarer makes a trump contract.

Moving on to the scoring system

The scoring system for Mini-Bridge includes the idea that the suits are not equal. Additionally, you may receive a big bonus if you bid and make a contract worth more than 100 points, known as *making game*. All other contracts are referred to as *part-score* contracts. (The scoring in Mini-Bridge partly duplicates that of Bridge. For more details, see *Bridge For Dummies, 4th Edition*, by Eddie Kantar.)

The point is that at Mini-Bridge (unlike Bridge) you start off by only having to pick your trump suit, you do not have to choose precisely *how many* tricks you want to contract for. You simply score the number of tricks you make times the value of the trump suit. Time for a wrinkle to that principle: As declarer, when you look at the dummy, you have to decide whether to aim high, for game, or low, for a part-score.

As I said, a *game contract* is one where the number of tricks contracted for, multiplied by the value of the tricks, comes to more than 100. A *part score* is where that value is less than 100. (And remember that the first six tricks you make don't count for this purpose.) Each trick at clubs or diamonds is worth 20 points, each trick at hearts or spades 30 points, and at no-trump, confusingly, the first trick is worth 40 points, and all subsequent tricks are worth 30 points.

In Mini-Bridge, all you need to know is that depending on your choice of trump suit, the number of tricks you need to win to reach 100 points and make game will vary. Only nine tricks are needed for a game in no trumps (40 + 30 + 30), ten tricks for a game in hearts or spades (4 × 30), and 11 tricks for a game in clubs or diamonds (5 × 20).

When you successfully make a contract worth 100 points or more, you get a 300-point bonus. You may already have discovered that making more tricks in a trump contract is easier than at no-trump, but the distinction between the major and minor suits is new and has important implications. You often have to make difficult decisions; for example, whether you want to aim for nine tricks in no trumps or 11 in a minor suit. Suddenly, no trumps become a lot more attractive — just like in Bridge!

When you *go for game* (by contracting for a number of tricks that will give you 100 points or more if you succeed), you position yourself to receive an additional 300-point bonus if you're successful. However, if you don't meet the game target, you not only score nothing, but also the defenders earn 50 points for each *undertrick*, or the number of tricks by which you fail to achieve your stated target.

With beginners, try for game with 25 or more points in the combined hands, using the 4-3-2-1 point scale for evaluating the high cards (see the section "Picking the declarer" earlier in this chapter). Some game contracts may fail, but they should still win more than they lose. Choose your longest combined suit as trumps, assuming the number of trump cards in your hand and the dummy hand consist of at least eight cards whenever you're not trying for game. When you have a long minor suit and game is an option, always consider whether game in no-trumps is a possibility.

Keeping the dummy involved

When you donate the dummy hand, make sure you stay involved in the play of the game. You can go around the table and sit with the declarer, playing the cards as a team. You can also stay in your seat but complete dummy tasks to stay involved in the play:

>> Watch the trumps as they're played, and say at the end of the hand how many each player held.

>> Count the cards played in each suit by the declarer so at the end of the hand you can say how many cards were originally held in each suit by the declarer (often referred to as their *original distribution*).

>> Watch the court cards played by one of the defenders (perhaps the one who announced the fewest points). Four tricks from the end of the hand, you should be able to calculate how many points are left in the remaining four cards.

TIP

Because everyone announces their high cards at the start, a canny declarer can often follow the play and infer where a vital missing card is. If the player on your right says they have five points and produce the diamond ace early on, they can't be holding a missing queen — but they must have that jack you are trying to locate, must they not?

The role of the defender

Another valuable aspect of Mini-Bridge play is defense. Defense is often glossed over when Bridge is being taught to any level of player. New players tend to switch off when they are defending, thinking that it is only declarer who has to do all the hard work. But this is, of course, far from the truth.

The first thing to remember is that against either a suit or a no-trump contract you do not want to lead a high card such as a king, queen, or jack unless you have a *touching honor* to it, the next lowest high card, respectively, the queen, jack, or 10. If you have to lead from touching honors, lead the higher card. The simple rule is to lead a low card from any suit not headed by touching honors (and while the king and queen are touching, as are the queen and jack, the king and jack are not). The lead of an unsupported ace in particular is something you should try to resist doing; an ace will take a trick later on in the hand, and may net a larger fish if you wait till someone else leads the suit.

As well as choosing the particular card in a suit you want to lead, it goes without saying that you also need to choose which suit to lead. Leading from your long suits looks right against no-trump; length is better than strength if in doubt. Leading from honor sequences of touching high cards against suits, or from holdings of one or two low cards, often works against a trump contract (but not if your short suit *is* the trump suit!). The idea is to try to let your partner get the lead and return the suit, to allow you to use a small trump to win the trick.

When defending, the third player to play on the trick (also called *third hand*) should usually aim to win the trick. When they have a choice of high cards to play that are touching one another — such as the queen-jack or the ace-king, they should select the cheaper of those equal cards. So the bottom of a sequence is the correct card to choose now, as third hand, rather than the top card, which is what you would play if you were leading to the trick. So holding QJ106, for example, the correct card to play as third hand is the 10, not the queen. But with KJ6, playing the king makes sense in order to stop the declarer from scoring a trick with the queen that they are not entitled to. However, look at what is in the dummy before committing yourself. Don't waste a high card if the sight of the dummy tells you a lower card will do just as well. When you win the lead as third hand if in doubt play back partner's suit, since they probably had a good reason to lead it, unless your own hand tells you that would be a mistake, or you can see something better to do.

Crossing to Bridge

After you have a good handle on Mini-Bridge, move on to Bridge.

The major difference between the two games comes in the bidding. The bidding phase of Bridge, sometimes called the *auction*, rather resembles those scenes you see on television where dealers in a stock market shout out competing prices. In Bridge, the process is marginally more decorous; players take turns calling out their bids. Speaking out of turn is just as much a faux pas in Bridge as it is in other walks of life.

During the bidding, the players hope to win the auction, and thus acquire the right to determine which suit is the *trump suit*, or the "boss" suit for the hand.

The bidding also determines how many tricks a partnership hopes to take in a hand. The minimum starting bid is seven tricks (just more than half of the 13 tricks available). As in Mini-Bridge, the first six tricks are taken for granted; for example, a bid of 1 spade is Bridge shorthand for "I intend to take seven tricks with spades as the trump suit." Every bid takes the form of a number and a suit (no-trumps counting as a suit here).

The dealer speaks first, and after the first bid is made, the auction moves clockwise, and the other players in turn may, if they want, make a higher bid, or they can discreetly stay out of the battle by passing if they prefer. Unlike at an auction, you don't need to fear that a severe nervous tic may force you to bid more than you intend.

A higher bid can either be for a higher number of tricks or for the same number of tricks in a higher-ranking suit. In Bridge, the suits are ranked as follows, no-trumps, spades, hearts, diamonds, then clubs, from highest to lowest.

The bidding ends when three players in a row pass after a bid. The last bid becomes the *contract* for the hand; the contract determines what the trump suit is for the hand and the number of tricks that the successful bidder must win in order to make good on their bid. One further wrinkle: Instead of passing or bidding a contract of your own, any player can "double" the opponents' contract. If there are no further bids after this, the double increases the score for the contract whether it is won or lost. If the most recent action was a double by the opponents of a bid by your side, you can "redouble," which further increases the score for good or ill if this becomes the final contract. The effect of the double or redouble is cancelled if either side makes a further bid.

If all four players pass at their first turn, the hand is thrown in, and a new hand is dealt by the next player.

PLAYING BRIDGE ON THE INTERNET

Another way to find out about Bridge is to go to the website of your National Authority — for example, the American Contract Bridge League at www.acbl.org/ or the English Bridge Union at www.ebu.co.uk/. Check out the site for your country of residence to find places to play. But, if you know the basics of the game and don't want a face-to-face encounter, the Net is the place for you.

Places where you can play free of charge are relatively limited, but the best of them is called Bridge Base. Go to www.bridgebase.com/ for the opportunity to play or to watch experts play in national or international competition. Bridgebase provides commentators who explain the action for all to understand. It also has some of the best educational software, which allows you to play through hands to gain a better understanding of the game.

You can also find Bridge on the Internet at OKBridge (www.okbridge.com/) and Swan Games (www.swangames.com/). Both these sites allow you to play duplicate tournaments — competitive Bridge events against people from around the world and to watch the best in the world compete in tournaments, from the comfort of your own home.

4

Scoring or Avoiding Points

When playing games in Part IV, such as Hearts, points are the hot potato. The focus is on not winning particular cards that rack up points. The bad news may be limited to a certain suit in the deck, or different cards may be the plague carriers, designated at the start of every hand by the dealer.

By contrast, Pinochle and Setback are games where the objective is to capture high-scoring cards (each game has its own ranking list, where different cards become more or less valuable).

Whatever the point of the game — to gain points or avoid them altogether — I give you the rules, details, and strategies in plain English.

Chapter **13**

Hearts

Hearts is a game of skill — to a certain extent. You're under the sway of whether you receive helpful or unhelpful cards, but good card sense and a good memory make an enormous difference in this game. Keeping track of the cards played in each suit helps you to master this game, and practice and experience have no substitute.

BEFORE HAND

To play Hearts, you need the following:

» **Three or more players:** Four are ideal, but you can play sensibly with any number up to seven.

» **A standard deck of 52 cards:** No jokers or wild cards come into play.

» **A pencil and paper for scoring:** Make a column for each player.

Getting to the Heart of the Matter

Hearts is a cutthroat game, meaning that you normally don't play in partnerships, no matter the number of players involved. The game I discuss here focuses on the four-player game, where all the cards are distributed evenly, 13 to a player. Later in the chapter, I discuss how to cope with fewer, or more, players.

The game revolves around *tricks*. In a trick, everyone takes turns playing one card. Whoever plays the highest card in the suit led (the suit of the first card played) picks up all the cards played. The person who wins the trick leads a card to the next trick, (they can lead anything they like — with one exception, which I discuss in a moment), and the process repeats itself until all the cards have hit the table.

Unlike most competitive games, the object of Hearts is to avoid scoring points. More specifically, the aim is not to win tricks that contain certain cards that score you points.

The name of the game holds the clue: The problem suit in this game is hearts. However, the ♠Q has a particularly unpleasant role in the game, too. Whoever wins a trick that includes one of the 14 *danger cards* picks up a penalty in the process; I discuss the scoring details in the section "Scoring: The time of reckoning" later in this chapter, but bear in mind that the ♠Q is as bad as all the hearts put together.

You play Hearts to a set score, and the winner of the game is the player who has the lowest score when another player goes over the top. Alternatively, you can play a set number of hands and stop the game at that point, with the lowest score winning.

Dealing the cards

At the start of the game, you cut for seating rather than just for the deal, because the seating positions matter in Hearts. Arrange the seating from the highest card to the lowest, with the player who cut the lowest card dealing the first hand. You stay in the same seats for the whole game. The dealer shuffles and passes the cards to the opponent on their right to cut.

HAVING A HEART TO HEART ON THE WEB

If you don't want to play a game of Hearts face to face, you can use a computer program to play against an automated opponent, or you can play online against real opposition.

You can access the necessary shareware at www.kerala-hotels.net/freeversecom/, and Thanos Cardgames offers a free Hearts game at https://thanoscardgames.jimdofree.com/.

You can find live Hearts play on the Internet at a whole host of sites detailed by John McLeod at www.pagat.com/reverse/hearts.html. Best known of the sites is the MSN Games at https://zone.msn.com/en-us/home.

Deal all the cards out in the traditional fashion — one card at a time, face-down, and clockwise. At the end of every hand, the deal passes to the left to the next player.

WARNING

Misdeals can arise in a number of ways. If a card appears face-up in the deck, the dealer gives out the wrong number of cards, or the dealer turns over anyone else's cards, the hand is immediately redealt with no penalties. If the dealer manages to turn over one of their own cards, the deal stands, with the only consequence being that the other players have a little extra information about the dealer's hand.

If no player spots that some players have the wrong number of cards before play begins, the deal stands, but the penalties are very severe. Play continues until the last possible valid trick, when the players with the wrong number of cards pick up the penalties for the unplayed heart cards as if they had won the tricks with those cards in them.

Passing your cards left, right, and center

After you pick up and sort your cards, you get to pass three of your cards to another opponent. The passing stage of the game gives you a chance to get rid of some cards that you think may score points or to get rid of a particular suit, thereby strengthening your chances of dumping high-scoring cards on someone else, or of discarding danger cards in another suit at the appropriate moment.

Passing methods

Getting rid of your bad cards involves a cycle of four passes:

>> **1st hand:** You pass three cards to the opponent on your left.

>> **2nd hand:** You pass three cards to the opponent on your right.

>> **3rd hand:** You pass three cards to the opponent across the table.

>> **4th hand:** You retain your hand without a pass.

To pass your cards properly, select your three cards, put them face-down in front of you, and then pass those cards before looking at the cards that you're about to pick up.

VARIATION

Two common additions to the cycle of passing on cards (making it a cycle of six deals rather than of four) are to pass one card to everybody — the *scatter* — and for each player to put three cards into the middle of the table, shuffle the cards, and then redistribute them at random — the *smoosh*. With the scatter, each player puts three cards face-down and passes on the cards without looking at what cards they receive. With the smoosh, all 12 discards are mixed together before redistribution.

Another alternative rule allows you to pass along the cards that you receive to the next player, as long as you don't look at the cards first. This procedure can result in getting back the cards you passed on, particularly if you switch with the player opposite you.

Passing strategies

TIP

When passing on cards, think carefully about the nature of your hand before making your move. You may assume that because hearts and the ♠Q score the points (and, by extension, the ♠K and ♠A, because they're likely candidates to capture the ♠Q), these cards are the hot potatoes that you want to pass on immediately; but this assumption isn't necessarily so.

On some occasions you want to pass your hearts and your top spades, of course; for example, if you're short in either suit, you want to unload the high spades (♠A, ♠K, or ♠Q) and your top hearts. However, if you have plenty of spades — say, at least five in the four-player game or four spades other than the queen — you can safely hold on to your high spades. If you do pass on the ♠Q, remember to whom you passed it. Doing so sometimes allows you to unload the ace or king of spades safely when a spade is lead.

Similarly, if you have a series of low hearts, you don't need to pass any of them on. Instead, throw away all the cards in a side-suit so that you can play whatever you like when another player leads the suit — however unpleasant it may be for your opponents. (The act of dumping an unwelcome present on an opponent is called *painting* a trick.)

REMEMBER

By the third or fourth time diamonds or clubs are led, you're just as likely to collect the ♠Q or a bunch of hearts by winning a trick as you are from leading hearts or spades. A side-suit containing the J, 10, 9, 8, 7 is a strong candidate to fetch the ♠Q, whereas a suit such as A, Q, 10, 9, 6, 4, 2 presents virtually no danger at all. Why? The answer is the control of those nice low cards. You should do your best to ensure that after the pass you do not saddle yourself with a long minor suit holding, unless you have small cards to protect yourself from being dumped on. The high cards in the minor suits don't cause problems as much as the lack of low cards in a long suit. Any suit (other than spades) in which you can't duck a trick leaves you exposed to collecting the ♠Q, or the *Black Maria*, at a critical moment.

Even the 3 may be a danger card; in a five-card suit such as K, J, 9, 6, 3, don't be surprised to discover that on the third round of the suit someone leads the 2, and you get showered with hearts from the other two players.

For an example, look at the hand in Figure 13-1. The spades are dangerous, but the hearts are useful, because you have so many of them. You should get rid of the ♠A, the ♠Q, and the ♣J in the pass. (If you are playing the variation that demands clubs be led to the first trick, being short of clubs can be good news.)

FIGURE 13-1:
Keeping your hearts may be the wisest decision.

Alternatively, check out the hand in Figure 13-2. The spades look safe enough, but you may want to get rid of all your hearts. Or you may keep the hearts and throw the ♦A, ♦Q, and ♣10 to create suits in which you have no or few cards.

FIGURE 13-2:
The spade suit spells the safest policy.

REMEMBER

Focus on what cards you get from your opponent. Doing so may help you guess what sort of hand they have by virtue of what they let go — and thus what their intentions are for the hand. You can usually infer what their possible danger suits are, too.

As soon as the cards have been appropriately passed, the play of the hand starts.

Starting the trick play

The player on the dealer's left starts by playing whatever non-scoring card they like.

VARIATION

The alternative version is for whoever has the ♣2 to lead it. If you play this variation, remember that having only a few clubs or even passing all your clubs before play begins may allow you to discard critical cards early in the game when a club is led. A sub-variation of this one prohibits the play of any penalty cards on the first trick, which makes this a good moment to dump your ♠A!

REMEMBER

In Hearts, the cards rank in regular fashion, from ace to 2, with the ace being high. You must *follow suit* (play a card in the suit led) if you can, and if you can't, you can play whatever you want.

Each player throws in a card, and whoever plays the highest card in the suit led wins the trick. You stack the tricks you take in front of you to facilitate the scoring at the end of the hand and you leave the penalty cards you unwillingly garner face-up in front of you (see the following section, "Scoring: The time of reckoning").

After the opening lead, where a club lead may be compulsory in some variations of the game, you have only one other vital restriction — and this condition is much more restrictive. Unless the heart suit has been *broken* — that is, a player discards a heart on a trick — you can't lead a heart unless it's the only suit you have left in your hand.

VARIATION

Some play that the discard of the ♠Q allows you to lead hearts thereafter, and some versions of the game allow you to lead hearts at any time.

If you have the ♠Q, you may want to get rid of it as quickly as possible, or you may want to pass it on to the opponent who's winning the game, to the closest pursuer behind you, or even to someone whose attitude you don't like! Whichever approach you choose with respect to playing the ♠Q is fine. It is up to you what you do, unless you play that you have no choice, and must pass on the ♠Q as quickly as possible. This version of the rule does make sense if playing Hearts for money.

TIP

As a general rule, the right approach in Hearts is judicious self-preservation first, spite and malice next. Throw the dangerous cards in your hand away first before painting tricks that your opponents win. If you never score any points, you're pretty sure to win, so try for that goal first and wait to upset your opponents until you feel safe.

REMEMBER

I can't emphasize how important it is to try to remember, if not all the cards, the cards in the suits that matter to you because your hand suggests they may be dangerous. You may not have to remember the diamonds if you have only the Q, 8, and 3 (you can be fairly sure your 3 won't win the third round), but with the Q, 8, 5, and 4, you need to keep a count of the suit and note if the 3 and 2 have put in an appearance. Otherwise, the third and fourth round of the suit may be more painful than you expect!

I suggest you don't try to count the hearts — players normally leave them visible on the table in front of them within taken tricks. Focus on the spades and whichever of the diamonds or clubs look worrying to you. Start by counting the number of times the suit has been led (assuming each time that four cards were played;

that is, unless you have noted someone show out). Far trickier is remembering to add one to your count of the cards played in a suit every time a player discards in that specific suit. After you feel confident you can keep count of the suit, try to expand your record keeping to remembering which small cards are still missing.

Say you have the Q, 8, 5, and 4 of diamonds that I mention earlier in this section. If the ◆K is led, you throw your ◆Q, and the ◆J and ◆9 show up. On the next diamond trick, your ◆8 comes in under the ◆A, and the ◆10 puts in an appearance along with the ◆3. When you see the ◆7 discarded, you know that two rounds of diamonds represent eight cards in the suit. The discard of the ◆7 makes nine, and your two remaining diamonds make eleven. Two diamonds still out — one being the ◆2, which you're watching for, the other being a higher one than your ◆5 (you don't actually care what card it is, although just for the record, it's the ◆6). The point: If one player has both diamonds, you might lose the next trick, but you would then be able to lead your last diamond and know the player with the diamonds will take the trick. Of course, it may be too late — someone may have passed you the ♠Q already! And note that the player with the ◆6 and ◆2 might win the first diamond trick with the 6 and lead back the 2, letting you win the second diamond trick, not the first.

If the missing diamonds are split, you can lead a diamond now and leave yourself with a safe card in diamonds. Playing a diamond yourself, as soon as you can, may be a better strategy than letting someone else discard that ◆6.

TIP

Leave yourself with low cards in each suit for the later tricks — the third and even the second round of a suit. Doing so allows you to lose tricks late in the game when everyone wants to unload their hearts and the ♠Q. Avoid playing on your safe suits (the ones where you have 2s and 3s that won't win tricks) until the end of the hand, but be aware that your opponents want to do the same thing. For example, when you have the Q, 9, and 3 of diamonds, lead the queen and follow with the 9, keeping the 3 for the third (more dangerous) round — unless someone has already discarded a scoring card on one of the first two rounds.

TIP

When you receive three cards in a suit from the player on your right, avoid leading a high card in that suit yourself. You can be fairly sure that something nasty may happen to you — unless the player in question was unlucky enough to pick up some cards in this suit from the player to *their* right!

WARNING

Hearts may not have the complex rules that other games have, but it does have rules. Keep yourself out of trouble by following these guidelines:

>> Playing out of turn has no formal penalty. If you finish and turn over a trick in which someone led or played out of turn, the game simply continues, but a player who still has to play on a tainted trick can demand that the lead and all the other cards played to that trick be taken back.

>> Failure to follow suit is called a *revoke*. A player may correct a revoke at any point until the trick ends. After that point, if someone draws attention to a revoke, the player who didn't follow suit takes all the penalty points on that deal.

Scoring: The time of reckoning

At the end of the hand, each player collects all the cards in the taken tricks, and the arithmetic begins. The simple version of the game doesn't tax your math skills unduly. Each player gets 1 point per heart, for a total of 13 penalty points possible in each hand. However, not many people play that way anymore, and when the ♠Q is involved, Hearts becomes more expensive.

The ♠Q, which has many names (the Black Lady, Black Maria, Black Widow, Slippery Anne, or Calamity Jane, to name a few), costs you 13 points on its own. Not surprisingly, therefore, you need to gear your strategy of both passing and playing to avoid taking this card. For that reason, you may want to pass the ♠A and ♠K, and also the ♠Q, before play begins if you have only a few spades. Conversely, if you have length in spades (particularly with some of the low cards), spades don't propose a danger to you.

You play to 100 points when 26 points are at stake. At that point, you can play that whoever has the fewest points wins. Or if gambling for stakes, you can play that you settle up with everybody paying or receiving the differences in score.

WARNING

Passing on low spades before play starts is almost certainly a tactical blunder because you help a player guard the ♠Q.

TIP

Because the penalty associated with the ♠Q outweighs that of the individual heart cards, leading spades early (if you can afford to, and as long as you don't lead the ace or king) often ensures that someone else takes in this card — not you. By leading spades early, you hope to flush out the ♠Q, and with the ♠Q out of the way, you can't be too badly hurt on a hand, even if you do win a number of hearts. So long as you don't leave either the ♠A or ♠K insufficiently protected by small cards, leading spades early is usually safe.

You do have one challenging escape if you get a really terrible hand stuffed full of high cards. If you manage to take all the penalty cards and thus collect 26 points, you finish up doing remarkably well: You have the option of reducing your own score by 26 points or charging everyone else 26 points. This accomplishment is called *shooting the moon*, and just like becoming an astronaut, it's a great deal easier to do in theory than in practice. The right hand rarely comes along for it, and if your opponents see you trying to take all the tricks, they'll save a heart or two for the end to take a couple penalty points and prevent you from achieving your aim.

WARNING

Shooting the moon is more dangerous than it may seem; in my experience, you lose more points in unsuccessful attempts to shoot the moon than you gain by making it. If you have a very good hand, you may choose to take an early trick with one or two points in it just to stop anyone else from trying to shoot the moon. Alternatively, you can give hearts to two different players to accomplish the same result with less discomfort to yourself.

VARIATION

Scoring variations in Hearts flourish as thickly as weeds on a lawn. Here, listed in descending order of frequency, are some of the most common additional scoring rules (you can play them simultaneously or not at all):

>> Shooting the sun, as opposed to the moon, involves taking all the tricks as well as all the penalty points. You get a 52-point bonus for shooting the sun.

>> Counting the ♦J — or, in some circles, the ♦10 — as a bonus card is quite common. Winning the trick with that card in it has real merit because it reduces your penalty points by 11 (or 10, in the case of the ♦10). If you have fewer penalty points than 10, you can even finish up being plus for the hand.

If you allow shooting the moon, you generally don't need to take the ♦J to shoot the moon, but some versions of the game require that you win this card, too.

TIP

Implementing the rule about the ♦J influences which cards you decide to pass on. You may want to keep the top diamonds in order to try for the prize. However, you may find capturing the ♦J is easier if you pass it on. In high-level games, you're unlikely to find players winning tricks in diamonds early on with this card. In practice, because players rarely get the chance to take an early diamond trick with this card, it tends to get discarded at the end of the hand.

>> If you manage to score exactly 100 points, your score is immediately halved to 50 points. Some versions play that if you avoid scoring any points on the next hand, you further reduce your score to zero.

>> The ♣10 can be a potentially lethal card if you play the rule, common in some circles, that the card doubles the value of the penalty points for whoever takes it. For example, capturing the ♣10 and three heart cards costs you 6 points, not 3.

>> The ♥A may be charged at 5 points, not 1.

>> Occasionally, the ♠Q carries a penalty of only 5 points, not 13.

>> Anyone who avoids winning a trick in a hand may be credited with –5 points.

> » In Spot Hearts, all the heart cards are charged at face value rather than at 1 point apiece. The ♥A ♥K, ♥Q, and ♥J are 15 (or according to some, 14), 13, 12, and 11 points, respectively, meaning that the deck contains 130 penalty points if the ♠Q counts for 25 points. Playing this game to a score of 500 or so is sensible.

Hearts with Three or Five-Plus Players

VARIATION

The rules of Hearts for three players or for more than five players differ from the four-handed rules because you can't divide the deck equally (refer to the section "Getting to the Heart of the Matter" for more information about playing with four people). But you can correct this problem by removing one or two surplus cards. For example, take out the ♣2 — clubs are traditionally the lowest suit — in the game for three players (which leaves 17 cards for each player), and remove the ♣2 and the ♦2 in the game for five players to even out the deck at 50 cards (at 10 cards apiece).

More interesting, however, is to start the deal with a full deck, giving an even number to each player. You leave the extra cards face-down on the table as a *kitty*. Whoever wins the first trick has to add the points in the kitty to their total at the end of the hand. The trick winner can look at the cards without showing anyone else until the end of the hand. This rule makes losing the first trick a very good idea!

VARIATION

A more generous alternative is to permit whoever wins the first trick to add the cards in the kitty to their hand and then discard an equivalent number of cards. Because this version can result in some significant cards playing no part in the hand, this rule seems unnecessarily generous to me.

The rule about forming a kitty has occasionally been extended to the four-player game — where it isn't strictly necessary. The idea is that you deal each player only 12 cards, with the remaining four cards forming the kitty.

The rules about passing cards change depending on the number of participants. The cycle of possible ways to pass and receive cards must expand with every additional player added into the game. You can add additional passes so that you exchange cards once with each of the other players — whatever takes your fancy.

Honeymoon Hearts

In Honeymoon Hearts, you play with two players, and each player gets 13 cards. You put the remaining stock of cards in a pile and turn the top card over. The non-dealer leads a card, the dealer (who must follow suit if they can) plays a card in turn, the winner takes the face-up card, and the loser takes the top face-down card. You turn the new top card over, and the sequence continues for 13 rounds until you use the stock up.

At the end, when the stock is exhausted, both players play out their remaining cards and score them up as you do in a regular game of Hearts (refer to the section "Scoring: The time of reckoning" earlier in this chapter).

Only the last 13 cards count for this game; the first 13 tricks are just an attempt to build up the hand.

Because the leader gets to dictate strategy, retaining the lead for the last few tricks is a good idea. That means getting rid of your middle cards early and retaining low cards for the last 13 tricks. Plan to lead with high cards for the last few tricks.

If the game appears to be going well, retain your penalty cards to try to dump them on your opponent. If it is going badly, do a damage-limitation exercise and get rid of your potentially expensive cards as soon as possible.

Black Maria

Black Maria, which was invented and popularized in the 1920s, is the most popular English variation of Hearts. Black Maria works well for three or more players and contains all the traditional Hearts rules (refer to the section "Getting to the Heart of the Matter" earlier in this chapter), but it has some additional penalty cards in the spade suit.

In this version of the game, you count the ♠A, ♠K, and ♠Q as 7, 10, and 13 points, respectively, making the spades more dangerous than the hearts.

This variation makes tackling the spade suit a priority if you don't get the ♠A, ♠K, or ♠Q. Admittedly, you may pick up a heart or two along the way, but in playing repeatedly on the spades, you eliminate the danger of a severe charge to yourself later on in the hand.

Cancellation Hearts

VARIATION

If a large number of players — say, six or more — want to play Hearts, playing with one deck means that you don't have enough cards. When each player has only eight cards, the risk of players having unbalanced hands, with only one or even no cards in a suit, becomes too high, and playing skillfully is difficult. To solve the problem, you can play with two decks, but that solution introduces a different question — what happens when two players play the same card on a trick? The final solution is an intriguing one: Matching cards can cancel one another out. When players lay two identical cards on the same trick, you treat both cards as not existing. So, for example, a trick that goes ♠2, ♠7, ♠7, ♠4, ♠4, ♠3 is won by the ♠3; the 4s and 7s cancel each other out.

Canceling cards allows for some interesting turns in the play. For example, with six players at the table, the first player leads the ♦2. Player two discards ♠Q on this card, and the next player tries the ♦4. Player four also plays the ♦4, player five puts on the ♦3, and player six, who has both the ♦2 and the ♦3 left, has the choice of torturing either player one or player five by canceling out one player's card and saddling the other player with the ♠Q. What a nice position to be in!

If a whole trick is canceled out, you carry forward any penalty points associated with that trick, and the winner of the next trick gets them. If the whole of the last trick is canceled, the penalty cards go to the winner of the previous trick.

Chapter **14**

Pinochle

P inochle is that rare bird, a game that works equally well with two, three, or four players. Most two-player versions of standard three-player games are only pale imitations of the real thing. However, Pinochle for two players is a game that stands on its own. Pinochle is especially satisfying because it allows a player with a good memory and imagination to overcome bad cards, and Pinochle has enough variety in its possibilities to make it a challenging game at many levels. It is a game that requires accurate assessment of your cards in the auction, and good card-reading skills in the play.

BEFORE HAND

All you need to play Pinochle are the following:

» **Two, three, or four players**

» **Two standard decks of 52 cards**

Actually, you only need the ace through 9 from the two decks, making two sets of 24 cards, or 48 in all. It's better, though not essential, if the two decks of cards have the same backs. It is relatively easy to find custom-made Pinochle decks of 48 cards in the United States. For the four-player game, you need two such decks.

» **Pencil and paper for scoring**

Pinochle for Two

Pinochle is a game of scoring points. You score points in two different ways during a typical hand of Pinochle: first by putting down *melds* from your hand, which can be *runs* (A-K-Q-J-10), *marriages* (any king-queen) or the special combination called the *pinochle*, the ♦J and ♠Q, or *sets*, such as ♦Q, ♥Q, ♣Q, and ♠Q. You score these melds during the first phase of the play of the cards — there are two such phases. The second way you score is to win tricks that contain scoring cards, which happens in both phases of the play of the cards. The winner of the game is the first to a specified total, which I discuss in the section "Finishing the game," later in this chapter.

Dealing to begin

Both players cut for the deal, and the player with the highest card deals first. They shuffle the deck and then offer the cards to their opponent to cut. Each player gets 12 cards, with the dealer distributing the cards four at a time.

WARNING

If the dealer exposes one of their cards, they must live with giving information away to their opponent. If they expose one of their opponent's cards, the player has the option of accepting it or calling for a new deal. If you find a card face-up in the stock, turn the card over and re-shuffle the stock.

After each player has 12 cards, the dealer places the remainder of the deck (24 cards) in the middle of the table. The dealer turns over the top card in the stock, which denotes the trump suit. After both players have a look, the dealer sets that turned-over card beneath the stock, where it stays until all the cards in the stock have been used up.

Because each player initially gets 12 cards from the deck of 48, that leaves a *stock* pile of 24 cards. The first element of the play involves each player in turn playing a card from their 12 cards, and then picking up a new one from the stock. This element of the game continues until no cards are left to pick up. You then move on to the second phase of the game, which involves playing out your cards from the remaining 12 until your hands are fully exhausted.

To begin the first trick, the nondealer leads out a card. The second player makes a play, and the higher card in the suit *led* (the suit of the first card played) takes both cards, or the *trick*. Whoever wins the trick picks it up and keeps it in front of them; they also get the opportunity to put down one meld if they have one. You're not required to play a card of the suit led, however — you may play any card from your hand that you like (see "Scoring the melds" for when you may not want to win the trick). The winner of the trick leads to the next trick, and the process continues in that way.

You play Pinochle with a *trump suit*, which means that one suit is the master suit. Any card in the trump suit beats any card from a *side-suit* (any non-trump suit) and wins the trick. You select the trump suit at random at the start of the game by turning over a card from the stock. Winning the tricks themselves isn't important; it's the point-scoring cards within those tricks that matter.

REMEMBER

Bear in mind that you're playing with two identical decks, so you may play the same card on a trick as your opponent. If you both play the same card, the first card played outranks the second one.

During the two phases of play, 250 points are up for grabs. However, you must be aware of the importance of scoring melds in Pinochle, as well as simply winning tricks, a process that I describe in the section "Scoring the melds" later in this chapter.

Ranking and valuing the cards

The cards rank the same way in all suits, trump or regular. The ranking, from highest to lowest, is ace, 10, king, queen, jack, 9. Table 14-1 shows the scoring for these cards.

REMEMBER

When you play the cards, the tricks won or lost have no significance. What matters is the point values of the cards won in the tricks, so before you start to play, you need to master the point values for each card. During the play, you aim to capture point-scoring cards in the tricks you win.

No less than three card-valuation scales currently exist: the streamlined, old-time, and revised valuation scales. Which scale you play is entirely up to you and your friends, but you need to agree on which scale to use before play begins.

Table 14-1 shows you how many points each card is worth in each of the three valuation scales. (My impression is that the Revised scale is the most common these days. The ace, 10, and king are referred to as *counters* in this game, and the queen, jack, and 9 are *non-counters*.) This simply means that only the ace, 10, and king are worth capturing, the other cards are valueless or nearly so.

Adding up the possible points

Because 30 points are at stake in each suit (adding the point values of ace through 9) and because you play the game with two decks, you have two sets of every suit, making for 60 points in each suit, which means 240 points are up for grabs in the play of the cards. Both players try to win as many points as they can, along with making scoring melds (see the next section).

TABLE 14-1

Pinochle Point-Value Scales

Card	Old-time	Streamlined	Revised
Ace	11	10	10
10	10	10	10
King	4	5	10
Queen	3	5	0
Jack	2	0	0
9	0	0	0

In addition, winning the last trick always gets you an extra 10 points, making 250 points the number of points available in the play in total, from the first and second phases.

Along with the card points, a series of awards for melds also come into play, which you may or may not claim, depending on whether either player actually has any scoring sequences to claim, or an opportunity to claim them. You don't always get to collect meld awards because the opportunity to score them depends on whether you're actually dealt (or get to pick up) the right hand.

Scoring the melds

You can score points for four different sorts of melds: the *sequence*, the *marriage*, the *pinochle*, and the *set*. You can score your melds during the play of the hand, and you can use any cards in your melds more than once to make a second meld in a different category at a later turn. For example, you can put down the ♠Q in a pinochle and then reuse it to make a set of queens.

Here's a list that scrutinizes all-things meld:

>> **Sequences:** Sequences are specific *holdings* (groupings of cards) in the trump suit (keep in mind that you turn over the top card of the stock to select the trump suit at random in the two-player game), and three holdings in the trump suit score you points, along with one equivalent holding in a side-suit: the A-10-K-Q-J, the K-Q, and the trump 9 all score points, as do the K-Q in a non-trump suit.

   • A-10-K-Q-J of the trump suit (a *flush* or *rope*) is worth 150 points.

   • The 9 of the trump suit (called the *dix*, pronounced *deece*) is worth 10 points.

- K-Q of the trump suit (a *royal marriage*) is worth 40 points.

- King-queen in a non-trump suit (a *common marriage*) is worth 20 points.

>> **Pinochle:** This meld is a combination of the ♦J and the ♠Q. One pair is good, but two are even better:

- Pinochle (the ♦J and ♠Q) is worth 40 points.

- Double Pinochle (both ♠Qs and both ♦Js) is worth 300 points.

>> **Set:** This meld brings together each of the four court cards: Aces, kings, queens, or jacks, but it has to be one of each suit; you can't make a set of queens including two spades and no clubs.

- Four aces (one of each suit), also known as *aces around* or *100 aces,* is worth 100 points.

- Four kings (one of each suit), also known as *80 kings,* is worth 80 points.

- Four queens (one of each suit), also known as *60 queens,* is worth 60 points.

- Four jacks (one of each suit), also known as *40 jacks,* is worth 40 points.

- Four 10s and four 9s are worth nothing.

If you get double sets of aces, kings, queens, or jacks (again one of each suit in each set), the score is 10 times what one set is worth. And a double rope in trump is worth 1,500 points.

REMEMBER

The *dix* of the trump suit (the 9) is worth 10 points. If the top card of the stock is a 9, the dealer scores 10 points immediately. Whenever either player wins a trick, they can exchange a dix they have in their hand for the turned-over trump card, and score 10 points for that. By doing so, you improve your chances of scoring melds from the trump suit.

Finishing the game

The object of the game is to be the first to score 1,000 points. If both players go past the winning post on the same hand, the player with the larger score wins. Other possible winning targets are 1,200 and 1,500.

VARIATION

If both players achieve the target on the same turn, you can break the tie in two additional ways. You can set the winning post at 1,250 (and if necessary, up to 1,500, and so on). Whoever reaches the new target first wins. You can also allow a player who has passed 1,000 points, or thinks they have, to announce it by *making a call.* If a player calls, the play of the hand stops, and the points scored thus far in the hand by the caller are totaled. If they're right, they win the game; if they're wrong, they lose.

Playing your opponent

The play of the cards affords you the opportunity to score points by winning tricks, and also to put down scoring sets. If you cannot manage the first task, you won't be able to attempt the second, so let us see how you should set about winning tricks.

Any card in the trump suit beats all the cards in the side-suits (non-trump suits).

REMEMBER

Phase one: Improving your hand and scoring melds

You aim for two targets during this phase of the game. For your first endeavor, you want to leave yourself with as many trump cards and high cards as you can for phase two so you can capture scoring cards and score points then.

In addition, and perhaps more importantly, you want to score points by putting down point-scoring melds from the cards remaining in your hand during phase one. The snag is that you can put down only a single point-scoring meld at a time, and only when you've won a trick (but see the roundhouse in *getting the most from your melds*). However, one big snag is that after you play a card to win a trick, you can't use it in a meld, so you have to avoid throwing away the scoring (or potential scoring) cards simply in order to obtain the lead.

During the first phase of the game, which lasts for 12 turns, both players exhaust the stock of 24 cards sitting in the middle of the table by playing out a card from their hands and then replacing it by picking up a card from the pile. The sequence goes like this:

1. **The nondealer leads to the first trick; they may select any card in their hand, as can the second player in reply.**

   Remember, the second player doesn't have to play a card in the suit led (or *follow suit*), even if they have a card in the suit. You may not want to follow suit if doing do involves playing a card that you want to keep for a high-scoring trick later on. Of course, if you don't follow suit or play a trump card, you lose the trick.

2. **Whoever wins the trick (by playing the highest card in the suit led or in the trump suit) takes the face-down card from the top of the stock. The loser takes the next face-down card.**

The procedure repeats itself until no cards are left in the stock.

3. **The winner of the trick can declare one piece of meld before drawing from the stock.**

4. **The winner of the trick leads to the next trick.**

5. **On the last of the 12 tricks in phase one, the player who wins the trick gets the choice of the face-down card or the trump card (the first card turned up that denoted the trump suit).**

REMEMBER

This last trump card is almost sure to be the dix, because one player has usually claimed their 10 points by switching their dix with the initial trump card.

Some play that the winner of the last trick gets the face-down card and must expose it, and the loser gets the trump card. Either way, the winner of the last trick has one final opportunity to score points by putting down a meld.

VARIATION

When the stock is exhausted, the second phase of the game begins.

REMEMBER

A card used in a meld does double duty: It stays on the table as part of your hand, where you can use it in the play to win or lose a trick. Just because it has been used to score points does not prevent it from being part of the 12 cards in your hand, albeit a visible part. So at the end of the hand you will pick up the remaining cards from the melds and put them back in your hand, to play them out during the second phase of the game.

Also bear in mind that though winning a trick in order to put down a meld may not be a problem in the early part of the game, getting the lead in an advantageous fashion toward the end of the first phase may be more difficult than it appears.

If you win a trick, put down any meld you want to score before picking up from the stock. After you pick up a card, your turn is over. Whenever you put down a meld, you record the score for it; you add the points you get in the play from winning tricks at the end of the hand.

TIP

Try to use 10s, if you can, to capture the lead; apart from being high cards, they serve little purpose in melding except for the trump 10 in the flush. However, winning tricks with 10s scores you trick points in the process. Conversely, you want to get rid of your jacks or 9s if you're looking to lose a trick. You want to give up low-scoring cards, which are of little use in scoring melds, rather than queens and kings. Losing tricks that you could win may often work out better than winning them if by doing so you preserve all your possible melding combinations in the process, especially in the early part of the game.

Bear in mind that if you lead a high card, such as an ace, early in the hand, you make it vulnerable to trump cards, and at best you pick up nothing of value from your opponent. The longer you wait to play an ace, the more likely you are to acquire something of value as your opponent may have fewer non-counters to throw.

In addition, when you have a choice, you should lead from a long suit (a suit you have many cards in) to make your opponent work harder to win the trick. Your adversary is likely to find that winning a trick in a suit that they're short in is difficult, and they may be forced to expend a trump card to do so.

Figure 14-1 lets you practice your strategy a little. The initial turned-up card is the ♣Q, making clubs the trump suit for the hand.

FIGURE 14-1:
A promising
sample hand.

As you look at this hand, you see that it has a marriage in spades (the king-queen), with the possibility — with a good pickup — of four kings and a pinochle (the ♠Q and ♦J). If you can pick up the ♣Q (by getting the dix and switching it for the ♣Q or by picking up the other ♣Q directly), you may get a run in clubs.

If you can pick up the ♣Q (by getting the dix and switching it for the ♣Q, or by picking up the other ♣Q directly), you may get a run in clubs — though you need the ♣A too, of course. Your strategy is lead the ♠9, hoping to put down the marriage in spaces quickly when you win a trick. Good cards to pick up from the stock are the ♣A, ♣Q, ♣9, or the ♥K.

Phase two: Playing out the cards

The sole aim of the second phase is to score as many points as possible by winning tricks with point-scoring cards in them.

Phase two is much more straightforward and less strategically complex than the first phase. You both pick up any of your exposed cards on the table in melds to bring the total of cards in your hand back to 12, and play out those 12 remaining cards from your hand. Each player (starting with the player who won the last trick) plays one card, as before, to a trick, and the player who plays the highest card in the suit led or the higher trump card takes the trick and leads to the next trick.

In this phase, you must follow suit if you can (a difference from the first phase). If the second player has no cards in the suit led, they must put a trump on the trick and win it (if they have any trump left). If a trump is led, the second player must play a higher trump if possible; having no higher trumps they must play a lower trump if they have one. The trump suit stays the same for both phases of play. If the trump suit is led, the second player can discard anything they want to get rid of, so long as they have no trump cards.

After both players play all their cards, each player looks through the taken tricks and adds up the trick points (refer to Table 14-1 to assign values to each of the cards). You add these trick points to the melds from the first part of the game to make your total for the hand.

In the second phase of the game, a failure to follow suit or a failure to try to win a trick by trumping leads to the player scoring nothing for their tricks for the entire hand — but they keep the points they score for melds. You can correct an error until you've played to the next trick.

In the sample hand I show you in Figure 14-1, at the end of 12 tricks, you collect 170 points in the melds. When you pick up the dix of the trump suit and switch it for the ♠Q, you score 10 points; when you put down four kings, that scores another 80 points; you put down a royal marriage and subsequently two common (non-trump) marriages of kings and queens and score 40 + 20 + 20 for those marriages. That all totals 170 points.

You also collect points in the first phase for winning tricks with scoring cards in them — maybe 50 points. You haven't totaled those points up yet; you add up all the card points at the end of the second phase.

Your adversary scores 100 points for four aces, a pinochle (the ♠Q and ♦J) for 40, and a common marriage for another 20, totaling 160 points. They also have 50 points in the play unrecorded.

Pretend that you have the cards shown in Figure 14-2 at the end of the first phase of the game.

FIGURE 14-2:
Ready for
the second
phase of play.

Your objective is to win as many tricks as possible in order to collect the scoring cards. Because you've been watching to keep track of the 12 trump cards and the six other aces, you know that your opponent holds five trump cards, including both aces, both ♦As, and one ♠A. You're lucky to have the lead, because now you can lead your long suit (hearts) and force your opponent to trump it. In return, you get to win tricks with your trump cards. If your adversary had the lead, they could take out some trump cards and neutralize your hand by leading diamonds (and maybe spades, too).

At the end of the second phase, each player adds up the points from the first and second phases; each player adds their score for the deal to their running total. Remember the game is played to 1,000 points.

Getting the mos.t from your melds

The key to the game is to put down as many combinations in the first phase of the game as you can; it's almost impossible to win unless you score with melds. You can use any card in more than one scoring combination, provided that you use it to score points with a combination from a different category of points. For example, you can put down four kings and then use the ♠K, which was already on the table, in a marriage by putting down the ♠Q. You can use the ♠Q with the ♦J for a pinochle, and then you can use that jack with three other jacks to make a set.

You can't, however, use a king with one queen for a marriage and then reuse the king with another queen for a second marriage. No bigamy is permitted in Pinochle! Also, just to complicate matters a little further, each meld that you score must include at least one new card from your hand that you have not previously melded. This implies, for example, that if you have already melded jacks around and a spade marriage, you cannot subsequently score the ♠Q and ♦J from those melds as a Pinochle.

TIP

The timing of putting down sequences may be important. For example, say you're looking at a king-queen in the trump suit (a royal marriage), which you have in your hand as part of a flush, the A-10-K-Q-J of the trump suit. If you put down the king-queen first, you can expand it by putting down the remaining cards in the flush later on for another 150 points. But, if you put down the flush first, you can't extract the king-queen from for another point-scoring move. As a rule, putting down marriages first gives you more flexibility in later play.

Another tip to keep in mind: Make sure that you meld any aces you may have into a set of 100 aces as soon as possible — that way, you ensure that you can use them to take tricks without worrying about losing the meld points.

You need to have the earlier scoring combination intact in order to embellish it. You can attain the 300-point award for double pinochle only if the first combination is still on the table in one piece.

Although you want to put down a trump marriage and then the flush, you must realize that doing so takes two turns. (You get to put down only one set at a time.) If the deck is fast running out of cards at the end of the first phase, you may have to settle for what you can get by putting down the flush and giving up on the secondary award. If you're worried about your opponent having the right cards for a high-scoring combination, such as a flush, at the end of the first phase, you should consider leading a high trump card — your adversary may not be able to win the trick without playing a high trump card, thus disrupting their flush. Simply winning the last few tricks — especially if your opponent leads a high card, indicating that they're keen to keep the lead — may be a good idea.

According to some people, one way to save a turn in scoring melds is by putting down a *roundhouse:* four kings and queens at the same time, scoring 240 points in the process. You get 80 + 60 for the kings and queens around, together with the four marriages for 100 points (one for 40 and three for 20). The attraction of this play is not in getting bonus points, but in the economy of effort in claiming melds. This represents the only exception to the rule that you can only put down one meld at a time.

Always try to focus on whether certain high cards still in your hand are ever going to be usable in a meld. As soon as your opponent puts down four aces, can your three aces ever make another set? Not if the eighth ace has already been played! In that case, use your aces to win tricks and take the lead.

If you hold two identical cards, one of which has been used in a meld and is on the table, visible to your opponent, make sure to play the one on the table first. No point in giving away information about your hand!

FOLLOWING THE CARDS

What separates the good Pinochle player from the moderate one is their ability to remember which cards have been played during the first phase of the game. Initially, try keeping track of the aces — all eight of them — and maintain an approximate count of the trump cards. Even this task is a tall order if you aren't used to following the cards, and you're likely to find your count of the hand straying because you have other things to focus on during the hand. But the task may be worthwhile, because you get a better feel for the hand, and you may find that you get to understand more about the way the cards work. The simple way to keep count is to track all the trump cards and aces as they're played. Don't include the cards in your hand in the count of the cards actually played.

Pinochle for Three: Auction Pinochle

Pinochle for three players brings in a whole different set of factors that you don't find in Pinochle for two. First, it reduces the need for careful study of the cards played, which is the characteristic of Pinochle for two. You also have an additional bidding phase of the game, which gives the opportunity for daring and judgment — as well as the opportunity for heavy loss through overbidding.

During the bidding, you compete for the right to name the trump suit — making you the *declarer*. The declarer takes on the other two players (the *defenders*) and is the only player permitted to score melds. This change introduces a different feel to the game; with only one person scoring melds, obtaining the right to do so through the bidding is an important element of the game.

VARIATION

Some people play that the defenders can score their melds as well.

Two additional factors make Auction Pinochle intriguing:

>> The existence of the *widow* (or *cat*), which consists of some undealt cards that give the declarer the chance to improve their hand through an exchange (see the next section for the mechanics of the widow).

>> The existence of the *kitty*, an extra pot of money, which adds an interesting gambling element to the game (if you want to play for stakes; it isn't required) to further encourage optimistic bidding. See the section "Feeding the kitty" later in this chapter for the details.

>> If you score the game rather than compete for stakes, play that the first player to get 1,000 (or 1,500) points wins the game.

Dealing out the widow

Pinochle for three players uses the same 48-card deck as the two-player game. After you cut for the deal and arrange your seating according to the cut, the dealer (the player who cut the lowest or highest card) distributes 45 cards among the players, three at a time.

After dealing 15 cards to each player, the dealer sets aside three cards face-down as the *widow*, which the declarer takes up as part of their reward for taking the contract. (See the next section, "Making a bid for glory," for more information.) In some variations, a card of the widow is turned up at this point to let everyone in on only part of the secret. Whoever becomes the declarer takes the widow, shows it to everyone after the bidding, and then throws away three cards face-down from their hand to reduce it to the same number of cards as everyone else. (Those three cards play no real part in the hand thereafter except that any points discarded count toward the declarer's target.)

The dealer must redeal if any card is exposed. Similarly, if a player has too many or too few cards, the error can be corrected if you spot it before declarer picks up the widow. If the error comes to light after that point, the declarer is given their contract if the error is in the defenders' hands, and the declarer loses double the value of their contract if their hand is wrong. (If the declarer doesn't make their contract, the failure is called *going bete*. Losing a double game is called *double bete*.)

Making a bid for glory

The bidding commences with the *eldest hand*, the player to the dealer's left, being the first to *speak*, or make a bid. The bid represents the number of points they think they can make on the hand if they're allowed to choose the trump suit to make melds and score points. You make your bid based on melds in your hand and on the high cards you have that can take tricks and score points.

In some circles, the eldest hand *must* make a bid; different people have different ideas about the bid, but 250 points is the normal minimum bid that you're allowed to make. The other players then have the option of passing or making a higher bid, but every increase in the bidding must be in multiples of 10 points. After two players pass in succession, the bidding ends, and the highest bidder plays the hand against the other two players (the defenders), who play in tandem.

The defenders operate as a single unit. It's two against one, so winning tricks may not be easy for the declarer.

Some people only allow a single round of bidding; this restriction seems too limiting to me. The continuous bidding is more interesting and tactically demanding. However, general rules state that after a player passes in an auction, they can't reenter the bidding.

If you permit the eldest hand to pass, and subsequently all the other players pass, too, throw in the hand and have the next player deal a new hand.

A bid out of turn can be accepted or rejected at the discretion of the player whose turn it is to bid. An insufficient bid may be canceled, in which case no further penalty is incurred, or the other players may accept it at their discretion.

After the bidding ends, the newly crowned declarer turns the widow face-up for all to see and takes the cards into their hand, throwing three cards back into the widow. Then the declarer puts down any melds, using all the cards at their disposal. The declarer is the only player entitled to score melds, and if they don't have any, they are certainly in trouble! The scoring table for melds is exactly the same as for the two-player version (see the section "Scoring the melds" earlier in this chapter).

If you force the eldest hand to bid, they may have to make a call with a wholly unsuitable hand. If this is the case, they can concede failure of their contract without looking at the widow. Conceding is in their interest, because if they have a totally unpromising hand, conceding can limit their losses. As soon as the declarer looks at the widow, they lose a larger penalty if they fail to fulfill their contract than they would have by conceding. Even so, the declarer still has the option to limit their losses by conceding after viewing the widow.

Here are the various penalties you incur for conceding or for contract failure:

>> If you concede without looking at the widow and you're playing for money, you pay the kitty and not the other players. If you're playing for points, you concede the value of your bid.

>> If you look at the widow and then concede, you pay a single stake to each of the players and to the kitty. If you're playing for points, you lose the value of your bid, and the other players get to score their melds, if any.

>> If you play out the hand and lose, it costs you a double stake to everyone. If you're playing for points, you lose double the value of your bid.

A successful bid lands you a single stake from all the players. And if you make your bid from your melds or you're close enough that you can claim with certainty that you'll succeed, you don't have to play the hand out and score up your bid.

When bidding, you classify your bids into three categories:

TIP

>> **Safe bids:** You have the melds in your hand and a near certainty of the points in the play to make your bid.

>> **Overbids:** You need specific cards in the widow and a little bit of help from the other players in the play of the cards.

>> **Psychic, or fake, bids:** These bids are designed to push up (or *run up*) the bidding, and you may have no chance of success if the second player pulls out of the auction — which may be referred to as *dropping the bidding*. You should limit this last category of bluff bids to the minimum — they become expensive if your bluff is called too often. But acquiring a reputation for experimenting in this way can be helpful; doing so may mean that you win the bidding more cheaply because nobody trusts you to have what you bid.

Melding and discarding as the declarer

All the melds that apply in the two-player game are available to the declarer in the three-player game (see the section "Scoring the melds" earlier in this chapter). One big difference, however, is that the declarer can put all their melds down at a single turn instead of having to make the plays individually.

Another minor distinction that arises in this form of the game: You can't first score points for a royal marriage and then for a flush. The marriage, which is worth fewer points, doesn't count.

After the declarer discards (or *buries*) three cards from their hand, they score their melds. The three discarded cards form part of their total points at the end of the hand, which gives the declarer a fair degree of flexibility to throw away vulnerable high-scoring cards, such as kings and 10s, that can be captured by aces. It may also give them the opportunity to throw away all their cards from a side-suit, which allows them to trump their opponents' leads and generate additional chances to score points. You can't discard anything into the widow and then use it in a meld.

After the declarer takes the widow, they nominate the trump suit.

WARNING Discarding the wrong number of cards or forgetting to discard costs the offending declarer twice their bid.

TIP When selecting the cards to discard, you should always try to keep as many cards from your two longest suits as you can and retain aces in the other suits if necessary. Try to discard from short suits. Throw away 10s — the most vulnerable high-scoring honor card — if they're unprotected by aces. All court cards in short suits — if not utilized in melds — are prime candidates for discarding. If you leave yourself with an ace with no other cards in that suit, lead it as soon as you can. Otherwise, you may lose it to someone else leading the other identical ace first.

Feeding the kitty

The *kitty* represents an extra player when it comes to paying out or winning bets. It starts with no money, and players pay into it, either a single stake or a double stake, whenever they fail in their contracts. You pay a single stake if you abandon the hand without playing it out, and you pay a double stake if you play and fail. If the declarer fulfills a contract, all the players pay them, but the kitty doesn't unless the bid is for 350 points or more.

Thus, the way to take money from the kitty is to succeed in a bid of 350 or more. The kitty keeps building until that happens. A successful bid of less than 350 leaves the kitty unchanged.

If you're playing for stakes, you should know that five different scoring tables are in use. You can use any of the five scales shown in Table 14-2 to pay off or get paid (and I have no doubt that many other such tables exist).

TABLE 14-2   ## Scoring Tables for Auction Pinochle

Bid in the Range Of	A	B	C	D	E
200–340	1	1	1	3	3
350–390	2	2	2	5	5
400–440	4	4	7	10	10
450–490	6	7	10	15	20
500–540	8	10	13	20	40
550–590	10	13	16	25	80

Here's how this scoring works in practice. A player who declares for 420 may abandon their bid before starting play if they pick up a hopeless widow — in which case they pay the value of their bid (somewhere between 4 and 10 units, depending on the scale in use) to the kitty and the same amount to each of the players. If they play out the hand and succeeds in their bid, they collect the same amount from everyone, including the kitty.

If you play out the hand and fail to score enough points, you pay double to everyone, including the kitty.

REMEMBER

If the kitty runs out of money, everyone except the declarer contributes an equal amount to build it up again.

Winning — in spades

For some variations of Auction Pinochle, the scoring system rewards a declaration in all suits equally, but these variations are in the minority. For the standard game, spades and hearts are generally worth more than clubs and diamonds. In fact, the mainstream position is to value all contracts in spades as worth double the standard amounts, which means twice the payout and forfeit. For example, if you go for a bid of 300 and choose spades as the trump suit, you stand to lose or gain twice as much.

You may also agree to play that hearts are worth triple the norm (agree to this scoring in advance).

Battling the declarer

Because you use and score all the cards in the deck, 240 points are up for grabs during play. And because the last trick scores an additional 10 points, 250 points are at stake on every hand in the play, together with all the melds, of course.

REMEMBER

Keep in mind that the points in the widow count for the declarer, so they aren't taken out of play. And even though the cards that the declarer discards don't feature in the play at all, they still count for them. Good to be the declarer!

Just as in the two-player game, when two equal cards appear on the same trick, the first one put down outranks the second one.

Generally, the declarer leads to the first trick. The winner of each trick leads to the next.

The rules of following suit are as follows:

» You can lead anything you like at any time.

» If you can follow suit, you must do so (and some play you must play a higher card if you can). If you're out of the suit led, you must play a trump if you can.

» If a trump is led, you must play a higher trump card to the trick if you can. This rule applies to both the second and third players. If you don't have a higher trump card, you can play any trump card that you like.

The rules about *overtrumping*, when the first hand leads a suit of which both the second and third hands have no cards, are conflicting. The second hand must trump if they can, of course. Some play that the third hand must overtrump if they can, but most modern versions of Pinochle rules state that the third hand must play a trump card but doesn't have to overtrump.

WARNING

The rules about following in the trump suit are very useful to the declarer, who can, for example, hope to force someone into playing two high trump cards by leading a middle card in the trump suit.

The defenders try to look for chances to weaken the declarer's trump holding early, if they can infer that the declarer doesn't have many high trump cards. (You may be able to deduce this information from their decision whether or not to play on the trump suit early.)

One defender can try to throw high-scoring cards onto their defending partner's trick (or *smear* the trick). By doing so, they give points to their partner and prevent the declarer from scoring the points. But you can't talk to your co-defender to tell them what to do!

WARNING

Pretty much any error by the declarer (failing to follow suit or failing to trump a plain suit when able to do so) costs them a double game, twice the points of what they bid for, or a double stake if playing for money. A *revoke* (not playing a card in the suit led) by a defender costs a single game. You have the opportunity to correct a revoke until the start of the next trick.

The defenders can accept a lead out of turn by the declarer if they want.

When playing out a hand as the declarer, bear in mind that you don't get any bonus awards for making more points than your bid. If you just concentrate on making your bid whenever you can, you'll do very well. You need to focus on the cards from two angles:

>> Try to remember how many trump cards and aces you've seen.

>> Try to keep a rough count on how many points each side has scored. Keeping count tells you how much more you require for your bid and indicates what you need to do to make it.

Bidding strategically

When you plan your bid, you can take a calculated risk on getting some help from the widow — but don't expect too much help.

For example, take a look at the hand in Figure 14-3. You count three useful cards that you could pick up: one in spades, one in hearts, and one in diamonds to complete a flush (A-10-K-Q-J). The ♠A would make four aces, but you can't count that possibility twice. In addition, either the ♣Q or ♣J would give you a set of queens or jacks. If you need one of three cards to improve your hand, you're a slight underdog to draw it from the widow.

FIGURE 14-3:
Weigh your
drawing odds.

The biggest mistake to make in bidding is to hope or assume that you'll pick up a useful card from the widow. Assume you'll get an average of 20 to 30 points from the widow. You can hope to use the widow to improve your hand a little in the play but not to make an additional meld.

Playing with spades and hearts counting extra gives an aggressive bidder an edge. Even if the declarer intends to bid in spades, they can make a concession after looking at the widow and just concede the single stake to the other hands and the kitty because they can concede in clubs or diamonds.

This quirk of scoring gives the declarer the option to intend to contract in spades (and even more so in hearts, if you play the triple-score rule) on more marginal hands because they can concede a single monetary unit on an unsuitable pick-up but play a double game with the right widow. The odds, therefore, move in the gambler's favor to win the bidding and hope for good news in the form of nice cards in the widow.

As a general strategy in estimating how many points you can win, assume that for every losing card you have, your opponents will be able to dispose of the two highest outstanding cards in the suit on that trick. So, for example, if you start the hand with the ♥10 ♥J ♥9 and you throw the 10 into the widow, you should assume that the jack and 9 will attract four of the remaining five high cards (the aces, 10s, and kings).

The ability to win the last trick is also vital; because of the defenders' desire to save up their high-scoring cards for a trick won by their side, you can assume that the last trick (and, to a certain extent, the one before that) will be critical in most hands, and therefore contain quite a few high cards. If you win those tricks, you'll be in good shape to make your contract.

Giving up without a struggle

The decision of whether to concede your hand when the widow hasn't proved especially useful is a tough one. Keep in mind that concession involves giving up a single stake to all; however, playing and losing require payment of a double stake. This principle applies whether you're playing for points or for money.

When you're faced with the decision of whether to play out the hand or concede, you need to have only one chance in three (or better) of succeeding to make it worthwhile to play out the hand. However, if you're a better player than your opponents (and how could that not be the case after reading this book?), you may go forward on slightly worse odds.

In the play, consider how you want the missing cards to be distributed so that you can make your bid. If you're missing an even number of cards, the suit figures not to *split*, or divide evenly in the opponents' hands, for you (except for the 1-1 split, which is even money). If you're missing an odd number of cards, a suit will split as evenly as possible — 3-2 or 2-1 most of the time. You don't need higher mathematics at this point in your Pinochle career!

The game ends when one player wins 1,000 points (or 1,500 if you prefer). If you're playing for stakes, tally the score after each hand and play until one player gets short on money or until you've played a predetermined number of hands.

If you're close to going out, you can often make a bluff bid to force another player to outbid you in order to stop you from getting the points you need to win.

TIP

Partnership Auction Pinochle

In the preceding two sections, I take you on a Pinochle tour where one player battles against the rest of the field (against one or two other players). However, in Partnership Auction Pinochle, you get to take on a partner to square off against another team of two.

You play with the same 48-card deck used in the two- and three-player versions of Pinochle (see the chapter introduction for specifics). Everybody cuts the deck, and the two players drawing the highest cards take on the players who draw the two lowest cards. The high-card team gets its choice of seats and deals the first hand. You can play with set partnerships, in which case the players simply cut for the deal at the start of the session, or with changing partnerships, where you cut for the deal and positions at the start of each game.

You play to either 1,000 or 1,500 points; the first team to hit the score wins. *Counting down* is permitted — you can keep a running total of points scored during the hand and claim a victory as soon as your total goes over the limit. Don't get too giddy, however: A false claim loses the game. If both teams go over the winning post on the same hand, some variations state that the declaring side wins; some play to a score of 250 points beyond the winning post — 1,250 or 1,750, as the case may be. If you play the game for money, the easiest way to do so is to allocate a stake per point, say 1 cent, or 5 cents if you are in a gambling mood.

Dealing and bidding

The dealer shuffles the deck and offers it to the opponent on their right to cut. Everyone receives a 12-card hand, dealt out in threes or fours.

When the deal is complete, the players, starting with the eldest hand (the player to the dealer's left), have the option of bidding or passing. After a player has made a call, the auction continues until three players pass in a row; at that point, the last person to bid has bought the contract, and they and their partner must make good on the bid or pay the consequences.

VARIATION

Some people play that everyone can make only one bid — which, to my mind, destroys the competitive nature of the auction. This variation is known as *Firehouse Pinochle*. Another common variation is that the dealer has to bid 250 if the first three players pass.

WARNING

When playing with a partner, the consequences of bidding incorrectly are more severe because of the fact that, in the process, you give your partner erroneous information about your hand. A bid made when it isn't your turn to speak is canceled, and it silences both members of the partnership for the whole bidding. You must increase any bid you make that isn't as high as an earlier call until it's the highest call, and that, similarly, silences your partner for the whole auction.

Bids start at 200 or 250 points minimum and must increase in multiples of 10. After a player passes, they're barred from bidding again.

VARIATION

The mode of bidding I describe in the preceding paragraphs is relatively simplistic. The partner of a player that passes has no idea whether their colleague can offer anything useful in the melding or play. To that end, some variations permit an additional bid at the first turn of any player to speak. They may bid "pass with help," which indicates that although they can't compete at the level that the bidding has reached, they have some cards that may be helpful eventually.

The standard rules from the other variations of Pinochle on misdeals apply concerning exposed cards or the wrong number of cards dealt out. In addition, some groups play the variation that a player with five or more 9s may call for a misdeal.

The two main varieties of Partnership Pinochle are Racehorse and Cutthroat. In Racehorse Pinochle, after the winning bidder has named trump, their partner passes four cards across the table. The bidder incorporates those cards into their hand and then passes the same number of cards back. In Cutthroat, the main variation of the four-handed game passing doesn't take place. The consequence of the pass is to give both players a chance to make more melds.

Melding

After the bidding ends, you can claim your melds; you claim points based on your own hand, which you then add to your partner's points to form your partnership's total score. This aspect of the game differs significantly from the three-player auction game, where only the declarer can meld and take assistance from the widow.

The fact that all four players can score on melds dramatically reduces the declarer's edge in the melding. They not only have no widow, but they also have to watch the other players score up. However, choosing the trump suit preserves an edge for the declaring side (keep in mind that flushes only count in the trump suit).

You can use any card more than once for melds, as long you use the card in a separate category of scoring (marriages with sets, for example). You can only use the cards in your hand — you can't co-opt your partner's cards.

Just as in the other versions of Pinochle in this chapter, after you count the melds, you pick up the cards and put them back in your hands before starting the play of the cards.

TIP Make sure that you remember what the declarer melded if you're a defender; track down their losing cards so that you can take full advantage of them by leading your high cards in suits where you know that they have to follow suit.

VARIATION Some people require that the declarer must make a minimum meld of at least a royal marriage, or 40 points (see the section "Scoring the melds" earlier in the chapter for point info).

If you're more than 250 points short of your bid before the play starts, you automatically *go set*, which means you don't have to play out the hand. You lose the value of your bid, whatever that may be. Your opponents do get to score for their melds, though.

TIP To determine how high you should bid, assume that you'll get no help from your partner and then compare that score with what may happen if you face a perfect hand. Bid somewhere closer to the lower level.

In Racehorse Pinochle (where you pass four cards to your partner), after trump is announced, the partner of the declarer should send trump so the declarer can make a flush if possible; aces so the declarer can make *aces around* (four aces); and, if the contract is in spades or diamonds, the other half of the pinochle — namely the ♠Q or ♦J. The declarer sends back anything that they don't want — particularly 10s, kings, and queens.

Playing out the hand

The full 250 points are at stake in the play of the cards, as in all variations of Pinochle: 240 for the scoring cards and 10 points for the last trick.

The eldest hand, or the player to the dealer's left, leads to the first trick, regardless of who the declarer is. The rules for following suit in three-handed Pinochle apply here, too: Following suit is mandatory, and if the lead is a trump card, you must play a higher trump if you can or a lower one if you cannot. If you can't follow suit, you must play a trump card, and you must overtrump if you can.

If you can't follow suit to a plain-card lead or if you can't overtrump a trump that's already played, then you must play a lower trump. These rules about trumping apply even if your partner is winning the trick at the point you have to play. Whoever wins the trick leads to the next one, and so on.

Just as in the other variations of Pinochle, the first of two identical cards played beats the second one.

Because this game involves a partnership, wrongly playing cards carries a stiffer penalty. For example, if you expose a card during the bidding, your partner is barred from bidding. In addition, the offender must play the exposed card at their first turn. The non-offenders may also be allowed to prohibit or demand the lead of that suit if the card isn't played on the first trick.

TIP

As declarer, if you can lead trump effectively at the start of the game, you should do so. Lead out lone aces as early as you can, or you run the risk of losing the trick when someone else leads the other ace, and you have to follow suit helplessly.

Picking up prizes and penalties

In comparison to the three-player game, the scoring for Partnership Auction Pinochle is relatively sedate — no bonuses for spades or hearts and no double penalties.

An unsuccessful declarer scores nothing on the hand for melds or tricks and simply loses the value of their bid. A successful declarer scores the points they took on the hand; in other words, scoring more points than you bid counts for something in this game. In turn, the strategy of playing conservatively to ensure that you meet your contract, which applies in the three-player game, has to be somewhat revised, because you may be sacrificing valuable additional points by a policy of caution in the play.

PINOCHLE ON THE WEB

The National Pinochle Association (www.npapinochle.org/) promotes the game and offers six sanctioned tournaments for members throughout the year. For an overview of Pinochle rules, check out https://pdfslide.net/documents/tournament-rules-national-pinochle-association-npa-when-conducting-a-national.html. To play Pinochle online for free, try www.playok.com/en/pinochle/. For details about a more complex version of Pinochle for four players, go to www.pagat.com/marriage/pindd.html, where an 80-card version of the game is discussed, using four decks with only the top five cards in each suit in play.

The defenders always score exactly what they win in tricks and melds on the hand, *unless* they fail to win a single trick in the play. After such a failure, the defenders score nothing, nada, zip, and zilch. Take your pick — it all comes back to the same round zero.

TIP

The ability to win the lead is vital; the leader dictates the direction in which the hand goes. Always try to win the lead if you know how you want the play to proceed. Similarly, the ability to lead your long suits and force out your opponents' trump cards is very important. If you don't have many trump cards, don't lead losing trump cards. Try to turn your side-suit cards into winners instead to force out your rival's trump cards.

Chapter **15**

Setback

Setback (which has more aliases than Prince and Sean Combs put together) is also known as Pitch, Cinch, or Smear. Some call it High-Low-Jack and a host of similar names. The game combines a relatively simple bidding phase with a thought-provoking phase of cardplay. The game is ideal for folks who are unfamiliar with the bidding techniques of more complex games such as Bridge (see Chapter 12).

Setback packs more variations to the square inch than most of the games I outline in this book, but don't let the options worry you; just concentrate on the main game initially. Most people play only a couple of the variations you see in this chapter, and I acquaint you with the most popular variations.

BEFORE
HAND

To play Setback, you require only the following:

>> **Between two and eight players:** The ideal number is four so that everyone has a chance to win the hand, but three players also pose an interesting series of challenges.

>> **A standard deck of 52 cards:** In some varieties of the game, you may need a joker or two.

>> **Pencil and paper for scoring:** As long as you can add up to five, you won't be overly taxed by the mathematics of Setback.

Getting Setback Savvy

Setback is a point-scoring game. All players (no matter how many are playing) get six cards, with the remainder of the deck being set aside, and then a single round of bidding determines who picks the *trump suit*. The trump suit is the boss suit, meaning that a card in the trump suit beats any card in any other suit (and a higher trump card beats a lower trump card).

Whoever guarantees the most points during the bidding is called the *pitcher* and gets to choose the trump suit. The pitcher has to fulfill their guarantee, or they lose the number of points they bid.

You score points by taking tricks that contain certain cards. You form a *trick* when each player puts down one card, and the player who plays the highest card in the suit that's led (or the highest trump card if one or more trumps are played) wins the trick.

After a series of hands, the first person to reach 11 points wins the game (or you can decide on any other number in advance).

REMEMBER

In Setback, you can play a trump card at any time, if you have one, and take the trick. In other words, you don't have to follow suit unless trump is led. However, when a trump card is led, you *must* play one if you have one. No suit outranks any other suit until the pitcher selects the trump suit.

Divvying up the deck

Setback uses the standard deck of 52 cards, with aces high and 2s low. At the beginning of the contest, each player cuts for the right to deal, and whoever draws the highest card deals the first hand.

TIP

Dealing is a distinct advantage in Setback because the dealer may have the last chance to win the bidding war and choose the trump suit if the other players pass. (Find out more about the dealer's advantage in the later section, "Dealer's choice?".)

The dealer shuffles the cards and then offers them to the opponent on their right to cut, if they want to do so, prior to the deal. The dealer passes out the six cards face-down, clockwise, distributing them out three at a time to each player. The dealer places the remainder of the deck off to one side. At the end of each hand, the deal rotates one place clockwise. Don't forget to pick up the unused portion of the deck!

WARNING

If the dealer forgets to offer the cards to the opponent on their right to cut, or if they expose an ace, 2, or jack during the deal (which, as you see later, are potentially significant cards points-wise), they lose the right to deal, and the deck passes one place to their left. If any other accident occurs during the deal, no punishment is handed out; the dealer simply gathers in the cards and deals again.

Mastering the bidding

The bidding begins with the player to the left of the dealer — also referred to as the *elder hand.* That player has the option of passing or bidding a number between one and four, which represents the minimum number of points they intend to win if they have the choice of the trump suit. You can make more than you bid, without penalty. (See the section "Knowing the score" to find out how much your hand may be worth.) Bear in mind that the bid relates to *points,* not *tricks.*

After the elder hand bids or passes, the bidding progresses around the table, ending with the dealer. Each player has one chance, and one chance only, to make a bid or pass. Any bid of four wins the bidding outright.

VARIATION

Quite a few people play that the smallest legal call is two because they think the bid of one is too easy to achieve. This variation isn't especially significant because a call of one is unlikely to win the bidding in any event, but you may want to keep this interpretation in mind.

For a bid to be legal, it must outrank the previous bid, or *call* — with one exception; see the following section "Dealer's choice?" for details. The suits themselves have no ranks, so a call of three from a player intending to use clubs as the trump suit, for example, isn't outranked by a call of three from a player who intends to use any other suit as the trump suit. You never mention suits in the bidding. A player's bid is based on how many of the scoring points they think they can get; you see in the section "Knowing the score" what wins you points.

VARIATION

One variation to bidding four is simply to lead a card on your turn to bid. This move implies that you're calling for four, the maximum, and are setting the trump suit with the card you play. Tough cheddar if you were about to make a call of four and someone gets there first — that's just the luck of the draw.

At the end of the bidding round, the highest bidder names the point number and has the right to nominate the trump suit. This player is known as the *bidder* or *pitcher.* The pitcher *leads,* or plays, to the first trick, and the card that they lead determines the trump suit for the hand.

WARNING

If anyone commits the error of making a bid out of turn or making an insufficient bid (one that doesn't beat a previous bid), the call is canceled, and the bidder doesn't get a second chance to make a correct bid.

The points that the pitcher undertakes to score have very little to do with the tricks themselves — the pitcher wants to collect certain cards that score points. However, at this point in the game, neither the pitcher nor anyone else necessarily knows what all these cards are.

Dealer's choice?

If the bidding comes back to the dealer (meaning nobody has reached the 4-point level), the dealer can take (or *steal*) the contract by equaling the highest bid. For example, if the last bid was two or three, the dealer can repeat the bid and steal the contract. However, in most circles — not everywhere — the dealer can't out-bid anyone who has gone for the maximum.

VARIATION

Some people consider that the dealer's privilege is outdated and no longer play this rule. Personally, I like the rule, and I feel that it doesn't prejudice anyone unfairly because everyone gets to be dealer an equal amount.

If everybody passes without a bid, the hand is considered dead, and the same dealer reshuffles the cards and redeals the hand.

VARIATION

Some people play that if everyone passes to the dealer, they must bid the minimum amount. If you adopt this rule, you may also decide that the minimum call is one rather than two because scoring 2 points is quite a difficult undertaking (which may prompt the dealer to think twice about passing the bid). The combination of forcing the dealer to bid and making them bid 2 points works together as a good strategic device to pull the dealer down when they're ahead.

Playing your cards right

The objective of the trick-taking phase of the game is capturing the tricks with the key cards in them (see the following section, "Knowing the score"). The high bidder has the lead for the first trick and must lead whatever suit they want to be the trump suit at the first trick. Normally, the pitcher leads their highest trump card, unless it's the jack, which is a card you try to retain for later.

After the high bidder pitches the trump suit, the other players must play a card in the trump suit (*follow suit*) if they can. In fact, if the trump suit is led at any point in the play, you must play a card in the trump suit if you have one. You don't have to try to win the trick — any trump card will do. If you have no cards in the trump suit, you can play whatever card you want.

After the first play, if any suit other than the trump suit is led, your options are more bountiful. You can follow suit, or you can play a trump card (it doesn't matter if you aren't out of cards in the suit that's been led). However, you can't discard on a plain suit if you can follow suit instead. If you *are* out of the suit led, you can either trump the trick or *discard* (throw away) anything you want.

Whoever wins the trick leads to the next trick.

REMEMBER

The rule that allows trumping while you still have a card in the suit led has a big impact on the strategy of play, so always keep it in mind. The pitcher wants to take care of all the trump cards as quickly as possible so that other players can't do any mischief with them; see the later section "Planning a strategy" for more information.

WARNING

If you catch the pitcher *revoking* (not following with a trump card to the lead of one or discarding on a plain-suit lead when they could follow), they lose the value of their bid; you play the hand out in full, and the other players score whatever points they make. If a *defender* (any player other than the pitcher) revokes, they lose the value of the pitcher's bid, and all the other players get to add the amount of that bid to their scores — including the pitcher, whether or not they would have made their bid.

Knowing the score

The tricks themselves are almost irrelevant (sorry for the disappointment). What *is* important are the locations of three key cards. Whoever wins the tricks that contain these cards scores points in the process. You may find that winning one trick can give you a series of points, whereas winning all the tricks but one may mean nothing — or less than nothing.

You tally scores at the end of the hand, when all the players inspect their tricks. Four points are awarded in the play (explained by the one-to-four bid); 3 of the 4 points are easy to work out, but the fourth point is less straightforward:

>> **High:** Whoever wins the trick with the highest trump card scores 1 point. The highest trump card may not be the ace, of course, because the ace may not have been dealt.

>> **Low:** Whoever wins the trick that includes the lowest trump card scores 1 point.

>> **Jack:** Whoever takes the trick that includes the jack of the trump suit scores 1 point. Being able to win this point depends on whether the card is dealt or not. If the jack is also the highest trump card, whoever wins the trick that contains it gets 2 points for their good fortune. (And yes, to satisfy the sea-lawyers out there, the jack can be the lowest trump, too!)

>> **Game (also known as the *most*):** Whoever has the most *scoring cards* in the hand wins 1 point. Each player goes through the tricks taken one by one and awards the following number of scoring points: aces are worth 4 points, kings 3, queens 2, jacks 1, and 10s 10 points each.

These scoring cards count in all four suits, not just trumps. Whoever scores the most wins the game point. If two players tie for the game point, no point is awarded.

VARIATION

Some people play that the low-trump point goes to the player who's *dealt* the lowest trump. My personal view is that you always want to give the award to the trick winner because the other approach introduces too much luck into the equation (in the sense that being dealt a card gives you a point without earning it as opposed to working at it, but not everyone agrees). Discuss this matter with your opponents in advance. The presence of jokers makes a difference in the interpretation of this rule — see the sidebar "Playing around with jokers" in this chapter for more details.

After all players complete the reckoning, your first chore is to check whether the pitcher made their contract. If they do, they score whatever points they collected, including any points taken in excess of their bid. If they make 3 points and only contracted for 2, they still score all 3 points.

If the pitcher fails in their contract, they're *set back* by the number of points equivalent to their bid — hence the name of the game. If the pitcher bids 3 and doesn't succeed, they lose 3 points, whether they finish up with 0, 1, or 2. If the pitcher fails in their contract and lose more points than they have, the player goes negative. This is recorded on the scoresheet by the scorekeeper circling their new score on the scoresheet. The pitcher has gone *in the hole*.

The defenders individually register their points, too, whether or not the pitcher succeeds in their bid.

Shooting the moon

Bidding and making all 4 points is a pretty rare feat. Anyone who bids 4 points successfully — which is also known as *smudging, slamming,* or *shooting the moon* — wins the game outright in most variations. However, most of the time, this rule applies only if the player involved isn't *minus* (or *in the hole*) at the time. If they are in the hole, the player has to be content with simply scoring 4 points.

VARIATION

If the joker is in play, a call of shooting the moon requires all 5 points, making it even more difficult to achieve.

REMEMBER

With four players, the chance of one of the other three players receiving a particular card is slightly better than 1 in 3. So, if you're trying to shoot the moon without the jack of the trump suit in your hand, you have only a moderate chance of finding someone else with that card.

Conversely, the chances of your king of the trump suit being the highest (or of your 3 being the smallest) should be about 2 in 3. In this situation, you're hoping that a card *isn't* dealt out. This bet represents decent odds, if you like a gamble. If you're more of a strategist than a gambler, however, read on!

Passing the winning post

You normally play to a fixed score, agreed on in advance. Whoever gets to that score first wins the *rubber*, meaning the whole contest. However, you may have a hard time finding much agreement as to what score you should play to. Playing to 7 yields a short game; playing to 21 can be a marathon. In between those extremes, you can play to 11, 15, or to any number that seems to fit the mood of the group.

REMEMBER

You don't have to pass the target as the pitcher to win; you can manage the task as the defender, too.

If two players pass the mark on the same round, follow these rules to break the tie:

>> If one of the players involved is the pitcher, the pitcher wins.

>> If neither player is the pitcher, you award the 4 points in the following sequence: high, low, jack, joker (if in use), and, finally, game point. Whoever reaches the target first, using this order of allocating the points, wins.

Planning a strategy

You can mosey on through Setback without giving much thought to how you play your cards, if that's your style. When playing with kids or in social settings, Setback is a perfect game to relax and have fun with. But if you play this way in a competitive match, don't expect to end up in the winner's circle too often.

VARIATION

PLAYING AROUND WITH JOKERS

In some parts of the United States, players add a wild variation to Setback by placing a joker in the deck, which introduces a fifth point into the game. Typically the joker counts as the lowest trump card, ranking below the 2, though some people treat it as ranking between the jack and 10. (Some versions of the game treat the joker as the highest trump card, which is a bad idea in my opinion because it can lead to a normal bid getting beaten by the presence of an unpredictable factor.) The joker point goes to whoever wins the trick with the joker in it.

Another variation, perhaps derived from Euchre, is to add the jack of the same color as an extra trump between the jack and the 10 (called the *jick*) and to treat the joker as the lowest trump, with a point to whoever wins the trick with either of them in.

The existence of the joker doesn't affect the status of the point for the low trump card, which still goes to the lowest trump in play other than the joker. However, playing with the joker provides an argument for saying that the low point goes to whoever is *dealt* the low trump card rather than whoever wins the trick with the low trump card in it. Otherwise, the point for the joker and the point for the low trump card are awarded in identical fashion.

If the pitcher leads the joker at the first trick, they can name whatever trump suit they want. However, leading the joker isn't normally a sound tactic because you want to save the joker to win a trick with it.

These strategies aren't for the faint of heart. To win at Setback, keep the following points of strategy in mind:

» The ace of the trump suit is always good for 1 point. The king of the trump suit is a favorite to get you a point as well. However, you must face the issue of whether to play the odds on a suit headed by the king. You have a good chance to win the high point with the king (see the earlier section "Knowing the score" for more information on the high point); your chances drop to fair with the queen of the trump suit. If you're desperate, going for the jack of the trump suit as your high trump card still gives you somewhat less than a 1 in 4 chance to have 2 points for the jack of the trump suit and the high trump card.

» With three trump cards, you can generally assume that you'll win at least one trick. Other players are unlikely to have three trump cards if you do.

» Don't play your aces in the side-suits until you extract as many trump cards out of your opponents' hands as possible. If you have trump cards to spare, lead the high trump cards. No point in saving them for a rainy day because you face a fair chance that your high cards in side-suits may be trumped by an opponent.

Losing an ace can affect your chances on the game point — and perhaps on the low trump card: Another player may use their 2 of the trump suit to take your winner and simultaneously score some points toward the game point.

» Don't lead your 10s as the first play in a suit unless you're absolutely desperate and think that doing so is the only way to get the game point. Other players may be able to trump the 10s, or they may get stomped by higher cards. Other players want to fasten onto your 10 because it scores so highly for the game point. Because, on average, no more than two 10s are out on any hand, the difference between winning a 10 and losing it to a rival may make all the difference to your chances of scoring the game point. At the very least, try to lose your high cards to the right opponent (one who isn't a threat to take the game point).

» As a defender, keep in mind that you still score the points you make whether the pitcher succeeds in their bid or not. However, when a player other than the pitcher is close to winning, you want to prevent them from picking up points in the play. Letting the pitcher score their low trump, the jack in the trump suit, or even the game point may be to your advantage if it keeps the points from falling into the wrong hands. Bear in mind that as long as no one has passed the post, the next hand may see you win outright, however bad your cumulative total is (if you shoot the moon). The saying "While there is life, there is hope" rings truest in Setback.

» Try to avoid leading the jack of the trump suit on the first trick. If someone else takes the trick — and the chances of this happening are good — you virtually write off your chances of winning the contract on the hand. If you have a trump suit without the ace, king, or queen, start with a middle card to try to get all the opponents' trump cards out of their hands.

» If you're the pitcher, be sure to lead more than one round of trump cards to try to collect the point for the low trump — unless someone else already acquired it on the first trick or unless you hold the card yourself. If you don't have the low trump, someone else can score up the point for the low trump by playing the card on a side-suit.

» As a defender, you can infer that a pitcher who leads one round of the trump suit and then switches to another suit has the low trump. In this case, playing trump cards to prevent them from scoring up the low trump may be to your advantage.

>> When bidding, be more aggressive when you're the first, or possibly second, to speak. Players with genuinely good hands are unhappy about dropping out of the bidding, and you may be able to tempt them into overbidding.

Grab a Friend: Partnership Setback

VARIATION

You play the partnership version of Setback with two teams (usually of two players each), where partners sit opposite each other.

The bidding proceeds the same way as the solo game (see the earlier section "Mastering the bidding"), with the dealer being able to steal the bid at their turn with a call equal to the previous highest call. If the first three players pass, the dealer must bid two, the minimum amount in this variation.

In the partnership game, you're working with your partner toward your goal. Each player pools the points they take for the side's total. You both want to pick your joint best trump suit, of course, and although you have the option of outbidding your partner by making a bid after they do, it's a fairly unusual thing to do. A long, strong trump suit of your own, which may be useless for your partner, may tempt you to outbid them.

Shooting the moon (see the section "Shooting the moon" earlier in this chapter) requires that the pitching side win all six tricks in addition to the 4 regular points. Shooting the moon is worth 5 points — winning all the tricks gets you 1 point. As usual, tricks made in excess of the bid by the pitching side count, with the exception of the additional fifth point for taking all the tricks. If you don't bid to shoot the moon, the maximum number of points for the pitching side is four; you don't get the point for taking all the tricks if you're not bidding for the moon.

VARIATION

One relatively common variation is for all four players to have a chance to improve their hands after the bidding is over. After the pitcher declares the trump suit, each player takes a turn to discard, face-down, all unwanted cards (which generally means non-trump cards) and picks up an equivalent number from the deck.

Scoring points is easier in the partnership game because one isn't fighting against the rest, so playing to 21 points doesn't produce an epic game. However, one of the requirements of Partnership Setback is that to win the game, you must pass the target by making your contract on a hand where your side is the pitcher. If you accumulate enough points as defenders to reach the winning post, you must wait to pitch a hand to win. You may find yourself in a position where you win the game but have fewer points than your opponents. If, for example, your opponents have 23 points, and you have 18, and you pitch for 3 points successfully, you win, despite being behind at the end of the game!

Setback for Three or Six

With two players, Setback drags unless you beef up the hands by using the draw I describe as a variation in the preceding section. The suggested number of cards you should put in play is eight.

With three players, eight cards is again the best number, although some perfectly good variations use six cards. With three, both the defenders gang up on the pitcher by trying to prevent them from winning tricks, or by dumping points where possible to the other defender. Three-Handed Setback tends to favor a conservative approach in the auction, because the odds tilt against the pitcher.

With six players, deal eight cards to everyone. After you use the standard auction process to announce trump, discard two cards from your hands. This route works as a substitute for the draw after the bidding.

5

Adding and Climbing

Adding and climbing? Sound like a lot of work, but I promise you that two of the main games I discuss in this part, Cribbage and President, are more fun (and less work) than the part title may imply.

One of the features that renders President and its related games unique is the idea that a successful performance at one hand entitles you to a higher status than players who performed less well. For the next hand, the poor performers have to subsidize the more elevated players by giving up some of the precious cards in their hand, thereby creating a vicious circle that makes it difficult for the lowlier players to break out from their peasant status.

By contrast, if you tire of taking on other players, create a feeling of solidarity by playing against the bank — a single entity — frequently in the shape of the casino. In return for a few percentage points in their favor, the casinos allow you to play Blackjack, and to spend as much or as little money as you want. Aren't they nice?

Chapter **16**

Cribbage

C ribbage is a game of numbers, in which you collect points by combining cards together to make runs, or scoring combinations. The mathematics is simple, but cribbage is a game of strategy and tactics. Sometimes you try to score points, sometimes you try to stop your opponent from scoring; every game is subtly different.

Cribbage relies on experience and intuition rather than strict mathematical calculation. In a given situation, one card may be the right one to play, and another may be the wrong card, and you may have no way to calculate which card is best. In Cribbage, you sometimes have to take a chance and sniff out the right thing to do. It's also a fast game; experienced players can complete a game in 10 or 15 minutes. You may want to start playing Cribbage with other relatively inexperienced players because slow play isn't encouraged.

That said, Cribbage is a finicky game that features many rules and regulations, and it may seem that a rule of etiquette governs almost every aspect of the game. The game also has a vocabulary all its own, which means that you need to know a few specialized words in order to play.

That's where this chapter comes in. I tell you everything you need to know to get started.

To play Cribbage, all you need are the following:

>> **Two players,** including yourself.

>> **A standard deck of 52 cards:** No jokers necessary.

>> **A pencil and paper for scoring:** Cribbage is frequently played with a Cribbage board, and some people think that using the board is an integral part of playing the game. You can purchase boards from all sorts of places, including https://www.amazon.com/. However, the pencil-and-paper version of scoring does equally well in a pinch.

Starting Off on the Right Foot

Cribbage is a game of scoring points, but in two distinct phases. First, there is the play of the cards, then scoring up the points in your hand. The issue to bear in mind is that the game is just as much about stopping your opponent from scoring points as it is garnering points yourself. You start out with six cards, from which you discard two, leaving yourself with four cards. You get opportunities to record points during two phases of the game — in the play of the cards and in the totaling up of your hand.

Dealing the cards and getting started

To start the game, both players cut the deck, and whoever draws the lowest card is the first dealer. The other player becomes the *pone*, which is just a crazy Cribbage term for nondealer. The deal alternates for each hand in the game thereafter.

For every hand, the dealer shuffles the entire deck and offers the cards to the pone to cut. The dealer then deals six cards face-down, one at a time, to both players and puts the rest of the deck, or the *stock*, in the middle of the playing surface.

Some people play that the pone doesn't get the chance to cut the cards before the deal, and if the dealer makes the mistake of offering the cards to the pone, the pone can take the cards, usurping the right to deal the hand. The logic behind this approach may be that Cribbage is considered a gentleman's game, so no one should be suspected of doctoring the cards, making the cut irrelevant. To me, this trusting attitude seems to assume too much. In the words of a Russian proverb, "Trust — but verify." Check which rules your opponent plays by before you start the game.

Each player picks up the six dealt cards and discards, or *lays away*, two cards face-down from the six. Those pairs of cards go into the *crib*, forming a third hand of four cards that gets scored for the benefit of the dealer. (However, the four cards in the crib play no part in the first phase of the game in which the cards are played out.) The dealer now has two hands with which to score points, as opposed to the pone's one hand. See the section "Choosing the right crib cards" later in this chapter for tips on choosing which cards to put into the crib.

WARNING

If a misdeal of any kind occurs, either because the dealer deals the wrong number of cards or because a card is exposed in the deal, you automatically redeal the cards, so long as you catch the error before both players make their discards. If the mistake comes to light after you both make your discards, the player with the correct number of cards can take 2 points and demand a redeal. Alternatively, they can ask the player with the wrong number of cards to take an additional card from the top of the deck or, if appropriate, to put their excess cards back into the deck.

If you intend to play a *rubber* (or a set) of three games, the players swap the right to deal the first hand on the second game. If, at the end of two games, each player has won once, the players cut again for the right to deal the first hand of the third game.

Cutting the deck

After both players decide which four cards to keep, the pone cuts the remaining cards of the stock, and the dealer turns over the top card of the cut deck to reveal the upcard, or *starter*. This card essentially becomes part of all three hands — the dealer's, the pone's, and the crib. See the section "Phase 2: Scoring the hand" later in this chapter for more information. The starter card doesn't take any part in the playing out of the hand, though.

After you reveal the starter, only the dealer can score the first points of the hand. If the upcard is a jack, the dealer scores 2 points, known as *two for his heels*. The dealer must claim and record these points before any cards are played (see the section "Recording the score" for more scoring info).

Phase 1: Playing the cards

After the dealer reveals the starting card and claims their possible 2 points, both players have their first serious chance to score points. During the play of the cards, you take turns playing one card from each of your hands. Your goal is to form certain combinations of cards that score you points.

During game play, you must keep track of the cumulative value of the cards that have been played. The cards have the following values:

» Aces are low and represent 1 point.

» All court cards — kings, queens, and jacks — count 10 points each.

» The numeric cards get their face value; for example, a 3 is worth 3 points.

Proceeding with play

Heard enough about pones already? Want to get the game started? Here's how to proceed:

1. **The pone leads by putting one card face-up in front of their position and announcing the cumulative total of the value of the cards.** In this case, the total is the value of their card. Incidentally, you can't score on the first play.

2. **The dealer then plays a card and calls out the combined total of the value of the two cards.** The dealer then marks up any points that they score in the process. See the following section for more information on which combinations score points.

3. **Play continues with the pone playing another card and calling out the cumulative total of that first, second, and third cards played.** The pone scores up points, if appropriate. This process continues throughout the hand.

REMEMBER

The crib plays no part in the play of the cards. And only the dealer can use the crib, in the second phase of the game.

Each player keeps the played cards face-up in front of their position instead of mixing the two hands, and all the cards remain visible during the hand. Although the played cards can form combinations with the other player's hand, both players keep their cards in a separate pile.

REMEMBER

You can play any card at any time, with the following exception: During play, the cumulative total of the value of the cards can't exceed 31 points. Sooner or later (usually sooner), one player finds themselves unable to play a card without taking the total over 31. When this happens, the player passes, saying "Go" to the other player, who must play any legal cards if they can. By playing the last card, they score 1 point, which is called 1 *point for go*. However, if either player can take the total to *exactly* 31 points, they get 2 points for doing so; if you have already scored 1 *point for go*, you only get 1 more point for bringing the total to 31.

When the total value of the cards reaches 31, or when neither player has a legal card to play, both players turn over their played cards, leaving them on the table, and start off anew with their remaining unplayed cards. The player that had to pass and conceded 1 point for go is the first to play, and both players take turns again to play their remaining cards. Again, the last to play scores 1 point — or 2, if they take the total to exactly 31 points.

As you can see, the dealer must score at least 1 point in the play, no matter what happens; because they play second, they're bound to score the 1 point for playing the last card during some phase of the play.

Spelling out the types of combinations

The idea of the play phase of the game I describe above is to score points by achieving any of the following combinations of cards:

>> If you bring the cumulative total of your cards and your opponent's cards to 15, you score 2 points.

>> If you match, or *pair*, the card played most recently by your opponent (or your own most recent card if you have just scored one for go), you score 2 points. For example, if the pone puts down a 10, you score 2 points by playing a 10 in another suit.

>> If you make a *pair royale* (play a third consecutive card of the same value), you score 6 points.

>> If you somehow manage to play a fourth consecutive card of the same value, you achieve the rare feat of a *double pair royale,* which scores you 12 points. I don't remember the last time I saw a double pair royale.

>> If you and your opponent play cards in consecutive order that form sequences, you score points for the length of the sequence. A *sequence* or *run* means, for example, 7-8-9, 4-2-3, or J-Q-K. If three cards are played consecutively (two by one player, one by the other), that can make up a sequence, and the player who puts down the third card scores 3 points. A fourth card in sequence scores four points, and so on.

REMEMBER

Be careful with sequences! The cards don't necessarily have to be played in sequential order for the sequence to register, and the suits of the cards are irrelevant. If player one plays a 7, player two plays a 6, and then player one plays a 5, it counts as a valid sequence, but so do the cards played in the order 5-7-6 or 7-5-6.

After the play restarts after the point for go or the total has been brought to 31, the old played cards are turned over, and you can't pair up or make a sequence from what has been played before.

Phase 2: Scoring the hand

After you finish playing out the cards, you pick up your hand (the cards you've been placing on the table in front of you) and move on to the main phase of scoring. For this scoring phase, both players treat the starter as a fifth card to supplement their hands for pairs, sequences, and combinations of 15, but during this phase, you can't use your opponent's cards as you can during the play of the cards.

First, you score up the pone's hand, and the dealer's follows. After you score both hands, the dealer scores up the crib.

The significance of this order of scoring is that toward the end of the game, each player scores three hands in a row (two as the dealer and then one as the pone), which can have a significant impact on the strategy of the game. Because Cribbage is a game of "first past the post," if both players are close to *pegging out*, or winning, you can score up your hand and win as the pone, while the dealer is impotently waiting to score up their huge hand.

The points that you score in the hand and the crib, as dealer, by and large, come from the same categories as those for which you scored points in the play, but a couple of modifications complicate matters. For example, you can use cards, including the starter, in more than one combination.

You score points according to the following criteria:

>> Each combination that adds up to 15 is worth 2 points (no matter how many cards are involved).

>> Each pair is worth 2 points.

>> The value of a sequence of three, four, or five cards is equal to the number of cards in the run. (Keep in mind that A-K-Q doesn't count as a run because aces are low.)

   So, with 8-9-10-10 your hand is worth 8 points; 3 for one run of 8-9-10; 3 for the run using the other 10; and 2 for the pair of 10s. But for 3-3-4-5 with a 5 as the starter card, you have no less than four different runs, two pairs, and two ways to make 15 points — for a grand total of 20 points!

>> If all four cards in your hand are of the same suit, you have a four-card flush worth 4 points. (The rules about a flush are more demanding; four-card flush do not count; see the next point.)

>> A five-card flush (five cards in the same suit), using the starter, scores 5 points for either player's hand. (A five-card flush can also apply to the crib but is quite rare.)

>> If you have the jack of the same suit as the starter, it's worth 1 point and is always referred to as *one for his nobs/nob* in the United Kingdom.

You score the crib hand in exactly the same way as your own hand, except for the restriction on four-card flushes. Consider flushes to be a last resort; unless you can't do anything else, let them go. With all the cards in the same suit, you have no possibility of making pairs. Plus, they don't count during game play.

TIP

Some numbers in Cribbage are impossible to score — 19, 25, 26, and 27. Because you can't score 19, referring to a hand as being worth 19 points is a humorous way of referring to a hand worth nothing.

Determining a strategy to score points

You can maximize your opportunities to score points during play by focusing on the following tips and hints.

Choosing the right crib cards

The first time you can affect your chances in the play comes when you select your cards to lay away in the crib. The points scored in the crib go to the dealer, and the pone and dealer score points for making pairs, combinations of 15, and sequences in the crib (see the previous section, "Phase 2: Scoring the hand," for the intimate details).

You can't reduce Cribbage to a series of mathematical rules, but a number of guidelines can help you maximize your opportunities when it comes to discarding into the crib.

Your first consideration should be to keep the best combination for your hand; however, at the back of your mind, remember that you want to help yourself in the crib if you're the dealer and avoid helping your opponent if they're the dealer.

If you're the dealer:

>> Try to throw away *touching cards* (a 6 and 7 or 9 and 10), a pair of cards totaling 5 or 15, or a pair of cards (a pair is slightly less attractive than you may think; it is worth points, but the chances of improving a pair into a pair royale is relatively slim). Especially promising non-pairs to throw into the crib are combinations such as 7 and 8 or 2 and 3, because they offer possibilities in at least two directions. The least promising options are distant high cards, such as a queen and 9.

>> The most promising card to lay away is a 5, because it combines so well to 15 with court cards or 10s. Lay the 5 away if you have no more than one total of 15, unless the 5 fits into a sequence in your hand. If, as the dealer, you have 5, K, 8, 6, A, 2, you may discard the king and 5 and hope that your opponent lets go of some high cards, too. You waste the 5 if you keep it in your hand because you can't make enough combinations of 15 if you keep the 5.

>> Throw cards totaling 15 into the crib. For example, if you have the 2, Q, 3, 10, 9, and 6, discard the 9 and 6. The combinations of 15 that you have left in your hand (the 2, 3, and 10 or the 2, 3, and Q) offer you some good chances in the play of the cards, and the cards you have discarded give you some promise in the crib.

As the pone, your first thought must be to keep a good hand together if you can:

>> If you have a choice of actions, try to discard extreme cards — that is, a high and a low one.

>> If you can possibly avoid it, don't discard a pair or cards that add up to 15 because those are guaranteed points for your opponent — although sometimes you can't avoid it. For example, what if you have a hand such as 7, Q, 8, 9, 7, 5? You want to keep the 9-8-7-7 combination, which is worth 12 points, but that requires you to let go of the queen and the 5, a highly volatile combination of 15. But what else can you do? If you keep 8-7-7-5, it can score you only 6 points, and although you may improve the hand with many starters, the 9-8-7-7 has so much potential that you should damn the torpedoes and throw the queen and the 5.

REMEMBER

You can utilize your opponent's cards when you're playing in front of you, but in scoring the hand, you use only your own cards.

>> When you have a choice between breaking up a pair of sequences and making another move, you should generally keep the sequences. However, disrupting the hand a little to ensure that you don't pass your adversary something on a plate is sometimes worthwhile. For example, if you have 3, 2, K, 7, A, 8, you can keep K-A-2-3 for 5 points, but letting go of the 8 and 7 is too much. Keep 8, 3-2-A for 3 points, and discard the king and 7, which don't hold much promise together. The best discard is a high card, such an 8 or 9, with another high card that's not a 10, for fear of the run.

TIP

A sound strategy when playing the pone position is reversing the strategy you employ as the dealer.

Leading to the first play

After both players make their discards, you need to make some strategic choices in the play. As the pone, you need to lead the very first play. Here are two strategies you can choose from:

>> **You can restrict your opponent's opportunities to score points.** Try to lead a card with a value less than 5, with 4 being ideal. If you lead a card with a face value of 5 or higher, your opponent can pair it off or make a total of 15. At the same time, you want to retain at least one low card for later on in the play so you keep the possibility of playing a card as the score moves toward 31. For example, with 8, 2, 2, 5, a lead of either 2 makes for a good start. But with 7, 7, 2, 6, you should keep the 2 for later use in the play and lead a 7.

>> **You can lead one card from a pair.** You invite your opponent to score 2 points by pairing up your card, after which you can play the third card and collect 6 points of your own. For example, if you start with 7, 7, 2, 6, lead a 7.

If you don't have either of these options, lead your highest card and take it from there.

Thinking about the whole hand

It may sound pessimistic, but planning for the worst is normally the right approach. As both pone and dealer, consider what play you can make to retaliate if your opponent matches the card you play or takes the cumulative total up to 15. Try to have a point-scoring reply available in any situation.

For example, as the pone, if you hold 7, 9, 7, 2, lead a 7, hoping to play your 9 to form a sequence if the dealer makes 15 with an 8 or to play your other 7 to make a pair royale if the dealer plays a 7.

If you're the dealer, bear in mind that pairing up the lead for 2 points is fraught with danger. You run the risk of allowing the pone to play a third card of the same rank to make a pair royale for 6 points. However, you have some insurance if you can reply to such a move with another score of your own. It's a sound move to pair up if you've already seen a third card of that rank as a card you put in the crib or through your opponent's earlier play. Leading a card in the hopes that your opponent will pair it up is an obvious strategy. So obvious, in fact, that when your opponent trusts you, they will rarely pair up on you; therefore, you can introduce some bluff into your strategy by not leading your pair.

So, if the pone opens by leading the Q, and you have K, Q, J, 6, you should play the 6 — not the king or jack — because of the risk of your opponent making a sequence. You probably don't want to play the queen because of the chance of a pair royale coming up.

In the same defensive mindset, try to avoid playing a 6 on a 4 or vice versa, allowing your opponent to score 15 and make a run simultaneously by the play of a 5.

However, on a lead of the 9, when you have 9, 2, 4, 3, you should pair up the 9, because you can play the 4 to make 31 for 2 points if your opponent plays a third 9. Always try to keep the big picture in mind when making your scoring decisions. By keeping a defensive mindset, you can anticipate your opponent's moves and switch over to offense with the flick of a card.

Always avoid taking the total to 21 if you can, unless you score points in the process by making a pair or sequence. Say, for example, that you hold 4, 9, 2, 4. When you lead a 4, your opponent plays an 8. Don't play the 9 to bring the total to 21, because doing so allows your adversary to peg 2 points easily if they have a court card in their hand. Even worse, if they have a 10, they make a 31 and a sequence. Instead, play your second 4, which takes the total past 15 and gives nothing away.

For the same reason, in a different scenario, you may avoid bringing the cumulative total to 26 — although if your opponent had earlier rejected the opportunity to play a 5 on your lead of a 10 to make 15, 26 probably presents no special threat because they do not have a 5.

Try to avoid giving your opponent a chance to make a three-card sequence — unless you can respond by scoring points yourself (such as with the fourth card of the sequence) or unless you score points in creating the opportunity for your adversary. If you have Q, J, 9, 10, and your opponent leads a king, play the 10 or 9 rather than the queen or jack to prevent them from being able to make a sequence.

If you have 8, A, 7, 6, you leap at the chance to play an 8 for a total of 15 and 2 points on your opponent's lead of a 7. (Note that you don't play a 7 because you have no reply to a third 7.) If you play your 8 and your opponent replies with a 6 for 3 points, you can play your 7 for another sequence of 3 points (better than pairing up for only 2 points). If they play a 9 on your 8, for 3 points from the sequence, you can play your 6 to make a cumulative total of 30 and a sequence of four cards, and with any luck, assuming your opponent does not have an ace themselves, you can then play the ace to make 31 total points, awarding you 2 more points.

Recording the score

Although it isn't essential for scoring, a Cribbage board can be useful. The board is a relatively simple device, with four rows of 30 holes. If you don't have a Cribbage board, you can draw some holes on a piece of paper, as shown in Figure 16-1. Keep score by using coins or other small objects as markers.

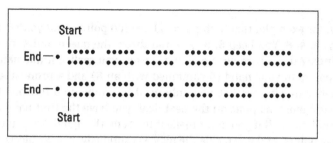

FIGURE 16-1:
A homemade
Cribbage board
in all its
simple glory.

Each player uses only one side of the board — either the top or the bottom. The object of the game is to go around the two tracks (or rows) the same way a horse goes around an oval, and, just as in a horse race, the idea is to complete the circuits before your opponent does. Beginning from the start point, the race involves going twice around your half of the circuit and then scoring 1 more point. Each point you score advances you one space, so you need 121 points to complete your journey and win the game.

Players each use two pegs (or coins or other markers if you're keeping score on paper) to record their points. When you score your first points of the game, you put one peg on the board, and as you score subsequent points, you hop over the leading peg with the *trailing peg* so that the board always shows how many points you recorded on your last score. Beginning from the start, you move up the outside part of the track and then back down the inside track.

VARIATION

For a short game, just go once around the course — in other words, to 61 points. The first player to reach or exceed the winning score takes the game, and play stops right there, even if the other player is panting to peg a high score.

VARIATION

Some people play that the dealer can't win the game by scoring 1 point for go. This rule ensures that the pone gets the chance to score their hand at the end.

In some versions of Cribbage (especially in the five-card variation I describe later in the chapter), the pone gets a head start of 3 points to compensate for the loss of the deal.

Reaching the finishing post

When you're nearing the end of the game, you often find that a general strategy for preventing your opponent from pegging out (winning) overrides what's otherwise the optimum strategy. If you're in the lead, you must play cautiously; if you're behind, you need to go all out for the win.

Say, for example, that both players have 100 points, and you're the dealer with Q, 8, 7, 2, 5, 8. You keep 8, 8, 7, 2 and throw the queen and 5 into your crib for 15 points. When a 6 comes up as the starter, you realize immediately that you have 14 points in your hand (6 combined with an 8) and a promising crib. You're the favorite to win, because you only need to scrape up a few points from the play. What's more, as pone on the next deal, you have the first hand of the next game to count as well if you don't make it to 121 on this hand. So, you must avoid giving away points, and you tackle the play as cautiously as possible. On the lead of an 8, you play your 2 rather than an 8, assuming that your adversary has another 8. If they could play an 8 to make a pair royale, the 6 points would be worth much more to them than the 2 points for the pair are worth to you.

Conversely, if you're in the pone's shoes at 100 points each, you have to plan your discards expecting that your opponent will reach 121 over the course of this and the next hand. Therefore, you must go all out for the big win, come what may.

For example, if you pick up K, 4, A, 6, 4, 6, the best combination may be to keep K, 4, 4, A — cards that may improve to a decent hand with an ace, king, or 4 as the starter. However, even turning up those cards isn't enough to give you a reasonable chance to win. Keep 6, 6, 4, 4 instead, which, with a starter of 5, give you a game winner.

As the game nears the end, if both players are close to pegging out, you may need to keep low cards to score points in the play — they dramatically aid your chances of scoring.

Playing Cribbage for Stakes: Lurches and Skunks

If you want to play Cribbage for stakes, an easy proposition is to play for a dollar a game. Alternatively, you can play for a penny a point — or a dollar, if you're a big spender!

VARIATION

You can also choose to introduce some additional gambles into the game. One such gamble is the ominously named *lurch* (or the even less-attractive *skunk*).

Lurching means you beat your opponent before they score 60 points, an almost impossible feat in practice. If you're lurched, or *left in the lurch*, you lose a double stake, so at a dollar a game, you'd lose $2.

Alternatively, some folks play that you can be skunked if you fail to reach 91 points, or *double skunked* (the same as being lurched) for failing to reach 61 points. Being skunked costs a double game (the margin of victory is doubled for the winner), and a double skunk costs a quadruple game (the margin of victory is multiplied by four).

You can also play a special scoring system for *dozens*, where you win a small additional stake for each hand in which you score more than 12 points. You get a similar amount for any *nineteens* (0-point hands) that as the dealer you manage to obtain in the crib. If you play these additional options, you need to keep a separate record of these elements on the score sheet.

VARIATION

If you play against tough opponents, you may occasionally fall foul of (or benefit from) *Muggins' rule*, which entitles one player to point out a failure by the other player to score all the points to which they are entitled. The player who spots the forgotten points can claim the points for themselves. If you're playing in a fast game, the occasional combination may get away from you, but the pain associated with Muggins' rule is enough to encourage you not to do it again! Not everyone plays this hardcore rule, and in games where one player is better than the other, handicapping the weaker player seems even more inappropriate.

REMEMBER

You can correct any error in your score during the play if you spot the error before any more cards hit the table. If you play with a board, marking the wrong pegging allows your opponent to call out Muggins' rule at once.

If you aren't playing Muggins' rule, you can fix a failure to score your hand correctly up to the moment of the cut for the deal of the next hand.

WARNING

However, if you claim too many points for yourself, your score is corrected, and your opponent gets points equal to the number you overscored yourself.

Five-Card Cribbage

Five-Card Cribbage is an earlier form of the traditional game that I outline earlier in this chapter. The two games are the same structurally; the main difference is that both players are dealt five cards each, leaving them with only three cards after putting two in the crib, which still has four cards in it. The deal becomes more important, relatively speaking, in Five-Card Cribbage, which may explain why it's standard practice for the pone (nondealer) to get 3 points right away in recognition of their handicap.

Laying the cards

In the standard version of six-card Cribbage I describe earlier in the chapter, the pone and dealer play out all their cards, and when the cumulative total reaches 31, the play starts again, with both players using up their remaining cards. In Five-Card Cribbage, you get only one time through of the cards; when the total gets to 31 or when neither player can legally play a card, the play stops. Consequently, it's very unlikely that you'll play all the cards, so the scoring is typically lower than in the six-card variety. All the scoring combinations are the same as in the six-card variety. See the section "Spelling out the types of combinations" for more information.

Scoring the hand

All scoring is the same, except that a flush only scores 3 points — a logical enough change, because it involves only three cards. The flush is worth 4 points if the starter card matches, though. See the section "Phase 2: Scoring the hand" for more information.

Reaching the finishing post

Because scoring opportunities are scarce with fewer cards in each hand, the game only goes to 61 points.

Cribbage for Three Players

The three-player game somewhat resembles the six-card variety for two players. The dealer deals out five cards to all three players and then puts one card into the crib directly. Each player throws only one card away, giving everyone (including the crib) a hand of four cards.

The player to the dealer's left cuts the cards to produce the starter. They then lead, and the subsequent players take turns to play. One player can score 1 point when neither of the other two can play, or 2 points for making 31. Each player plays on their own, although you often see trailing players ganging up against the leader.

The player on the left of the dealer is the first to score, followed by the other nondealer and then the dealer.

Scoring for three on a regular Cribbage board is close to impossible, so you probably have to resort to pencil and paper or make a specially designed board.

CRIBBAGE ON THE WEB

The American Cribbage Congress (ACC) website (www.cribbage.org) is the place to go for online Cribbage news and information. You get it all here: Master Rankings, a list of tournaments in the United States organized by date or location (with telephone numbers to contact organizers for more information), and details about joining the offline version of the ACC. In addition, you find lists of clubs in the United States by region, a library of playing tips, and a set of links to other Cribbage and gaming sites. And don't leave this site without visiting the gallery that features pictures of Cribbage boards!

For other sites to play Cribbage online, try www.gamecolony.com. John McLeod's website at www.pagat.com/adders/crib6.html lists a whole host of other options. You can also find details of Cribbage software there. Visit https://hobbylark.com/card-games/top-5-cribbage-tips-and-how-to-play-cribbage-strategy for tips on improving your performance.

Chapter **17**

President

P resident may come as an interesting surprise: It has very little in common with any of the other games I discuss in this book. Unlike almost every other game you may have come across in your card-playing travels, the results of a game of President extend beyond the scoring — the winner of the previous deal is entitled to improve their hand for the next game at the expense of the loser. Much good-humored abuse of privilege can take place in President.

Many people know President by a different name. Rich Man Poor Man, Landlord and Scum, just plain Scum, or Warlord and Scumbags are all popular names for the game. President is also popular in Hungary, where the natives know it as Huberes (meaning *vassal*). However, for those of you who played in the game in school, the most common name is a seven-letter expletive that I can't print here; think of it as a "fundamental" problem. So, President it has to be, at least for the time being.

BEFORE HAND

You need the following to play President:

» **Four or more players**

» **A standard deck of 52 cards** (if you have more than seven players, add a second deck).

» **Pencil and paper for scoring**

Lobbying for the Basics of President

President is a *climbing* game — your plays are determined by whether you can beat the previous player's card. Each play must equal or outrank the previous one. The peculiarity of President is that it isn't obvious whether you should play at all on your turn, and if you do, what card you should put down.

You achieve success in President by getting rid of all your cards before everybody else. You avoid humiliation by not being the last player to get rid of them all. Everyone receives approximately the same number of cards. At each of your turns, you have the option of *following* the cards that have been played by playing cards of your own or *passing* by not playing a card. If you play first, you can make any legal play you want. Sounds easy, doesn't it? Well, it is — up to a point.

The rank of the cards is straightforward enough: 2s are the highest cards, and then the regular sequence applies from the ace down to the lowly 3. In the standard version of the game, suits play no part.

Dealing and playing the cards

The dealer for the first round, selected at random, deals out all the cards in the deck face-down, clockwise, and one at a time. For subsequent rounds, the dealer depends on the results of the previous round. See the following section "Starting over: Go fetch, scumbag!" for more information.

Due to the number of players at the table, some people may get an extra card, but this doesn't really present a problem. Because these players are the first to play, the inequality evens out.

The player to the dealer's left plays first, putting one, two, three, or four cards of the same value face-up on the table.

VARIATION

One fairly common variation for the first lead is to have whoever has the ♣3 put it down, either on its own or with other 3s. Whichever rule you play, the hand continues in the same fashion.

After a player lays the initial card, the opportunity to play progresses in a clockwise direction. However, for any other player to put down a card, they must put down the same number of cards as the previous lay down — for example, if the first player puts down three cards, all subsequent players must put down three cards. And to make it even tougher, the cards you put down must have a higher rank than the cards already played. At each turn, you can follow with the same number of cards of a higher rank, or you can pass.

For example, say that you're playing with six players, and player C puts down the first card. The play may take this form:

A	B	C	D	E	F
		3, 3	Pass	5, 5	Pass
6, 6	Pass	J, J	All Pass		

All pass means that everyone passes after this point because nobody is willing or able to make a play. Legal plays here would be a pair of queens, kings, aces, or 2s. Remember, 2s are always high.

When you play a card (or cards) that nobody can or wants to top, the trick is over. You sweep the cards away, and whoever played last on the previous trick starts the sequence of plays again, playing whatever card or cards they want to play.

VARIATION

President abounds with variations. Discuss the variations before you begin playing to make sure everyone follows the same set of rules. Some of the most common variations (and my humble opinions on them) are:

>> You can play that a single card is only beatable by a higher card of the same suit. This rule makes the game considerably harder — probably too hard.

>> Some folks play that only one time around the table is permitted per trick. (In my preceding example, play would have stopped when player B passed. Because player A was last to play, they would lead to the next trick.) This option seems inferior to me because it leaves the last person to play in too favorable a position — they know that if they play on this trick, they get to lead the next trick, which is a huge advantage. The point is that the winner gets rid of their difficult holdings, such as 3s or 4s, whether singly or in pairs, which would otherwise be next to impossible to do in mid-trick. In the mainstream variety of the game, a player doesn't know whether their play of anything but a 2 is sure to win the trick — a difference that has a big impact on strategy.

>> Some people play that you can play *triplets* (three of a kind) on *doubles* (two of a kind), which you can play on *singles* (one card). These people maintain that a higher-ranking card is still necessary, so you can play a pair of 5s on a 4 but not on a 6. Some even play that you can lay triplets of a lower number on a pair; for example, you can play a pair of 7s on a queen. Both of these versions take some of the fun out of the game because they give you too much flexibility with your doubles and triplets. Remember, in the normal game, you must play the same number of cards (so the only way you can play a pair is if someone else led a pair), *and* the cards you play must outrank the previous cards.

TIP

You can pass even if you have a legal move — and you may well want to. For example, say that someone leads a single card, and you have a high pair and a low card. If you would have to split up the pair to play, you should pass. The logic is that if you get to play your high pair later on, you may force everyone else to pass. You win the trick, and you can get rid of your awkward low card by leading it on the next trick. Playing just one of your high cards reduces your chance of winning a trick. Also, as a separate tip, when you're the player leading to the trick, letting go of your lowest cards first is almost always right. The problem with keeping a low card, such as a 3, is that you can never play it *on* anything. You have to wait to get the lead, and you can't win the lead if you have nothing left of value.

Ending a hand

The card-playing phase continues as normal until one player runs out of cards. (If a player goes out when they are the last to play on a trick, they obviously can't lead to the next trick, so the player to their left starts up the next trick.) Whoever runs out first wins and becomes the *president* on the next hand.

But play doesn't end at the first person out; you continue until only one player is left holding cards. The unlucky cardholder becomes the *scum*. The finishing order determines who plays first, second, third, and so on for the next hand.

After the scum surfaces, the scoring kicks in. The winner, and president for the next hand, gets 2 points, and the runner-up, or *vice-president*, gets 1 point. The scum, or *beggar*, loses 2 points, and the second-to-last player, the *worker*, loses 1 point. All players in between (the *congressmen* [or women] and the *citizens*, titles which are not used in a four-player game) score nothing and lose nothing.

TIP

When nearing the end of a hand, you need to plan your strategy. Try to recall how many high cards are still out. Keep track of the aces and 2s if you can. When players are down to only a few cards each, you may have difficulty deciding whether to split up a pair in order to try to get the lead. Say, for example, that you're left with ♠K, ♦K, ♣4, and the last play was a single jack. Most of the other players have two to five cards left. You may not want to split up your kings if plenty of aces and 2s are still out. Your kings are very powerful together, because no one is likely to have a higher pair. However, if you can tell that your king is likely to win the trick, play it. You can lead your 4 and have a good chance to get rid of the other king on one of your next turns.

Starting over: Go fetch, scumbag!

All players acquire a social status, as well as points, based on the results of the first hand. After the scorer does the arithmetic, the players title themselves according to their finishing positions.

Before the next hand starts, everybody switches seats. The president gets to sit in the most comfortable chair, and the other seats follow a clockwise order of importance: The vice-president gets the next best chair (to the left of the president), the congressmen and citizens follow, and so on. The scum is left to kneel on the floor or sit on a box or something equally uncomfortable. None of the above rituals are strictly necessary, of course, and you often don't go through with them — though you may threaten to. At this point, you deal the next hand, a ritual performed by the scum.

WARNING

Only the scum is allowed to handle the cards; they shuffle and deal the cards and clear away the cards at the end of every trick. No one can interfere in the scum's duties, and the penalty for forgetting is that you become the scum for the next hand, regardless of the finishing order. (Some play that the president deals the cards for the new hand after the scum prepares them, but that rule doesn't seem right to me: The scum is supposed to do all the work!)

Before the new hand starts, the poor scum's humiliation increases. The scum must give the president their two highest cards and receive any two cards from the president's hand in return. Similarly, the worker must give the vice-president their highest card and receive any one card in return. No one else exchanges cards. As in life, the exchanges weight the odds heavily in favor of the status quo (poetic, no?).

VARIATION

Just as the lower players must give up their best cards, some people demand that the top dogs must give up their lowest cards — even if it means splitting a pair to do so, rather than giving up any card or cards that they choose. The consequence of infringing the rule is becoming the scum on the next hand.

Probably because they don't have to worry about any elections, it's considered right and proper for the president to abuse their power over the lower players. Although the day of reckoning is always potentially around the corner, you should make the most of your role as president while you can. Even if you get unseated as president later, you can look back happily on your day in the sun. Requests to fetch drinks, empty the ashtrays, or shine your shoes are entirely in order.

After you exchange the appropriate cards, the play of the hand continues as I describe in the section "Dealing and playing the cards" earlier in this chapter.

The first player to reach 11 points wins.

FOLLOWING WITH AN EQUAL CARD

The rules that I set out for President require that each card played be higher than the previous one and in the same amount (one card on one card, two on two, and so on). However, one school of thought allows you to play an equal card or pair of cards.

If you play the equal-card rule, it allows an additional twist: When you play an equal card, the next player has to miss a turn. In fact, the number of equal cards played — one card, a pair, or a triple — represents the number of players who have to skip a turn.

Some people restrict the play of equal cards by allowing the play only if it's a card of the opposite color. For example, you can follow the ♥7 with the ♣7 or ♠7 but not the ♦7.

Conversely, some people introduce the idea of *suit ranks,* taking the Bridge (see Chapter 12) valuation of spades as the top suit, followed by hearts, diamonds, and clubs. For example, you can follow the ♥7 only with the ♠7, not the ♦7 or ♣7. If you play this rule, any pair of cards that contains the spade ranks above the pair of the same rank that doesn't.

Two variations are associated with the play of any four of a kind:

- Four jacks can appear consecutively on the table in a number of different ways, and playing the cards in two pairs produces no excitement. However, when the leader puts down four jacks (say) at one time, it turns the game upside down — it inverts the ranking of all the cards for the rest of the hand. When you follow suit, you must do so with a *lower* card or set of cards rather than a higher one.

  When the ranks are reversed while playing the suit-ranking rule, the rank of the suits reverses to clubs, diamonds, hearts, and spades (in that order), and the superior pair is the one containing the club. A reversal almost certainly unseats the president and makes them finish last; they generally have the best hand in terms of high cards, so when the "best" is reversed, they suddenly have a poor hand. The reversal lasts for only one hand. Moreover, if another four of a kind appears on the same hand, it restores the ranking order of the cards to normal.

- If four players play four single cards of the same rank consecutively, it produces an even more active revolution: You have to follow with lower rather than higher cards, and the order of play is reversed to counterclockwise. This reversal applies only for the single hand. (Playing the four single cards is uncommon but not impossible, particularly if you don't follow the suit-ranking rule.)

Running wild with jokers and 2s

VARIATION

If you play with jokers, you can use them in two ways:

>> **As the highest card (above the 2):** If you include more than one joker as a high card, make sure their markings allow you to distinguish which ranks higher.

>> **As a wild card:** You can use a joker to make two 3s into a set of three 3s, for example. If you play the rule about allowing equal combinations (see the sidebar "Following with an equal card"), a pure combination of two 9s beats a joker-9 combination.

You can also bless the 2 with extra powers. In the mainstream version of the game, 2s rank as the highest cards, so to beat two aces, you need to play two 2s. However, if you aren't using jokers, you can play that a single 2 beats a combination of two, three, or even four of a kind. (Other people use other cards, such as the ♣3 or ♦J, as wild cards in this way, but these groups are in a distinct minority.)

VARIATION

In the Hungarian variety of President, all jokers, 2s, and 3s are wild.

Palace

Palace is also known as Karma, but most people know it by a name that makes it onto comedian George Carlin's list of words that are unacceptable on television.

Palace adheres to the standard theme of trying to get rid of all your cards as quickly as possible (like President), but it introduces a number of elements that complicate the strategy, making the game both delightful and infuriating.

BEFORE HAND

To play Palace, you need the following:

>> **Three to six players**

>> **A standard deck of 52 cards:** Jokers are necessary for the six-player game and are recommended, but not compulsory, for smaller groups.

>> **Pencil and paper for scoring**

The object of the game is to get rid of all nine of the cards you're dealt. How you get rid of these cards is what makes Palace distinctly different from President. You get three sets of three cards:

>> **You get three cards in your hand,** which you must get rid of first.

>> **You get three cards face-up on the table,** which you must get rid of second.

>> **You get three cards face-down,** which you must get rid of last (yes, without knowing what they are!).

Unlike President, the regular order of cards, from ace to 2, applies here. Jokers are wild, meaning you can play them at any time, but they also have a special significance in this game; see the section "Unleashing the special cards" for more details.

Dealing and setting up

You select the dealer at random for the first hand, and then the deal rotates clockwise thereafter.

The dealer gives each player nine cards. They start by giving each player a parcel of three cards face-down. You spread out the cards into a horizontal row without looking at them. Next, the dealer deals another three cards, which they turn face-up, one on top of each of the face-down cards. Finally, they deal three cards that you pick up as your hand.

The dealer puts the balance of the deck (no cards remain when you have six players — all 54 cards, including jokers, are dealt out) face-down in the middle of the table as the *draw pile*, or *stock*. Players can pick up these cards during the course of the hand.

Before play starts, all players have the option of doing a swap, and exchanging any or all of their own three face-up cards, but not their face-down cards with the three cards in their hands. Players can make this exchange in any order; you don't have to take turns.

TIP

Making your face-up cards as high as possible is a good practice. Pick up the low cards from your face-up cards and put them in your hand, and put down high cards as your face-up cards. Doing so gives you more flexibility in the later stages of the game and is a particularly good idea if you have a draw pile to work with. This strategy may lose you time in the short-term, but trust me, you will be happy you did so in the middle of the game.

Reaching the Palace through card play

The player to the left of the dealer is first to play, and they start the ball rolling by leading from the three cards in their hand. You can use only the cards in your hand at this point in the game.

The leader can play any number of cards of the same rank, generally the lowest card or cards in their hand, putting them face-up to form the discard pile. Throughout Palace, the *number* of cards led is irrelevant — all that matters is the *rank* of the cards. The leader ends their turn by refilling their hand with up to three cards from the draw pile in the middle of the table, as long as there are any cards left in that pile, and the turn moves clockwise.

The next player must either play one or more cards of the same rank, which must be equal to or of higher rank than the last play, or they must pass. The number of cards they can play is not affected by what the previous player did. If they pass, they must pick up the whole discard pile, and their turn is over. If they make a legal play, they pick up a card or cards from the draw pile, if they can, to replenish their hand, and the next player has the same options. If a player passes and picks up the discard pile, the player to their left starts the ball rolling again by leading.

This phase of the game takes some time, as players play, then pick up from the stock, or pass and pick up the discard pile. But eventually, you use up all the stock, and the game reaches a point when a player has no cards left to play and cannot pick up from the stock. At that point, and only then, you may play from your three face-up cards.

If you want to play one of your three face-up cards, you do so, and play continues. (This is why it is an advantage to have high cards now; it increases your chance of being able to play.) If you can't or don't want to play one of those cards, you put one of your three face-up cards onto the discard pile and then pick up the whole pile as your hand. By transferring one face-up card to your hand, you've reduced the number of face-up cards, perhaps making it easier to make a play the next time around. Of course, before you can get the opportunity to play a face-up card, you have to get rid of your new hand — which may take a while.

Eventually, a player works their way through their three face-up cards. On their next turn, they turn over, at random, one of their three face-down cards. If they can legally play the card, play continues, but if they can't play legally, they pick up the discard pile and the newly turned-up card as their new hand. Again, they have to work their way through the process, but at least they disposed of one of their face-up cards.

When you reach your last face-down card and play it legally, you win the game. Alternatively, if your last face-down card is an illegal play, you must pick up the discard pile and use it up before you can win. In a game with three or more players, the game continues. After all, this is a game about not losing rather than winning!

Unleashing the special cards

Some cards have special roles to play:

>> The 2 is both high and low. You can play a 2 on any card legally, but when it hits the table, it reverts to its role as the low card. The next player can play anything they want on top of the 2, because any card outranks a 2.

>> When someone plays a 10, it removes the whole discard pile from play. You set the cards aside for the duration of the game, and the same player who played the 10 gets another turn. Now, of course, they can play any card they want. Generally, 10s are treated as wild cards and can be played at any time. However, some people say that you can't play a 10 if the discard pile is at jacks or higher. In other words, 10s retain their status as a normal card, not a wild card.

TIP

The 10 can be a lifesaver, but it can save your opponents' bacon, too. If you have a choice of plays, you may want to keep the 10 if you know that you're less likely to be in trouble over the next few turns than your opponents. Conversely, if the 10 is the highest card in your hand, you may want to play it and clear the decks rather than pick up the discard pile.

>> You can play jokers at any time. Jokers are *transparent* — that is, they have no value as a card. The pile keeps the value of the card played just before the joker.

Jokers, however, reverse the direction of the game, from clockwise to counterclockwise or vice versa. Playing a joker forces the last player to beat their own card, giving you an opportunity for sadistic merriment, which is only outrivaled when the tormented one plays a second joker and returns the favor. If you do not have jokers, you can use 8s to take on the same role.

>> When you play a set of four cards of the same rank (either singly or as a combination of plays), the whole discard pile is removed as if someone played a 10, and the player who completed the set of four gets to play again.

VARIATION

>> In some variations, you must follow a 7 with a lower card rather than a higher card. These cards aren't wild; you can only play them if the previous card was a 7 or lower. And they don't cause a permanent revolution — after the next player plays a card lower than 7, the player after that must beat the low card by playing higher, and the natural order of things resumes.

Tabbing a winner — and a loser

You can play Palace until one player wins by getting rid of all their cards, where-upon the hand stops. But if you want to keep with the spirit of President, you can continue until you determine a loser, too (the last player with cards remaining).

This loser (because I can't call him by their real name, I'll just call him the *scum*) takes on the role of the scum in the game of President, and they must handle the cards, buy the drinks, and generally abase themselves (see "Starting over: Go fetch, scumbag!" for the humiliating details).

Chapter **18**

Blackjack

Of all the gambling games of skill you can play, Blackjack is the easiest to grasp. You can play it at home, as a pure gamble, either for stakes or for fun, or you can take it seriously. (In which case, if you take the advice in this chapter, you stand a good chance of at least breaking even.)

You can play Blackjack in two similar ways, depending on whether you want to play a social game at home or grind it out in a casino. In this chapter, I deal with the friendly, at-home variety of Blackjack first, and then I tell you about the more formal casino version of the game.

BEFORE HAND

To play Blackjack, you need the following:

» **At least two players:** You can play with up to 10 or 12 at home, and typically up to six in a casino.

» **At least one standard deck of 52 cards without the jokers:** Standard Blackjack requires only a single deck of cards, but if you have more than seven players, add a second deck.

» **At least 20 chips per player:** You can use matchsticks or bottle caps to keep score, just as long as you can count with them.

Social Blackjack

In Social Blackjack, the person you select as the dealer (who is also known as the *banker* because they occupy both roles) gives each player two cards to start, with the option to acquire as many additional cards as you want. The object of the game is to make your cards total as close to a score of 21 as possible without going over that total. If you do go over 21, you *bust* and lose the hand automatically.

You compete solely against the banker in Blackjack. Although other players sit at the table, their performances are technically irrelevant to you because from your point of view, it is your hand against the dealer that matters.

REMEMBER

The suits of the cards mean nothing. You are only interested in the numerical values of the cards. Fortunately, this area of the game has no complexities — well, virtually none:

>> Each card takes its face value from 2 to 10.

>> An ace can be worth either 1 or 11; each player has the option, depending on their hand, of choosing either value.

>> The court cards — the jack, queen, and king — are all worth 10.

Setting the game parameters

After you organize your starting chips (or matches, or peanuts, or whatever you use to keep score), the group needs to agree on minimum and maximum bets. If everyone wants to play a friendly game, a minimum of one and a maximum of three units — thus allowing bets of one, two, or three chips — make sense.

Next, you need to select the banker, who deals the cards and plays against all the other players. To select the dealer randomly, deal out cards face-up to each player in turn. Whoever gets the first jack is the banker. Or you can just nominate someone from the group.

Burning and turning

The banker *cuts the deck* (by splitting the cards into roughly equal portions and putting the bottom half above the top half) and then takes the top card and turns it face-up. Next, they transfer the face-up card to the bottom of the deck, a procedure called *burning the card*. The purpose of burning is to alert the players when the deck is fully used up and when the banker must shuffle the deck. You follow this same procedure, regardless of the number of decks you use.

LOUIS XV LIKED JACK

Blackjack derives from Vingt-un (French for 21 and pronounced *van-turn*), a French game popular at the court of Louis XV in the 18th century and also favored by Napoleon in his exile at Saint Helena. Blackjack may have acquired its modern name from a casino promotion that offered special odds on an ace plus a black jack. Blackjack also goes by the names Vingt-et-un and Pontoon, especially in the United Kingdom.

VARIATION

Some people play that if the card turned over is an ace, the banker puts the card back in the deck and cuts again to find a new card.

The banker now deals one card face-down to all the players, starting from the player on their left and moving clockwise. When everyone, including the banker, has a face-down card, the betting commences.

WARNING

If the banker omits a player during the deal, that player can demand a card at any time until the second round of dealing begins. After that point, the player is out for the duration of the hand. If the banker deals a player two cards rather than one for the first round, the fortunate player has some options. They can either discard one of the cards and carry on as normal, or they can play both cards as the first card of two separate hands — in which case they must put up an extra unit. Any other time that a player gets an extra card by mistake, the player has the choice of which card to take, but they must discard the unwanted extra card.

Placing your bets

After all players peek at their face-down cards, you can bet any amount from the minimum *stake* (bet) up to the maximum stake, both of which you agree upon in advance (see the section "Setting the game parameters" earlier in this chapter).

Betting as a player

You want to bet as much as you can on your first card if you have a suitable one or bet the minimum if you don't have a good prospect. So what kind of card makes for a good bet? The best card is an ace, followed by the court cards and 10s, and so on down to the 7. Next best after the 7 is the 2 and then the 3, and on up to the 6, the worst card.

REMEMBER

A high card, coupled with another high card, gets you close to 21; a low card may give you more options in the play; but a middle card can leave you stuck in the middle with nowhere to go. If you draw a high card, you're left with a hand that's too small to stay for 21 and too big to allow you to draw another card safely.

The standard Social Blackjack system suggests that you put the maximum stake on an ace or court card and a moderate stake on a 9 or an 8 — and perhaps on a 2, 3, or 7. Put the minimum on a 4, 5, or 6.

After the group takes a moment to consider their cards, the player to the left of the banker gets the first chance to bet. They place the units they want to bet in the middle of the table, and then the next player gets their chance to bet, and so on, until the action makes its way to the banker.

Betting as the banker

After the players make their initial bets, the banker looks at their card. If they like their chances, they can double the stakes for everyone by simply saying "Double!" If the banker doubles, everyone who stays in the game plays to win or lose twice the amount of their original bets.

If the banker doubles, you and the other players can do any of the following:

>> You may withdraw, which is probably the right move on a 5 or 6, but players must know the banker's temperament to make this decision. If you withdraw, you lose your initial stake.

>> You can accept and play for double stakes.

>> You can accept and say "Redouble!" to quadruple the stakes — in which case someone gets taught a sharp lesson!

Doubling the stakes is probably the right strategy if the dealer has an 8 or higher, although they may vary their strategy depending on whether the players have bet high or low on this hand. The higher they bet, the more cautiously the banker should bet. As a player, you should probably only redouble if you have an ace; unless you can see that the banker's judgment may be temporarily impaired by previous losses.

If the banker doesn't like their cards enough to double, they say nothing, and you play for your initial stake.

As the banker, you can draw some inferences from other player's bets, which may prove useful to you later on. Your decision as to whether to double may be based on whether the players bet aggressively or put up the minimum, as well as on your own card.

Splitting pairs to double your winnings

If your first two cards are the same denomination, you have the option of *splitting* your cards.

After the banker declares their bet, the splitter turns their cards face-up and separates them into two hands, putting out one additional stake so that each hand has an amount equal to the original bet. The banker deals one face-down card for each hand, and the player plays each hand separately. The player now has two hands with a stake in each one. They can win both hands, lose both hands, or win one hand and lose the other.

Dealing the second round

After the first round of betting, the dealer gives everyone a second card face-down.

VARIATION

In some games, the banker turns their second card face-up, a huge advantage to the players; and in some circles, the dealer puts the players' second cards face-up, too. These variations have a huge bearing on strategy (see the later section "Deciding on a drawing strategy").

Should you stay or should you go?

After the initial hands of two face-down cards come out, play proceeds clockwise, starting with the player to the banker's left. They look at their hand, hoping to see a *natural*, which is an ace and a 10 or court card, totaling 21.

If the player doesn't have a natural (and one rarely does), they have two options, depending on how their total compares to 21:

>> If the player is happy with their score (which usually means that they have 17 or more), they shouldn't take any more cards. The player *stands* or *stands pat*. (Standing is also known as *sticking*, especially in England.) They can say, "I'm good" or put their chips on top of the cards to indicate that they want to stand pat. After indicating their choice, the player's turn is over, and the banker switches their attention to the next player.

>> If the player decides that they want another card, which they certainly do when their total is 14 or less, they can say, "Hit me" or "Again" (or "Twist" in England). The banker gives the player another card — face-up this time. After that, the player can receive more face-up cards until they're satisfied with the total they achieve.

If the player accepts another card and takes their cumulative total over 21, they *go bust* and lose. They must give up their stake, no matter what the banker does subsequently.

Anyone caught not surrendering a busted hand must pay a forfeit of an additional stake.

You keep your first two cards face-down so the banker knows some but not all the story at this point. You turn over your hand only when the banker completes play.

Each player has the same options until everyone completes a turn. The banker then turns over their cards and has the same options as the players — to take more cards or to stand.

If you want an extra card, you don't have to receive it face-up; you have a more risky option if you like your hand, called *buying a card*. If you follow that policy, you put in an extra stake and can get just one more card. This is also called *doubling down*.

Breaking (or depositing into) the bank

After the players and the banker have their turns, you flip the cards to determine winners, losers, and payment options.

Paying the players

If the banker busts, they must pay every player who remains (they collect the stakes of the players who go out either by choice or by busting). When the banker decides, at some point in the hand, to stick, all players turn over their hands. The dealer pays off all the players closer to 21 than they are and collects the bets from players further away from 21 than they are.

If a player ties with the banker, the banker wins. All the players who go bust automatically lose their stakes, no matter what the banker does. And this is where the dealer's big edge comes from. They collect from players who go bust before they have a chance to make their own decision as to whether to draw a card or stick — and they win out even over the players who have the same hand as they do.

Facing natural consequences

If the banker gets a natural, they collect twice the stake bet by everyone — except from a player who has a natural, who has to pay only a single stake.

If you get a natural and the banker doesn't, you get twice their stake in return and, more importantly, take over the deal for the next hand. You, the new banker, reshuffle the entire deck before dealing the new hand.

If the banker gets really unlucky and two players pick up naturals on the same hand, the player who received their cards first takes precedence and acquires the deal. The banker has to pay both players the double stakes, however.

VARIATION

Two other treatments for the transfer of the deal are common. The first is that the deal passes after a certain number of hands. The banker can also *sell the bank* to the highest bidder if they calculate that they can't afford to pay out the field. Whoever bids the most takes over the deal. Because the bank generally has a big edge, selling the bank is something you do only in the case of a dire emergency.

Landing a special payoff

If you have a hand of five cards that total less than or equal to 21, you make a *five-card trick*, or a *five-and-under*. A five-card trick is an automatic winning hand, no matter what the banker's cards total (unless the banker has the same or a natural, in which case they win), and it pays double stakes. A *six-card trick* pays out four times your stake. And if you get seven cards that total below 21, it pays eight times your stake.

TIP

The possibility of a five-, six-, or seven-card trick is what makes a starting card of a 2 or 3 a reasonable beginning at Social Blackjack (see the section "Placing your bets" earlier in this chapter for tips on starting hands).

Social Blackjack has two other special hands:

>> If you get to 21 with a hand consisting of a 6, 7, and 8, the banker pays you a double bet.

>> If you get 21 via three 7s, you get a triple payment.

Both these hands are an automatic win, even over a natural, but do not entitle you to take over the bank.

REMEMBER

All bonus awards apply only to the player, not the banker. The banker wins the hand with the bonus combinations, of course, because each means that they have 21, but they don't score anything special for them.

Starting over

At the end of the hand, the banker puts all the used cards face-up below the burnt card and then deals the next hand with the remaining cards. When the banker comes to the burnt card in the middle of the deal, they shuffle the remaining portion of the deck, burn another card, and then complete the deal. You don't shuffle the cards at the end of each hand, only when you reach the burnt card.

Planning Your Basic Blackjack Strategy

Much of your success at Blackjack has to do with the cards you receive. However, you can influence your chances of success by knowing how to respond to the cards you're dealt.

When two is better than one

If you have a pair of aces or a pair of 8s, you should always split, whether the banker doubles you or not. Aces are potent cards, but not in pairs. Meanwhile a total of 16 is about as unpromising as you can get, so splitting 8s gives you a chance of having at least one decent hand by drawing a 10.

The question of whether to split is different in Social Blackjack (where you don't know the banker's cards) than in Casino Blackjack (where you know one of the banker's cards). See the later section "Splitting cards — when to stay together and when to break up" for more information. Don't split 2s, 3s, 4s, 5s, 6s, 9s, or 10s under any circumstances. Split 7s only if the banker hasn't doubled you.

REMEMBER

If you split a pair of aces and subsequently turn one into a natural, you're *not* entitled to take over the bank. And you only get paid a single stake, not twice the stake.

TIP

If you're playing the variation where the banker turns up one of their cards, you know much more about their hand, but you should still never split a pair of 4s, 5s, 6s, 9s, or 10s. 4s, 5s, and 6s are the worst possible starting cards, so do not voluntarily increase your chances of having a bad hand. Conversely, with two 9s and 10s you already have a good hand, so do not gamble by splitting them up. You should still always split aces and you should split 8s unless the banker has a 9 or 10 showing. Split 2s, 3s, and 7s whenever the banker has a 5, 6, or 7 up.

Doubling down, to up the stakes

After you look at your first two cards and if your cards total 10 or 11 (they don't have to, but these are the smart bets), you can double your bet and receive precisely one more card face-down. Just say "Double down," and the dealer gives you an additional card.

You only want to buy a card when your cards total 10 or 11 because your chance of drawing an honor card and getting a good total is pretty reasonable.

The downside to this approach is that you can't draw or buy an additional card thereafter, and by increasing the stakes, you leave yourself exposed to a bigger loss. So wait for a good hand to buy a card.

Casino Blackjack

Blackjack in a casino closely resembles the social form of the game (see the "Social Blackjack" section at the beginning of this chapter) — except that you always play Casino Blackjack for money. Casino Blackjack also has a degree of formality that doesn't apply to the social game.

When you arrive at the casino, the dealer is there waiting for you and your money. You find the following items at hand in the casino:

>> **At least one deck of cards:** Most casinos play with at least four decks. Some have automatic shufflers, and some require the dealer to shuffle. Pick your personal preference; the odds are pretty much the same whichever format you opt for.

>> **A casino table:** You play at a semicircular green baize table with space for at least six or seven people to sit down.

The professional banker (and dealer), known as a *croupier* (pronounced *crew P.A.*), has a *shoe* (a device from which to deal out the cards that avoids the risk of the cards getting turned over or accidentally seen) for the decks of cards. (A few casinos still play with single or double decks, but these places are now the exception rather than the rule.) The banker plays on behalf of the *bank* (the casino itself), which naturally wants to see you lose. In the background, to the rear of the table, the *pit boss* (or supervisor) stands behind the banker and casts a watchful eye over the proceedings.

Casino betting: Playing against the bank

Most casinos place a minimum and a maximum bet on the Blackjack tables that you can find written on a sign at the table. You may see a table with only a $5 minimum, and you can play for less at many places, particularly in Reno, Nevada. As for upper limits . . . well, after you finish this chapter, your confidence may be high, but you may never have to worry about breaching the bank's maximum bet rules.

The critical distinction between the casino game and the social one is that players make all bets in advance of the first card, so you don't have any extra information.

VARIATION

In Europe, betting on a hand isn't limited to the players who pick up the cards: Any spectator (also known as a *kibitzer*) may bet in advance on the hand. You may be able to find this variation in some casinos in the United States.

How good a bet is Blackjack at the casino? The answer is not *too* bad. The banker's edge comes from the fact that you have to commit yourself to drawing a card — which introduces the possibly of going bust (going over 21) — before the banker plays out their hand, unless you make a Blackjack with your first two cards. Even assuming good play, this factor converts to about a 2 percent edge for the banker. Furthermore, the payouts for your really good hands aren't so generous at the casino — no bonus hands exist, and a natural (a Blackjack) pays three to two odds, not double odds.

On the other hand, several factors weigh in on your side at the casino:

>> You get to see the banker's first card.

>> The banker doesn't get to double the table like they do in Social Blackjack.

>> The banker's natural only pays them single odds — to even things out, I suppose.

>> The banker doesn't win ties; they're a standoff. This factor is the biggest one affecting the gambler's chances by comparison to the social game, where the banker wins out on ties.

Overall, you, the gambler, are pretty close to even money with the bank. A good Blackjack player can hope to at least break even in the long run if they can develop the card-counting skills, as I discuss later in this chapter.

Casino formalities: Dealing up and getting started

At the start of a game, the banker shuffles all the decks together and asks a player to slide a marker into the bottom half of the decks. Bankers normally use only 75 percent or so of the decks before they shuffle the cards again. The banker reshuffles the decks early because some expert players can take advantage of their mathematical skills by figuring out when the decks are more suitable for the player than for the bank.

Before the deal, each player puts a bet down on the table. You can't reduce your bet thereafter, but the banker doesn't have the option to double the bet either, as they do in Social Blackjack.

After all the bets hit the felt, the banker doles out a face-up card to each player and to themselves. No further betting is permitted. The banker deals a second card face-up to the players but face-down for themselves.

When you have your cards, only one further action can take place before you play out your hand. If the banker deals themselves an ace, they can offer insurance to everyone to protect against a natural they may deal themselves on the hand. Insurance allows each player to make an additional bet that pays off if the dealer has a natural but loses otherwise — a gamble that pays odds of 2 to 1 if the dealer gets their natural.

WARNING

Insurance is a bad bet — ignore it unless you know that many of the remaining cards in the deck are 10s. How can you know that? Well, if I tell you, I'll have to kill you! Seriously, though, counting the cards in Blackjack is a skill that can make you both rich and unpopular with the casinos. After you master the basics of Blackjack, you may want to look at a website such as www.888casino.com/blog/card-counting-trainer for more information.

Playing the cards

After the deal, you now proceed to play as you do in the standard social game (see the section "Social Blackjack" earlier in this chapter). Each player in turn gets paid for a natural if they have one, stands pat, or calls for another card.

TIP

To stand pat, wave your hand in front of your cards. To call for another card, make a raking motion with your index finger, like you're scraping dirt off the table. Most casinos require hand motions for your decisions so that no confusion arises, but if you speak clearly, they will also understand.

If you go over 21, you have no option but to concede, because everyone can see your cards. You suffer no disadvantage from having your cards face-up in this version of the game because the banker's plays are *forced* — they have to make the plays I describe in the following list.

After all the players make their choices, the banker turns over their second card. They then must make one of the following plays:

>> If they have 21, they collect all the bets from players who haven't gone bust (gone over 21) — but not at the double rate that applies in the social game.

When the banker shows an ace, they look at their second card to see whether they have a natural. If play continues, you know that they don't have a natural.

>> If the banker has 17, 18, 19, or 20, they must stick, and they pay all the better hands.

REMEMBER

Ties are a standoff in Casino Blackjack. In the case of a tie, the dealer returns all the bets on the table to the players who made those bets.

>> If the banker has 16 or less, they must take another card until they get 17 or more or goes bust. This rule has a significant impact on your strategy, which you can read about in the following section, "Deciding on a drawing strategy."

VARIATION

One variation, which is by no means universally played, allows players to surrender (by simply saying "surrender") when faced with particularly bad hands. When you surrender, you lose only half your stake. If the banker has a 10 or court card showing and you have 15 or 16, surrendering is probably your best option because the banker's chance of beating you is more than 2 to 1. If the banker doesn't have 21 on an ace, surrendering becomes a less attractive option.

Deciding on a drawing strategy

The banker's plays are compulsory, but your strategy isn't. In fact, the values of the banker's first and subsequent cards lead to some fairly complex analysis.

Seeing one of the banker's cards makes a huge difference. Think about it this way: If the banker has a high card showing — say, a 9, 10, jack, queen, king, or ace — their chance of having a good hand from their first two cards alone is pretty high, because any 8, 9, 10, court card, or ace as their face-down card (they have more than a 50-percent chance of having one of those cards as their second card) gives them at least 17. Conversely, if the banker turns over a 4, 5, or 6, they can't have a good hand off their first two cards unless they have another low card and get a lucky drawing card.

The sight of the initial card may affect your decisions on marginal hands — hands ranging from 12 to 16 — when you aren't sure whether to stay or draw a card. If the banker has a 2 or 3, you're in fair shape as well because they're unlikely to have a great hand and may well have a poor one.

Of course, most hands aren't marginal at all; they have pretty clear-cut actions. You should never take a card on 17 or more (unless you have an ace and a 6 — *a soft* 17 that you can't go bust on), and you should never stick on 11 or less. But on hands ranging from 12 to 16, what you see in the banker's hand affects your strategy:

» If the banker has an ace, court card, 10, 9, 8, or 7, take an extra card if your total is more than 11 but less than 17.

» If the banker has a 4, 5, or 6, stick on any total of 12 or more.

» If the banker has a 2 or 3, stick on any total of 13 or more.

Here's an example to help you see the logic behind these guidelines. Say that you have a 10 and a 6 for 16, a lousy hand. If the banker has a 10, a court card, or an ace up, you're a heavy underdog, but the odds (I won't go into the calculation) say that your best shot is to take another card and hope to improve your hand. If the banker has a low card up, however, your best chance of winning the hand is for the banker to bust. You should stay where you are and hope that the banker gets a bad second card (a 10 or court card) and then busts when they are forced to draw a third card.

REMEMBER

Unlike Social Blackjack, 2s and 3s don't offer any special possibilities because most casinos don't have five-card trick or special payoff hands, although you may find rare exceptions for five- or six-card tricks (see the section "Landing a special payoff" earlier in this chapter).

The hands I've discussed up until now allow you to win the equivalent to your bet. But that's not how you (or the casinos) make the big money in Blackjack. Some hands allow you to double down or split your cards, and aces allow you more flexibility to beat the dealer.

Doubling down

In Casino Blackjack, the bank is always happy for you to invest more money so you can *buy a card* (or *double down*), which means you double your stake and receive an extra card face-down (or face-up if the casino doesn't like drama). Because the dealer's strategy is mandatory, no matter what you have, there is no edge for the dealer to see your cards. You can buy a card regardless of the total of your cards.

Most Reno casinos don't allow doubling down on any number except 10 or 11.

When you buy a card, you must double your original stake, and you receive only one card, at which point your turn ends. Doubling down reduces your options, but it may be very much the right play. Buying a card is another strategy that's heavily influenced by the banker's card; you only double down when the information in front of you makes you the heavy favorite to win.

Follow certain guidelines helps you decide when to double down. Always double down

>> When your two cards total 11, no matter what the banker has up

>> On a 10 or a court card, unless the banker has a 10, court card, or an ace showing

>> On a 9 when the banker has a low card (anything from a 2 to a 6)

>> When you have an ace and a low card (anything from a 2 to a 6) or two cards totaling 8 when the banker has a 5 or a 6

The logic dictates that you're the favorite whatever you draw, so you want to double the stakes if you can. This move may be less obvious than the relatively straightforward advice of the preceding three bullets, but doubling down in this case makes sense.

Splitting cards — when to stay together and when to break up

You can split your first two cards into separate hands and receive new cards for each hand whenever your first two cards are a pair. The casino is always happy to see a player invest more money, and you're happy to double your money when the odds are in your favor.

The one splitting restriction is that if you split aces, you get only one extra card for each hand. In addition, if you make a natural, it pays only single odds. But splitting a pair of aces is still clearly the right play.

At most casinos, if you split a pair and then draw the same card to form another pair, you can split your new pair again to form three hands.

The general approach to splitting a pair goes along the following lines:

>> **Never split a pair of 4s, 5s, or 6s.** Number totals like 8 and 10 are good for you because the chances of drawing an ace, king, queen, or jack are quite

good. You don't want to break up good drawing hands. And because a 6 is the least promising drawing card, why voluntarily saddle yourself with two of them as the nucleus of a hand? A total of 12 may not be such a great number either, but it's the best you can do under the circumstances.

>> **Never split 10s or court cards.** By splitting 10s, you give up a likely win in the hope that you win on both hands — not, by any means, the right thing to do because you are not a big enough favorite to win both hands after splitting.

>> **Split a pair of 8s (because 16 is such a bad total) unless the banker has a 9, 10, court card, or ace.** When the banker has a high card, you're likely to lose, and you don't want to concede twice your stake. (Take a deep breath and draw a card with your 16 in these circumstances.)

>> **Split 7s if the banker has a 5, 6, or 7 showing.** When the dealer has a bad hand and you figure to be able to improve your total of 14 by splitting, go for it.

>> **Split 2s or 3s if the banker has a 7 or lower card showing.** With the dealer having a bad hand, it makes sense to play more than one hand if you can.

>> **Only split 9s if the banker has an 8 showing.** In this case, you figure to get 19 on one hand, and the banker figures to get 18, so you improve your position. If you don't split, the hand is likely to be a standoff.

Going high or low when you have an ace

When you have an ace and another card, your hand has two possible values: a *soft* one, counting the ace as low (1), and a *hard* one, counting it as high (11).

What the banker has showing affects your soft or hard strategy:

>> When the banker has an 8, 9, 10, court card, or ace, only stick on 19 or higher. For example, when you have an ace and a 7 and the dealer has a 10, draw a card because you're likely to lose if you don't. If you don't get a good card, you can draw another card or hope that the banker draws a bad card and goes bust.

>> If the banker has anything less than a 7, stick on 18 or higher.

>> Never stick on a soft 17, no matter what the banker has showing.

>> When the banker has a 5 or 6 up, you should double down and buy a card.

Doubling down gives you two chances to win. Either you can pick up a good card, or the banker can go bust.

BLACKJACK ON THE WEB

You can practice your Blackjack strategy in several places on the Web; here are a few that caught my eye. You can play online for free at www.casinoworld.com/fx/?alt=3 or www.247blackjack.com/. You can also tap into a virtually unlimited number of websites that teach you everything you want to know about Blackjack at www.pagat.com/banking/blackjack.html.

REMEMBER

If you draw a card and go over 21 by using the valuation of the ace as 11, you revert to the other valuing scale and follow the appropriate strategy.

6

Playing Poker

Playing competitive card games is all well and good, but nothing is more fun than winning money — especially from your (former) friends and neighbors.

Some gambling games you don't play against the casino. Some games are everyone for themselves. That's the case with poker, and I discuss several of its most popular versions in this part of the book.

Chapter **19**

Shuffling Through Poker Basics

T rying to cover Poker, a game with at least 200 variations, in a few pages may seem like a futile endeavor. This chapter is an overview of the basic terms and rules that you encounter while exploring a range of specific Poker games. In subsequent chapters, I cover some of the most popular versions of Poker.

BEFORE HAND

To play Poker, you need the following:

» **At least five players:** Somewhere between six and ten is ideal, but you can cope with fewer than five.

» **One standard deck of 52 cards:** In some versions of the game, you also need the jokers.

» **Chips or counters:** Ideally, you can use chips of at least two different denominations, such as ones and tens (different colors or sizes) to make the accounting easier. Money is a perfectly acceptable alternative to chips. In fact, Poker is almost always played for money. As a general rule, bring a reserve of at least 80 times the minimum bet.

Covering the Poker Bases

Almost every game of Poker shares some common elements. To start with, Poker is a gambling game, which makes it a game of money (or chip) management. The aim on each hand is to win money — or, at the very least, to avoid losing too much money. Your personal goal may be to have fun, but if that's your sole aim, it may not come cheap!

To be successful, you must achieve a hand of higher rank than any other player at the table who remains in the hand. To win, though, you don't actually have to have the best hand — you just need to convince the other players that your hand is better than theirs. You can win by forcing the other players to drop out of competition, or by outranking their cards in a showdown. If you win, you collect all the bets — commonly known as the *pot* (or *pool* in England).

Ranking the Poker hands

Almost all Poker games, regardless of how many cards you get, require you to make the best five-card hand. The player who can construct the highest-ranking hand wins the pot (or splits in the case of a tie).

REMEMBER

In Poker, the suits have no rank, making all suits equals. It's the rank of the cards that counts.

The following list details the various hands from the highest-ranking (the royal straight flush) to lowest (high card), along with the odds of catching such a hand:

WHAT IS THE WORLD SERIES OF POKER?

The World Series of Poker (WSOP) started as an invitation-only event for seven people, but when ESPN began televising the event 20 years ago and amateur player Chris Moneypenny won the big prize of $2.5 million in 2003, it mushroomed into the global phenomenon it is today. Sponsored by Caesars Entertainment, this series of Poker tournaments is held annually in Las Vegas and traditionally takes place in June and July (the 2021 tournament was postponed until September 30 due to Covid-19). The World Series of Poker Circuit gives players all over the country the chance to participate in Feeder Tournaments, where the winner is entitled to a place at the table. The combination of extensive media coverage, the huge field it presents every year, the $10,000 buy-in, and its multimillion-dollar first prize makes it a must-see event. For more information, visit the WSOP website at www.wsop.com/.

>> **Royal straight flush:** The top five cards of the same suit; in other words, the A-K-Q-J-10 in one of the four suits. Achieving royalty isn't an easy achievement; your chances of hitting a royal straight flush are 650,000 to 1.

>> **Straight flush:** Any sequence of five cards from the same suit (such as the 2-3-4-5-6 of clubs). In comparison to the royal straight flush, this hand comes up every day, clocking in at 75,000 to 1. If two players have straight flushes on the same hand, the higher sequence outranks the lower one (K-Q-J-10-9 outranks 8-7-6-5-4, whatever suits the cards are in).

>> **Four of a kind:** Four of any one card — for example, four 7s or four queens. The fifth card in the hand can be anything. If two players have four of a kind at the same time, the rank of the four cards determines the better hand; four 8s beat four 7s, for example. The odds of getting this hand are 4,150 to 1. Where two players have the same set of four of a kind by virtue of a game that uses shared cards, the highest kicker wins.

>> **Full house:** Three of a kind matched with a pair — for example, three 10s and two 9s. If two players both have a full house, the higher three of a kind determines the better hand — three queens and two 4s outrank three 10s and two 7s, for example. Full houses have odds of 700 to 1.

>> **Flush:** Five cards of the same suit, no sequence required. When two players have flushes, the highest card in each flush determines the better hand; aces are always high in flushes. If the top cards are the same, you look at the second card, and so on. Thus, ♦A, ♦8, ♦6, ♦4, ♦3 outranks ♠K, ♠Q, ♠9, ♠8, ♠3 (aces are always high in flushes). Flushes come up with odds of 500 to 1.

>> **Straight:** Five cards of consecutive rank (in numerical sequence) in any suit. If two players have straights, the top card of the straight determines the winner — ♠K, ♦Q, ♠J, ♣10, ♣9 outranks ♣J, ♦10, ♥9, ♥8, ♦7. The ace can rank high or low to form a straight, but around-the-corner straights (Q-K-A-2-3) aren't permitted. Straights have odds of 250 to 1.

>> **Three of a kind:** Also knows as *triplets, trips,* or a *set,* this hand consists of three cards of the same numeric value, together with two unmatched cards. As you may expect, the higher-ranking three of a kind wins. The odds are 47 to 1 against being dealt three of a kind.

>> **Two pair:** Four cards in two pairs with an unmatched fifth card. Ties are broken by the value of the top pair, followed by the value of the second pair, and finally by the spare card; thus, K, K, 4, 4, 6 outranks K, K, 4, 4, 3. Two pairs have odds of 20 to 1.

>> **One pair:** One pair with three unmatched cards is the second-lowest hand. The rank of the pair, followed by the unmatched cards, splits the tie — K, K, A, 6, 4 beats K, K, Q, J, 7. You pick up a hand with a pair two out of every five hands.

>> **High card:** The weakest hand, *high card* means you have five unmatched cards. The top card in the hand determines the better collection. If two hands tie, such as two hands with ace-high, you move to the second card, and so on. Your chances of picking up a hand with no combination are 50-50; in other words, the average hand of five cards has no pair.

Poker hands consist of five cards only. If you and an opponent tie with the best five-card hand you both can make, you do not go looking any further to try to split the tie.

If you play with wild cards, *five of a kind* (four of a kind plus a wild card) takes over as the highest hand possible, above a royal straight flush. If two players both have five of a kind, the hand with the higher value wins — 6s beat 2s, for example.

Spicing up the game with wild cards

Many unconventional games of Poker feature *wild cards* — certain, predefined cards that can represent absolutely anything the player wants them to.

The most common wild cards are

>> **The joker:** Any time you play with a joker, it's wild. You can use it to represent any card, although most people play it cannot duplicate a card already in your hand. If your flush consists of joker-A-7-3-2, the joker stands for a king, not a second ace.

>> **The 2s, or** *deuces:* 2s represent whatever card you want them to, just like a joker.

>> **One-eyed jacks:** If you look at all the jacks in a standard deck of playing cards, you notice that the ♣J and the ♦J look at you face-on, but the ♥J and the ♠J appear in profile. That means that the ♥J and the ♠J are *one-eyed jacks.* Some people also play the one-eyed king, the ♦K.

>> **The bug:** Some people play with a *bug,* using the joker. If you do, the holder can designate it as any card they choose, with no restrictions. Under this rule, for example, a hand with any natural pair and a wild card becomes three of a kind. The common rule in casinos is that a bug has the rank of ace unless designating it as a different card completes a straight or flush; for example, a hand such as J, J, joker, 7 is only worth a pair of jacks with an ace on the side, or an ace *kicker,* but any four cards of the same suit with a bug make a flush, and a hand such as 7-bug-5-4-3 make a straight.

Getting Started: Basic Play

Before you can bluff, go all-in, or head for the hills, you have to assemble the chips or money you need to bet. Players use either money or, more typically, chips (also called *checks*). At a casino, where Poker is one of the more popular games, you can buy chips from the casino and replenish your stock whenever you run out (the casino will gladly oblige your request) though not in the middle of a hand.

When all the players have their chips and drinks in hand, you're ready to start by cutting for the deal and the seating rights. The player with the highest card deals the first hand, and the other players seat themselves, in order of the cards cut, around the table. The second-highest player sits to the dealer's left, and so on.

In a social game, most groups play *dealer's choice,* which means that the dealer chooses what version of the game to play and what cards are wild, if any. The deal rotates after every hand, allowing a new player to choose the game.

In American casinos, you rarely get to choose the game. Even at a table that features multiple games, the casino typically rotates the games every 20 to 30 minutes instead of letting the players choose. In English casinos, whichever of the players is designated to be the dealer frequently has quite a bit of choice as to how you play the game. The players mark the dealer by passing a little plastic button around the table, and the dealer keeps this button in front of them. Sometimes the button has the permissible choices of games printed on it, and the dealer turns the button to reveal the relevant game.

Ante up!

After you designate a dealer and divvy up the chips, players throw in the *ante.* Antes go hand in hand with betting (see the following section, "The mechanics of betting," for more information).

You don't have to bet on a Poker hand if you don't want to. However, to prevent a player from just sitting quietly, being dealt a hand every deal, and then throwing the hand in without cost until they get the perfect hand, you implement the ante. The *ante* is an advance bet, usually the minimum bet, that you have to pay in order to be dealt a hand. The ante may be a quarter at most in a social game, and it could perhaps be a dollar in a casino.

At most games, everyone has to *ante up,* meaning that everyone throws the ante into the center of the table before the deal. The ante serves the double purpose of making everyone contribute something and starting to build the pot for each hand.

Alternatively, the player to the left of the dealer may have to put in one chip, and the next player may have to post two chips. This is known as the *straddle*, or the *small blind* and *the big blind*. The next player to bet must put in at least two chips if they want to stay in. The blinds come into play in games such as Texas Hold 'Em and Omaha. For Draw and Stud Poker, the ante is nearly always used.

The mechanics of betting

After you put in the antes or blinds, the dealer deals the cards, you assess your hands, and the first opportunity to bet goes around the table. The player to the dealer's left or to the big blind's left gets the first chance to bet.

Each game has a certain number of rounds of betting. This is the period in which the players take turns to check, bet, call, raise or fold, terms that I define in a moment. The game ends when the bets made by the players who have not dropped out or bet all of their money in are equalized. Draw Poker has two such rounds of betting — one before and one after the draw; Hold 'Em has four rounds. Other games may have different numbers of rounds.

Everything in Poker takes place in strict rotation, on a clockwise basis. Never do anything until the player on your right has acted.

If, when your turn arrives, you aren't too excited about your cards, you can do either of the following:

>> **You can check.** Players can *check*, which means to stay in the game without making an additional bet. You can't check in the middle of a betting sequence — only if you're the first to bet or if all the bettors before you have checked. This does not necessarily imply you are about to drop out, or will not match a bet if a later player makes one.

>> **You can fold.** If you don't want to stay in the hand (perhaps if the stakes have gotten too high or your cards are hopeless), you can *fold*, in which case you quietly (or raucously, depending on the mood of the game) drop out. Put your cards face-down in front of you or push them in to the middle of the table, or the *muck*, where the dealer can collect them and wait for the next hand to be dealt.

However, if you still like your cards enough to want to stay in when the action gets to you, you can remain in the hand by doing any of the following:

>> **You can bet.** To bet, put some chips or money into the pot. If the other players want to stay in the game, they must bet the same amount or raise.

>> **You can call.** Calling involves betting an amount equivalent to the previous bet, less any amount you have already put in toward that bet in the form of a

blind bet. Calling the bet is also referred to as *seeing* or *matching*. After another player makes a bet, if you want to stay in the game, calling is your least expensive option. Incidentally, since the mathematics of the betting can be quite complex, this is why you should not push your bets into the pot when you make them. Instead keep the bets in front of you during the round of betting; at the end of the round the dealer will collect the money together.

>> **You can raise.** An aggressive approach is to *raise* the previous bet (also called *raising the stakes*), which means betting the amount of the previous bet, plus any extra amount you feel your hand is worth.

Be careful not to make a "string raise" when you want to up the betting. When raising the bet, announce your intention as you call the previous bet rather than saying you intend to call, and then adding the raise as an afterthought. In other words, your wording should be "I'll raise the bet 5 dollars" not "I'll call the bet and raise you 5 dollars." If you take the latter approach, your opponent may force you just to see them and cancel the raise.

For example, say that you're the third player to bet. The first player bets two chips, and the second player raises the bet by five. On your turn, you can call, which involves putting in seven chips (the original two plus the five chips), or you can call the bet of seven and raise again, say five more chips, if you really feel like your hand.

Some games stipulate that between them they can raise the bet only three times in total on any round of betting after the opening bet.

>> **You can go all-in.** If you're running out of money and can't meet the last bet, you can go all-in. On the flip side of the coin, if you really like your hand and want to clean out your opponent's clock, you can bet all you have (provided that this does not exceed whatever betting limits are in force). Going all-in means that you put all your chips on to the table, and everybody's bet for this round must meet yours. If two or more players remain in the hand, they can start a separate pot that only they compete for and you have no interest in.

The hand is over when only one player is left betting because everyone else has folded, or when the showdown occurs after the last round of betting is complete. If there is only one person left standing, they take the pot. If two or more players are left in, the player who has been called shows their hand, and the other player either shows their hand if they have won, or can concede, with or without showing their cards.

One of the interesting things about Poker is that you don't have to bet if you don't want to; you can concede, or fold, whenever you like. Of course, by folding, you lose all your investment thus far — but you don't risk losing more. Remember, the worst beatings at Poker come not from having bad cards, but from holding the second-best hand!

TIP

After you decide what you want to bet, put the stake down on the table instead of throwing it into the pot. This is good etiquette, because everyone can see what you're betting. Don't expect everyone to take your word for it!

The first round of betting comes to a stop when someone makes a bet (or a raise) that everyone else calls or that makes everyone else drop out. In games like Draw Poker, a second betting opportunity comes later in the hand. Check out Chapter 20 for more information.

Sandbagging is the practice of betting nothing, or checking, in the early part of a round to encourage others to bet and then raising when bet comes. Nothing is wrong with this form of deviousness, although some home games don't allow sandbagging. A player who's first to bet frequently goes for this approach when they're worried that a direct bet may scare the other players out of the hand. Of course, checking and then raising may scare the other players out, too.

Making the minimum and maximum bets

VARIATION

Limit Poker is very popular in the United States. The minimum bet in home games may be as low as 5 cents or even a penny; you also frequently play a limit of one chip for the bet or raise in the early stages, with a maximum of two chips in the later stages. In casinos, the minimum is generally at least a dollar.

You can also play an alternative system in which the maximum bet is limited by how much money is already in the pot, a popular system in the United Kingdom and in the United States with games such as Omaha. A limit of half the pot restricts the maximum bet even more. For example, say that six people are playing, and everybody puts in one chip as an ante. If the first bet is for two, you can call that bet (making the pot 10 chips at that point) and, if you want, increase the bet by 10 if you're limited to the amount in the pot or by 5 if you have a half-pot limit. When you're just starting to play Poker, I suggest that you stick to the chips limits, not the pot limits! The point is that the stakes go up far more predictably at Limit Poker, so you never find yourself getting in over your head.

If you play *table stakes,* you may not go get new chips or take out more money after a hand starts. If a player has insufficient money to match the last bet, they put all they have into the pot, creating a *side pot* for any further bets from the remaining players.

You can also have a financial upper limit (no bet larger than $100, for example), or you can set a range, such as $1 to $50.

VIDEO POKER

You can play Draw Poker on the Internet, although most casino or online Poker these days is Texas Hold 'Em. However, you can play Video Poker at casinos. Most Video Poker machines give pretty close to even money, but you need to investigate the specific machine you want to play quite carefully. Check out www.casino.com/videopoker for more information. One of the keys to playing Video Poker at a casino are the comps, or the rewards the casino gives you for playing. These comps may come in the form of snacks, meals, or accommodations. Believe me, this should help you decide where to play and at what stakes. Check out www.casino.org to see what I mean.

WARNING

If you bet out of turn, you must leave the bet in the pot. If the stakes don't increase, your bet stands, but if someone raises the betting, you can't recover your misplaced wager if you decide to fold; however, you can stay in by contributing the extra chips needed. As a point of both etiquette and strategy, don't be too eager to contribute your bet, particularly with a good hand. Try to disguise your excitement if you can — or fake it, if you prefer bluffing.

Winning ways

The betting and the hand as a whole can end in any of the following ways:

» One player makes a bet or a raise, and everybody else folds. The player left is the undisputed winner, and they're not required to show their hand. They simply collect all the bets.

» Everybody can check during the final round of betting, in which case all players must show their hands immediately in a *showdown*. The highest-ranking hand wins.

» One player makes a bet, and all the remaining players in the game call the bet. The player making the bet shows their hand first, allowing the other players to put away their hands (or fold) if they can't beat it or to show their hands if they can beat it or just for show.

REMEMBER

When it comes to the pot, other players' chips, or other players' cards, you can look (if they show you), but you better not touch! Don't touch anything but your own bets and cards. If you're at a casino, let the dealer pass you the pot if you're fortunate enough to win it.

Bluffing Dos and Don'ts

Bluffing entails betting on bad or moderate hands or drawing fewer cards than you should in an attempt to represent a good hand.

Keep the following points in mind as you develop your bluffing strategy:

» **Don't be too stolid.** Keep in mind that you have to speculate to accumulate, and if you aren't caught bluffing occasionally, you're not doing it enough.

» **Do study your opponents' actions at the table.** Try to work out how often they bluff, and try to get a read on their body language during their bluffs. In fact, if you can, try to watch a group of players before joining them. You can read their behavior much better when you're not tied to one position at the table and you don't have to worry about a hand. If you don't have this opportunity, make sure to pay attention after you fold your cards.

» **Do try to work out the strengths and weaknesses of your fellow players before and during play.** If you notice that someone is unprepared to surrender any pot to a potential bluff, make sure that you exploit that weakness in them. However, don't try to bluff them out, because know in advance that bluffing won't work. Make them think you're bluffing with the best hand.

» **Don't try to bluff against multiple players still in the hand.** If more than three players are still in the pot, the odds are that one of them can beat whatever bluff hand you're pretending to hold. Keep your bluffs for the smaller number of players.

» **Don't bluff against the evening's big winner.** Such high rollers have more money to burn and are likely to invest it in seeing the hand through to its conclusion.

» **Don't show your bluff.** Try to avoid showing your hand after a successful coup, unless you don't intend to bluff much more that evening.

» **Don't get caught bluffing too often.** If you get caught bluffing more than 50 percent of the times you try it, change your strategies and possibly your opponents. You may be cavorting with too tough a crowd.

TIP

You can also utilize a *semi-bluff*, which means that although your hand may not be a winner right now, it has the potential to turn into a cash cow — for example, betting with a flush draw and a pair of aces.

No matter what variety of Poker you are playing, if you are competing in a game where players only stay in with sound hands, you have a good chance of driving the others out of the pot with a well-timed bluff on bad cards. On the other hand, if your opponents often call even when their hands don't justify it (a strategy exemplified by the approach "you can't fool me, I'm too ignorant!"), you can't bluff successfully against them and you don't need to — you can win by only playing when you have a good hand.

Reading Your Opponents

Any Poker player worth their salt deliberately tries to mislead you about what they have. So how can you tell for sure whether they're bluffing or revealing the truth? You can't! But depending on how subtle the clues are, you may be able to draw out information as to whether your opponent has a good hand or not. Clues can come in the form of body language and physical responses known as *tells*.

TIP

Consider keeping records on the people you play against (as well as on your own performance). After all, if money is at stake, do anything you can to improve your game. If you play in a casino or in home games, you can wait until after your session to scribble notes on a pad, or you can run to the bathroom to jot down notes if you can't wait. If you play online, your site should have a note-taking feature.

A word of warning before you start to interpret the signals: The weaker the player, the more likely they are to try to simulate weakness or strength. In fact, most players instinctively follow this strategy. Players try to act the opposite of the way they really feel because they think Poker is all about pretending. The less interested and involved they appear to be, the better their hands. My suggestion: If the signal is unambiguous, it's a lie; the more subtle the behavior, the more accurate it is. If someone appears visibly disappointed, they probably got what they needed.

Facial clues

Your face may reveal nervousness when playing a weak hand if you display obvious unhappiness. Conversely, you may display a show of confidence when your hand is strong.

What's giving you away? The eyes are a common culprit. Many players cover their eyes with dark glasses, visors, or low-brimmed hats to prevent players from seeing where they're looking and how long it takes them to check out their cards.

TIP

When you start playing Poker in casinos or at home, consider wearing dark glasses if you're comfortable in them; other players will be watching you.

Watch out if someone appears to be taking a little longer than usual to check their cards; they may have a decent hand and may be planning their approach. Conversely, if you noticed a player watching the other players before their turn to act, they may be planning to steal or raise with a good hand.

Body language

In Poker, when players have big hands, they typically act like they're ready to take on everyone else, so they exhibit some aggressive characteristics. You may see their chests expanding abnormally, or you may notice their voices become slightly higher as they make comments. Some of the top Poker players in the world make a habit of staring at the veins on their opponents' faces and necks for blood pressure changes. But, as always, be wary of a player with a bad hand deliberately acting aggressive so that the other players fold.

During a bluff, a player may demonstrate anxiety, but if they know they'll fold the hand if gets re-raised (a non-confrontational end), they may look quite comfortable. Also beware of a player whose hands are shaking — this nervousness can represent a big hand or a big bluff.

It's difficult to fake relaxing or slumping with a weak hand, but if a player mentally stands to attention when looking at their cards, be on guard.

Watch how the players organize their chips and their cards. The more neat and organized the player, the tighter they are likely to be. Being a neat freak is a difficult thing to fake; no matter how hard I try, no one will think I'm a tidy person!

Even the physical motion of putting in a bet may shed light on the degree of confidence the player has, which may reflect on the quality of the hand. An instantaneous call or raise may also be revealing.

TIP

Don't be too quick to throw your chips in. Give every decision some consideration so when you do have a tough decision to make, other players can't infer what you're thinking about.

HITTING THE ONLINE FELT

The Web offers numerous sites that cater to the Poker player's every whim. Visit `https://us.888poker.com/how-to-play/strategy/` for strategy tips, and `www.pokerlistings.com/online-poker-rooms` for links to dozens of Poker sites. Visit `www.pokernews.com/poker-rules/` for Poker basics. You can also check out the online tutorials at `https://poker.com`.

Before you put down any real money, you should make sure the site you want to use has a good reputation. `www.thepokerproject.com` and `www.pokerlistings.com` are sites that provide you with this service.

For an idea of how to navigate the murky Internet Poker waters, I also suggest you use *Winning at Internet Poker For Dummies* (Wiley) by Mark Harlan and Chris Derossi as your map.

Chapter 20

Draw Poker

D raw Poker is the game that serves as the best introduction to all other varieties of the game of Poker. It is simple and skillful, embodying virtually all elements of the game found in more complex varieties of Poker. Indeed, I can safely say that almost every serious Poker player has cut their teeth by playing Draw Poker. You can play Draw Poker at home or in a casino, and you can teach the game to everyone from young children to your maiden aunt!

BEFORE HAND

To play Draw Poker, you need the following:

» **At least three players:** Somewhere between four and seven is ideal, but you can cope with three or up to seven.

» **One standard deck of 52 cards:** In some versions of the game, you also need the jokers.

» **A table, chairs, and some chips or counters:** Ideally, you should use chips of at least two different denominations (different colors or sizes) to make the accounting easier. Money is a perfectly acceptable alternative to chips; in fact, you almost always play the game for money. As a general rule, bring a reserve of at least 80 times the minimum bet.

Five-Card Draw

In this romanticized, Old Western version of Poker, you get to *draw*, or trade in, some of the five cards you're dealt for new cards, after the initial round of betting. You can change up to four cards, but you get only one such chance. This distinguishes Draw Poker from all the other versions of Poker I discuss in this book, where cards are dealt out one at a time (and you only get two or four to start), and upcards are a big part of the game.

VARIATION

One of the more popular versions of Draw Poker, particularly in the United States, is Jackpots (or Jacks or Better), which requires the first bettor to have at least a pair of jacks to make the initial bet. This is the only variation from the standard game of Draw Poker, described in the following sections.

In the other standard variety of Draw Poker anything goes with betting — a player can make the first bet with a high card or three of a kind, a style of play that increases the potential for *bluffing*, which means pretending that you have a better hand than you do (see Chapter 19 for bluffing tips).

The objective of Five-Card Draw is to make the best five-card hand so as to beat any player who stays in the pot until the end. For a complete list of hand rankings and other Poker basics, see Chapter 19.

Dealing and putting in an ante

After you cut the deck for the deal (the player who draws the highest card deals, and thereafter the deal rotates clockwise), everybody puts in an ante. (A less common alternative is for the dealer to put in the ante for the whole table; offer this option up to one of your high-rolling friends.) See Chapter 19 for more information about the ante.

The dealer passes out one face-down card at a time, clockwise, to each player until everyone has five cards. The betting also starts at the dealer's left, and if you play the Jackpots variation, you must have a pair of jacks or better to place a bet. (A player with jacks or better doesn't have to bet if they don't want to; they can also pass.)

If the first player passes or *checks*, the next player to the left has the same options of betting or passing. If everybody passes, you gather the hand up, reshuffle and redeal it, with everyone placing an additional ante. As you can see, the point of this is that you never get to change your cards and draw new ones for free; someone has to bet, or else the hand gets thrown in.

Some people play that if a hand is redealt, the minimum holding required for the first bet also increases from a pair of jacks to a pair of queens. If everyone passes on the next hand, the minimum holding required jumps to a pair of kings and finally to a pair of aces. Sometimes the stakes also increase when this sort of thing happens. If no one can open with a pair of aces, some variations play that the requirements for opening start coming down; others play that the requirement for opening goes up to two pair.

Determining a strategy for the first bet

The first decision you need to focus on is when (and if) to make the first bet, or *open the betting.* The key issue is how many players haven't yet had the opportunity to open the betting and which players may have much better hands than yours. In fact, apart from the quality of your hand, your location at the table is the single most important thing about betting in Draw Poker. You have to think about who had the chance to bet, and did not, and who might be about to bet. When thinking about the first bet, keep the following factors in mind:

>> If you're one of the last three players with the option to make a bet, go ahead and do so on a pair of jacks or better.

>> If four players can still make a move, only bet if you have at least a pair of queens.

>> With five or six players yet to bet, wait until you have a hand better than a pair of kings.

>> If seven players are still to bet, wait to make the first bet until you get a pair of aces or better.

And, of course, if you don't have a good enough hand to bet, simply pass and fold if another player bets.

Deciding whether to stay in or to fold is more difficult. First, consider how many other players are betting. The more players who stay in or, worse, raise the betting, the stronger your hand needs to be to remain in the game:

>> With one other player betting, you should have a pair of kings or better to stay in.

>> With two players betting, you need any two pairs to stay in.

>> With between three and five players still in, you again need two pairs, but the more players in, the better your top pair should be.

>> With six players in, only remain in the game with three of a kind or better (see Chapter 19 for more information on the ranking of hands).

The only other hands you need to consider staying in with are those that can't win at the moment but are close to becoming good hands — for example, hands that are one card removed from a straight or flush. I discuss this type of hand in the following section, "Surviving the luck of the draw." The general rule is that you shouldn't stay in the hand unless you have at least a pair or four cards to a straight or flush. And remember: You can't start the betting with these hands if playing jacks or better, but you can stay in with them.

TIP

When you're one of the first few people to bet, try not to *limp in*, or call a minimum bet before the draw in the hope of improving your hand. You should either raise or fold, because if you stay in with a poor hand on a draw, you're simply throwing good money after bad odds.

If you have a really good hand, you may consider the check-raise. This involves checking, then re-raising when someone has the audacity to bet. At jacks or better, this strategy is very dangerous; the hand may get thrown in if you check.

REMEMBER

The guidelines I give in this section are just that — guidelines. As you begin to feel more comfortable with the game, you may introduce a little psychology into your decision making. As you get to know the mannerisms and habits of the people you play against, you can use that information to help you make decisions about how good your hand may be in comparison to the other players' hands. The sounder your opponents appear to be, the more you need to have to stay in with them.

Surviving the luck of the draw

After a player makes a bet, each player in turn has the option of folding, calling, or raising (see Chapter 19 for more on these options). As soon as the initial phase of the betting ends, you have your one and only opportunity to improve your hand.

The dealer starts with the first player remaining in the game to their left by asking that player how many cards they want. They keep the cards they want out of the five that they were dealt and discard the rest face-down. They call out the number of new cards that they want or say that they are *standing pat*, meaning that they don't want to trade in any cards. The dealer passes the correct number of cards to the player face-down and then moves on to the next player, offering that player the draw and receiving an equivalent number of cards in return. At their turn, the dealer also calls out how many cards they want.

In most variations of the game, you can change as many or as few cards as you want. With five players or more in the game, you may be permitted to change no more than three cards.

If a player wants to change cards and none are left in the deck, you shuffle the last remaining card of the stock card together with all the previous players' discards, to make a new deck and continue from there.

Still can't decide whether to keep the flush draw or go for the three of a kind? If you want to make a sound decision for the draw, knowing the odds helps.

Looking at the odds

One of the key areas of draw strategy is knowing what drawing hands are worth staying in for in hopes of creating a winning hand. Table 20-1 shows you just how likely — or unlikely — it is that you can improve your hand at the draw in certain situations.

WARNING

Before you read Table 20-1, keep in mind that if you don't hold at least a pair or four cards to a straight or flush, you should drop out of the bidding immediately rather than pay for the dubious privilege of attempting to improve an unpromising hand. Damage limitation is one of the most important arts of Draw Poker. Remember that you have an even-money, or 50/50, chance of not improving your hand — no matter what it is!

Keep these terms in mind as you read Table 20-1:

>> An *inside straight draw* means you have four cards to a straight, with one inside card as the missing link (giving you four cards to hit the straight, or *outs;* four 4s). For example, you have 3, 5, 6, 7, so you need the 4.

>> An *open-ended straight draw* means you have four consecutive cards, such as 3-4-5-6, and two different cards can complete the straight — either the 2 or the 7 (giving you 8 outs).

>> An *inside straight flush draw* means you have four of the cards needed for a straight flush, minus a specific inside card. For example, if you have ♦4, 5, 7, 8, you need the ♦6 to complete your straight flush (leaving you with 1 out for the straight flush and 8 outs for a regular flush).

>> A *kicker* is a high card, such as an ace. If two players put down a pair of kings at the showdown, whoever has the higher kicker wins the hand.

As you can see from Table 20-1, your chances of drawing to a straight aren't all that good — even on an open-ended straight. Drawing for a long shot isn't a good idea unless you want to make a charitable donation. And drawing with three cards to a straight or flush is grounds for institutionalization in 35 states.

The chances of improving a pair and a kicker are less than the chances of improving just the pair because you trade in only two cards.

TABLE 20-1   Your Drawing Chances for Draw Poker

You Stay in With	You Draw This Many Cards	You Want to Get	Your Chances Are
An ace	4	Two pairs or better	Slim — 1 in 14
An ace and a king in the same suit	3	Two pairs or better	Slim — 1 in 14
A pair	3	A better hand	Good — 2 in 5
		Two pairs	Pretty good — 1 in 3
		Three of a kind	Fair — 1 in 8
		Full house	Almost non-existent — 1 in 100
A pair and a kicker	2	A better hand	Good — 1 in 3
		Two pairs	Fairly good — 1 in 5
		Three of a kind	Slim — 1 in 12
		Full house	Almost non-existent — 1 in 120
Two pairs	1	Full house	Slim — 1 in 11
Three of a kind	2	Full house or better	Slim — 1 in 16
		Four of a kind	Poor — 1 in 22
An inside straight	1	Straight	Slim — 1 in 10
An open-ended straight	1	Straight	Fairly good — 1 in 5
Four cards to a flush	1	Flush	Pretty good — 1 in 4
Four cards to an inside straight flush	1	Straight or better	Good — 1 in 3
An open-ended straight flush	1	Straight or better	Quite good — 1 in 2

TIP

When you're known to follow the strategy of drawing two cards when you hold a pair and a kicker, and then you're dealt three of a kind later on and again draw two cards, the other players may assume that you hold a pair and a kicker. Developing this pattern has given you an opportunity to bluff. (You can find out more about bluffing in Chapter 19.)

WARNING

If you call for more cards than you actually want, you must make an extra discard before picking up so that your hand has the right number of cards. If you pick up the wrong number of cards, you're out of the game. If you ask for too few cards, your hand is *fouled*, because you no longer have enough cards for a valid hand.

REMEMBER

Most hands aren't won on a pair. Because drawing three cards gives away so much information about your hand, staying in with a pair against more than one other player isn't such great strategy. A pair of aces is the top hand half the time (before the draw) with seven players in. With four players in, assume that jacks are usually the best pair. (All this information argues for betting the maximum with two pairs, because you want to drive the other players out before they have the chance to improve their hands.)

Knowing what to get rid of

You may occasionally face the dilemma of what to discard on a hand with more than one reasonable option. This situation arises most often when you have a high pair and four cards to a straight or flush — for example, ♠Q, ♦Q, ♦8, ♦6, and ♦5 or ♦K, ♣K, ♣Q, ♥J, and ♠10.

You must determine whether enough money is in the pot and enough players are left in to get at least 5 to 1 odds. But when you have straight and flush possibilities, the odds are with you to keep it and try to complete it.

Assume, for example, you have a four-card flush draw — and to remain in the hand, you have to call a $10 bet. Should you call? First you must assess your chances of drawing what you need. Drawing to a flush, your chances are 1 in 4.5; drawing to an inside straight, your chances are 1 in 11; and drawing to an open-ended straight, your chances are 1 in 5.

In other words, if you want to stay in to go for the open-ended straight, you will fail to make your hand 5 times for every time you make it once. You will lose an extra $10 four times and win the pot once. So if you put up $10 five times, the pot must pay you $50 or better (5 × $10) to compensate for your losses, and that is after you deduct your ante and your own bets thus far from the equation. If you follow any other strategy, you're bucking the odds, which isn't a good way to make a living!

WARNING

You don't have to be too worried about other players trying to look at your cards. Nobody wants to run the risk of acquiring a "peeker reputation." However, you should avoid voluntarily exposing your cards to another player — they may feel less reluctance to look at your cards if you show them to them! Don't show your cards to spectators or to players sitting out, either.

Continuing after the draw

After everybody still in the game draws cards, a second and final round of betting takes place. The second round starts with the player who opened the betting in the first round. The betting limit, if you're playing with one, is generally doubled at this point.

The betting still goes clockwise around the table until everyone left in has called the final bet or until only one player remains. Whoever makes the final bet shows their hand, and anyone who can beat that hand must show; you don't need to reveal what you have otherwise. The cards speak for themselves — because you use all five cards, everyone can see what you have, so you don't have to claim the hand by stating what you have.

After the hand is over, the deal passes clockwise to the player to the dealer's left, and the whole process begins again — at least until you clean out all the other players, or everyone loses interest.

VARIATION

The website www.pagat.com/poker/variants/draw.html offers information on the many variations on Draw Poker.

Chapter **21**

Stud Poker

S even-Card Stud is possibly the second-most common Poker game played today. Texas Hold 'Em has surpassed Seven-Card Stud and every other Poker game in terms of popularity, but Seven-Card Stud remains a popular tournament game, and bigger tournaments like the World Series of Poker host a few Seven-Card Stud events every year.

Stud Poker exists these days in two main varieties: Seven-Card Stud and the less popular Five-Card Stud. Different modifications of the same strategies apply to both games. Stud Poker differs from other Poker games in that you get to see part of your opponents' hands during the betting. That may take away some of the romance and intrigue provide by games such as Hold 'Em and Draw Poker, but it brings a whole new level of gamesmanship into the picture. Unlike Hold 'Em, where you have to guess your opponent's hand from their betting strategy, here you get to see part of your opponent's hand, and draw more concrete inferences; but there is always an unknown element to the game, and that is where the skill in reading your opponent comes in.

BEFORE HAND

To play Stud Poker, you need the following:

» **At least five players:** Somewhere between four and eight is ideal.

» **One standard deck of 52 cards:** No jokers are necessary.

>> **Some chips or counters:** Ideally, you should try using chips of at least two different denominations (different colors or sizes) to make the accounting easier. Money is a perfectly acceptable alternative to chips. In fact, the game is almost always played for money. As a general rule, bring a reserve of at least 80 times the minimum bet.

Seven-Card Stud: Betting Down the River

Nobody can level the charge of predictability against Seven-Card Stud. The uncertainty inherent in the game arises because the pattern of dealing out the cards creates so many unknowns. This is what makes it such a challenging game. At every turn, more of the pattern is revealed, but never enough to know for sure what is going on. As the cards are turned over, rounds of betting persuade the weaker hands to drop out; but are the others staying in because they have a good hand, hope to get one, or are just bluffing?

Starting with the ante and the limits

Most low-limit Seven-Card Stud games require no ante (a bet made by all players before the deal to get the pot started; see Chapter 19 for more Poker basics). However, if you're playing in a high-stakes game, you may have to post a modest ante before the hand begins. Before beginning play in a casino, you may want to ask the dealer about any procedures. In a home game, all players agree to the rules before they start.

If you do have to post an ante, stick the small bet into the middle of the table before the deal. Most $2/$4 limit games have a $.50 ante. The higher the stakes become, the higher the ante rises.

REMEMBER

Most games of Seven-Card Stud are defined by the size of the *limit-bet*, which comes in two separate quantities. For example, a $1/$4 limit game has these restrictions:

>> **First betting round:** On the first round of betting, the initial bettor must put up at least $1 (they have the choice of betting $1 or $2), and other initial bets are for that same amount. Raises, on the other hand, may be anywhere between $1 and $4.

>> **Second betting round:** Typically, the minimum bet on the next card goes to $2. Again, raises may be for up to $4 at the player's discretion.

>> **Following betting rounds (up to the seventh card):** The minimum bet becomes $4. Raises must then be in increments of $4; normally there is a limit of three to the number of raises.

Betting in the early stages

The dealer (chosen by a cut or whatever method you prefer in home games) deals clockwise, starting to their immediate left. They deal one card at a time around the table until each player has two pocket (or *hole*) cards lying face-down and a single upcard for all to see. The player with the lowest upcard showing is required to open the betting — a bet known as the *bring-in*. The low player has no option but to make at least the minimum bet. If two players have identical low cards, the alphabetical order of the suits — clubs, diamonds, hearts, spades, with clubs being the lowest — determines who opens the betting.

VARIATION

Some people still play that the high card bets first on the opening round of betting.

The player immediately to the left of the bring-in now has the option to call the bet, raise, or fold (see Chapter 19 for more information on these actions, and what a round of betting consists of). If they fold or call, they leave the person immediately to their left with the same options. However, if they raise (in our example $1/$4 game, they may put in an extra $2 to make the total bet $3), every player to their left must match that raise, raise further (again by up to $4), or fold. The game proceeds clockwise until every player makes their choice of how to act and everyone has either seen the last raise, or has folded.

REMEMBER

Stud typically features a three-raise limit on each round. Check with the dealer if you are playing in a casino and you aren't sure of the rules.

Each player receives three more cards face-up, one at a time, and the final card comes face-down. A round of betting follows each card, and in these subsequent rounds, the player with the best hand showing has the responsibility to act first. If two hands are of equal value, the first player to the left of the dealer acts first. The round of betting after the first upcard is dealt is known as betting on *third street*, the next round is *fourth street*, and then *fifth* . . . well, you get the picture! The final card is known as *the river*.

On fourth street and all subsequent rounds, the player with the high hand isn't required to bet. They can *check*, which means that they don't bet and pass the option to bet to the next player. If another player makes a bet, the players remaining in the hand must at least call the bet to stay in the hand.

After fourth street, if any player has a pair showing, any player can bet for the maximum table limit. For example, in a $1/$4 game, the normal limit on fourth street is $2, but with a pair showing, anyone can bet $4. After that first bet, anyone can raise by $4, whatever they have showing.

When the showdown takes place in Seven-Card Stud after the last round of betting on the river is complete, you announce your hand value. Unlike, say, Five-Card Stud, the selection of five cards out of a total of seven means that you have an element of choice, so it may not be immediately obvious what you have. So make everyone's life easy by announcing your hand.

Passing the first pivotal moment: Third street

The card structure of Seven-Card Stud creates two critical moments. The first is when you receive your first upcard on third street. (The second crucial decision comes on fifth street; I cover this decision time in the following section, "Staying in on fifth street.") When you can see your two hole cards and everyone can see your third card, your hand generally falls into one of three categories: good, promising, or bad. You don't need me to tell you what to do with the bad hands, do you? This section considers hands that are already good or that may become so.

In order to make your decision easier, here's a list of the best starting hands in Seven-Card Stud:

>> **Three of a kind (also referred to as *trips*)** is the best possible hand on third street. This happens when you start with two concealed cards of the same rank as your visible card. Although you only experience this situation a little more frequently than 1 in 500 times, you want to exploit this hand to the full — but don't give your hand away by betting too aggressively too early. However, with high trips, you can often bet freely without giving away the show, because players will assume you have a pair. Hey, they know the odds, too!

>> **Any pair of matching court cards** is the next-best start. Preferably, you want both high cards hidden for deceptive purposes, but you'll take this hand any way you can get it. The size of your kicker (the accompanying single card) may also affect your hand — the higher the rank, the better.

WARNING

Any time a player has a pair showing, be ready to drop unless you have a good or very promising hand (such as a pair yourself or connecting suited cards). If the pair comes on fourth street, you know that player presumably had a reason to stay in the game after their first upcard, and now their hand has improved. You better have a good reason to stay in.

>> **Three connected high cards in the same suit** (♠A, ♠K, ♠Q, for example) is also a very powerful hand, giving you good options for a flush or straight and other possibilities if those boats don't come in.

>> **Any medium-sized pair or three medium-value connecting cards in the same suit** is the next-best option.

>> **Three almost-connecting cards in the same suit** are next. For example, you may have the king and queen of diamonds together with the 10 of diamonds.

>> **A small pair or three cards to a straight or flush** can also be of some value.

With anything less, go away at once — unless you want to bluff!

TIP

Some hands play better in *multi-way pots* (hands that feature many players remaining in) and some in *shorthanded pots* (where only a few players remain):

>> **The hands that play well in multi-way pots** are drawing hands — three cards to a flush, three cards to a straight, or a combination of the two. If you complete your hand, you may be a favorite to win whatever the other players have. So you are happy to have them all stay in.

>> **The hands that play well in shorthanded pots** are big pairs. Even if you don't improve your hand, you may still win if the other player doesn't get what they need.

WARNING

You must look around at the other cards showing on the table to see whether your hand is *live*, meaning that you can complete it with cards still left in the deck, or if your hand is *dead*, meaning your opponents have already been dealt the cards you're hoping to receive. Most of the smaller pairs or hands requiring a favorable draw to complete a straight or flush are playable when the cards you need to improve your hand are completely live. But the more cards that you can't receive because someone else has them, the worse your odds become. For example, if you have the ♦7 and ♦8 together with the ♣6, the last cards you want to see hit other players' hands are the three 9s and two 5s. Your chances of making a straight have dropped considerably — time to give up and wait for the next deal.

Watching the dead cards is critical to calculating the mathematical odds correctly. If you want a 3, and you see two of them hit the board, only two 3s are left for you, not four, so your chances of getting one are cut in half.

With three cards to a flush, your chances of completing are about 5 to 1. If you see a couple of cards in your suit visible in other players' hands, the odds move against you, so it may be wise to drop out. A straight is far tougher to complete than a flush. If even one of the cards you need is dead, you're probably playing against the odds to continue unless you have high cards that may win you the hand if you pair up.

When deciding whether to stay in or drop, you not only need to check what cards are out, but also how many players are in the pot when your turn arrives. The more players who remain, the better or more promising your hand should be to stay in. Equally, you must ask yourself: "Have the players in the game indicated that they're likely to bluff, or do they always have the goods when they stay in on a hand?" The issues of who, if anyone, raised the pot and where they're sitting in relation to you may also be relevant to your decision. Your best position is sitting after the active players, not in front of them, so you have much more information to work with.

Staying in on fifth street

In Seven-Card Stud, fifth street (your third upcard) is another critical decision-making time, because the betting limit increases. You may be forced to pay more to stay in the game to see your last upcard (sixth street) and final downcard (the river, or seventh street). Accordingly, fifth street is the right moment to fold a poor hand that you haven't been able to improve, especially against aggressive betting, where drawing to the card you need becomes too risky. If you stay in, be sure you can (and that you're willing to) play your hand out to the end. If an opponent's exposed cards beat your whole hand, it's best to fold.

Here are a few general tips on how to survey the table to assess your chances on fifth street:

>> **If you want to complete a straight,** look to see if other players are showing the cards you need before you bet. You really need to have four cards to a straight still to stay in, and hopefully you're drawing to an outside or *open-ended* straight (one that you can complete at either end) rather than an *inside straight,* which needs a specific draw to be completed.

>> **If you want to make a flush,** check to see how many of the suit cards have been dealt to the other players and adjust your strategy accordingly. For example, if you're going for a flush in hearts and you hold four of that suit (if you don't already have four cards to a flush, time to fold!), you know that nine hearts remain in the rest of the deck. However, if seven of those nine cards are visible elsewhere, only two hearts are left — and your chances of receiving one of them are slim.

In the exceedingly unlikely event of all eight players staying in a hand until near the very end, you won't have enough cards left in the deck for everyone to receive the final downcard (8 players times 7 cards apiece is 56, not 52). If this happens, everyone gets to share a community river card, turned face-up.

Surveying the Stud Landscape: Table Strategy

If you could manage to be dealt good hands all the time in Stud Poker, you'd be a big winner. Unfortunately, you can't, so you need to concentrate on getting the most out of your good hands, not wasting money on the bad hands, and not being burned by the moderate hands — which are far more dangerous than the miserable hands.

Reading the table

The interesting thing about Seven-Card Stud is the fact that you can predict virtually nothing about anyone else's hand without looking at the betting patterns. For example, if all you can see up in another player's hand is ♦7, ♣9, ♥K, ♦4, that player can literally have almost any hand at all, from a king-high array of odd cards, to one or two pairs, to three or four of a kind, to a straight. And the hand also has room for a flush or straight flush in diamonds. What you must realize is that even if that player has a great hand, they've had no reason to bet strongly so far. If their first two hole cards are the ♣4 and ♠4, and a 7 was the last hole card, their hand was bad enough in the beginning to have been folded in the face of strong betting. How's your mind so far?

TIP

You must consider whether the chances of the other players making their hands have been affected by the cards in other hands. In the previous hand, if you're holding a full house with three aces and competing against this player, you may be cheered to see the ♦6 and a 4, 7, and king among the other players' cards. You know that you're exposed only to the risk of four 9s; you can beat any other hand automatically because a straight-flush in diamonds is already ruled out. (See Chapter 19 for more information on hand rankings.)

But what do you do when you're showing a high pair or trips on the board and another player still bets huge? Are they bluffing? And how can you add the trick to your bag? Read on!

Bluffing

The best time to bluff in Seven-Card Stud is on third street when you have a high card showing or when you're one of the last players to bet and the early players haven't entered the pot. Representing a pair or better with your bet may scare other players with a strong hand out of the game. An even better situation is when you don't have a pair, but you do have some other possibilities to win the hand if someone else stays in. With the downcards ◆7 and ◆9 and the upcards ♠6 and ◆A, you may bet as if you have aces while hoping to complete either a flush or straight.

However, remember that who you're trying to bluff is critical. If you're up against an aggressive player or one who stays in on every hand, you may be wasting your money on a bluff. Also, if you represent a high pair, you don't want to see too many of that card visible on the table in other players' hands.

TIP

You may be tempted to stay in with bad hands (just in case something good happens). Don't do it! Over the course of the evening, on average, you'll lose more money by staying in on nothing for a couple of rounds and then going out than in any other way. You can lose your money on moderate hands easily; why surrender money on bad hands? Drop out after the first three cards unless you have the makings of a straight or flush, have a pair, or have three (or perhaps two) high cards.

The same advice also applies midhand, when one of the other players has you beaten with their face-up cards. If you can't beat them now without a ton of luck, why stay in and donate? What if they have something big in the hole?

Winning (or not losing) at Seven-Card Stud

The easiest way to win at any game of Poker is to stick to playing only when the odds are in your favor — which means playing when some of the players are weaker than you. When you start out in Poker that may not be too easy to accomplish, so you should play for the smallest stakes you can manage until you feel confident. After you get comfortable, try to play in games where you have an edge. You want at least a couple of weak players at the table when you sit down. If you can't identify the weakling — it may be you!

If you sit down in a new game, *play the players*, or try to assess the opposition as quickly as possible: Who plays inferior hands? Who folds at aggression? Who bets on the hope of getting a good draw? Who calls bets with weak hands and long-shot draws? Who can be bluffed, and who bluffs? Don't lose interest in a hand when you bow out of the betting; try to work out the other players' betting strategies. It may pay to fold a few hands early on, no matter how anxious you are to get going.

REMEMBER

The typical winning hand at Seven-Card Stud, if play continues to the river, is a flush — that should be good enough to win most hands. A straight is much more problematic, but it's better than an even chance to win. However, most games don't go down to the river for chances at straights or flushes; most hands are won with just two pair or trips, because all the other hands drop out when one player bets strongly in midgame.

Staying in and dropping out

With three of a kind early on in a hand, almost nothing can persuade you to drop out. But other hands aren't so easy to play:

>> **With a high pair only,** fold if you're obviously outgunned by a player with a better hand on the board or if multiple players with higher upcards than your pair have bet.

>> **With a low or medium pair,** the size of your kicker (and whether it may give you the chance of a straight or flush) may be relevant, but equally vital are the number of players remaining in the game and the relative sizes of their upcards.

>> **With three cards to a straight or flush,** stay in the deal initially unless the price of doing so is unacceptable. Remember, if all your flush or straight cards are live, the hand is almost always playable. If you have high upcards showing, you should consider raising with the first bet because you can combine your bluff with the chance of winning the hand legitimately if others stay in. This also works well as an ante- or blind-stealing strategy, because it adds deception to your play.

WARNING

Even if your first three cards are suited, your chances of completing the flush are only 5 to 1 against. With three cards to a sequence, your chances of completing the straight are 6 to 1 against. So, make sure enough money has hit the pot to justify playing on if you decide to go for it.

REMEMBER

More hands are decided by the ranking of a pair (or two pairs) against a similar hand than are decided by a flush against a straight. So, if you start with a straight or flush draw, you want to have at least one — preferably two — high card larger than anything you see on the board. Drawing hands, like low-pair starting hands, need to improve or turn a high pair quickly to justify continued play. Bet early when you have high hands that may be able to win without improvement in order to thin out the competition, but don't automatically raise on hands where you need a draw to turn what you have into a good hand, such as a straight or flush, because the idea is to keep other players in the game. Keeping other players on the hook while you draw increases the pot odds in case you get lucky.

Five-Card Stud

Five-Card Stud, although no longer as popular as it once was, is by far the fastest poker game. In Five-Card Stud, which can be played with up to ten players, you don't get to draw to replace any cards; what you're dealt is what you get, and that's that. However, instead of picking up all five cards dealt to you face-down, at one turn, you get your cards one at a time, with opportunities to bet after receiving each card.

After paying the ante, each player is dealt one card face-down. This *hold card* remains down for the course of the game. Your other four cards are dealt face-up. When everyone has received one face-up card, the person with the highest face-up card has the first opportunity to bet, and then the betting progresses clockwise. If two equal cards are showing, the player nearest the dealer's left makes the first bet.

When every bet has been called, the third card is dealt out, face-up, to the players remaining in the game. At the end of the final bet, all the players left in the game show their hole cards, and the best hand takes the pot.

Five-Card Stud is mostly a game of high cards and pairs. Remember the average five-card hand includes no pairs. Don't play for straights and flushes unless you have three cards to a straight flush on third street, or it looks like you may luck into a straight or flush on fourth. Similarly, don't pay out good money to stay in a hand when you have three cards to a flush; the chances of completing it are very slim. On the other hand, bet the limit whenever you have a pair showing that out-ranks any other pair visible at the table. And when you have a concealed pair, bet on it immediately, if you're not beaten by a visible pair in someone else's hand.

Chapter 22

Texas Hold 'Em

The popularity of some card games rises and falls, but unquestionably, the flavor of the moment is Texas Hold 'Em Poker. The reason for this is that improvements in camerawork have suddenly allowed the television viewer to appreciate what a fine game Texas Hold 'Em really is.

Although many varieties of Poker feature bluff and money management skills, Texas Hold 'Em is preeminent in this. And the game is easy; well, maybe not easy to play well, but easy enough to grasp the basics of. This all adds up to compulsive television watching, and it is even more fun to play both at home or in a casino.

BEFORE HAND

To play Texas Hold 'Em (referred to for the rest of this chapter simply as Hold 'Em), you need the following:

» **At least five players:** Somewhere between seven and ten is ideal in a game of Limit Hold 'Em, but you can cope with fewer.

» **One standard deck of 52 cards:** You don't need jokers.

» **A table and some chips or counters:** Ideally, you should use chips of at least two different denominations (different colors or sizes) to make the accounting easier. Money is a perfectly acceptable alternative to chips; in fact, you almost always play the game for money. If you play at a small limit table, such as $2/$4 (see the following section for more information on limits), you should have roughly $100 in chips.

Holding 'Em Up — Texas Style

Hold 'Em is one of the most popular gambling games in the world. It takes 5 minutes to learn and a lifetime to master. The object of the game is to combine two face-down cards you receive (*downcards* or *hole cards*) with five face-up community cards (*upcards*) that are available to everyone to make the best possible five-card hand.

After each player gets two cards face-down, a round of betting (see the definitions in Chapter 19) takes place. After players call, raise, or fold, the dealer *burns* one card (or places it face-down, not to be heard from again) and places three cards, which are common to everyone, face-up on the table, and then another round of betting takes place. After the best, another card is burned followed by another face-up card, with another round of betting. Finally, the dealer burns the last card and places a fifth and final face-up card on the table, and the last round of betting follows.

If there are two players left in at the showdown, whichever of them is called on the last bet shows their hand, and the other player either concedes (in which case they do not need to show their hand, or reveal their winning collection). Sometimes the last player standing wins the hand; if a player makes a bet that no one calls, they take the pot without having to show their hand.

REMEMBER

Hold 'Em has quite a few technical terms. After you get some hands under your belt buckle, however, you'll have no trouble not only remembering the terms, but also tossing them out like an old saloon pro. The first three communal cards are called the *flop*; the fourth communal card is the *turn* or *fourth street*; and the last communal card is the *river* or *fifth street*. Throughout this chapter, I offer up some other terms — mentioned for the first time in italics to put you on guard!

The objective of Hold 'Em is to make the best five-card Poker hand — see the rankings in Chapter 19. You can use any combination of your hole cards and the community cards to make the optimal Poker hand. If the *board* (the five community cards) is the best possible hand for everyone, the result is a tie for all players remaining in the game. Alternatively, you must use one of your hole cards if you want to use four of the cards from the board. (See Chapter 19 for more information on ranking Poker hands.)

You usually play Hold 'Em without any wild cards.

VARIATION

The three most common betting structures for Hold 'Em are:

>> **Limit Hold 'Em:** Limit Poker is the most popular betting structure, whether you play at casinos and card rooms or in social games. The amounts that any

player can bet or raise are predetermined. For example, at a $10/$20 limit Hold 'Em game, you bet and raise in amounts of $10 for the first round and after the flop (*the small bet*), and then the bets go up to increments of $20 for the turn and river (*the big bet*). You can occasionally find $1/$2 tables in most casinos, and you can almost always find $2/$4 tables, which allow you to play without breaking your bank. As such, it is ideal for beginning players.

>> **No limit Hold 'Em:** The hyper-aggressive no-limit Poker is perhaps most widely known because it's the variety of game you see on the World Poker Tour, ESPN, and other places. Other than the initial blind bets (see the following section), you don't have a predefined limit to follow in regard to what you can bet (except you can't bet more money than you have in front of you when the hand starts). You can bet all the chips in front of you any time you like. If you're playing head-to-head against a player who has less money than you, you can only bet that amount. Putting all your chips at risk is known as *going all-in*. Putting up all your chips is one of the biggest adrenaline rushes you can experience at a card table. Will you double your money or lose it all?

>> **Pot limit Hold 'Em:** Pot limit Hold 'Em is somewhere between limit and no limit. The maximum bet is the amount of money currently in the pot, and the minimum is determined by the big blind bet at the time (see the following section). The size of the pot thus restricts the size of each bet or raise. The way it works is that after you have put in the appropriate amount to call the last bet, you can raise by whatever is in the pot at that moment. As a result, on each additional round of betting, the limits rise sharply. Pot limit Hold 'Em is mainly played in Europe — although pot-limit events take place each year at the World Series of Poker in Las Vegas — and the strategy is broadly similar to no-limit Hold 'Em.

Making blind bets

Unlike many varieties of Poker, Hold 'Em generally doesn't have antes outside of high-stakes tournament play; in other words, all players don't have to put in a bet before the cards are dealt. Instead, the two players to the left of the dealer are forced to put in bets for the first round. The second player to the dealer's left puts in a bet that's typically double the size of the bet of the player to the dealer's immediate left (these two bets are the *small* and *big blinds*, respectively). The size of the bigger bet represents the minimum bet on the first round for all the other players.

The blinds are considered part of your initial bet, so the small blind must eventually double their bet just to stay in the game, unless another player raises the big bet; if the small blind wants to fold, they lose the forced (smaller) bet. If no one raises the initial bet, the big blind has the option of calling — in which case they put no more money in — or raising. (For more information on these basic Poker actions, see Chapter 19.)

In tournaments, the blinds start small and then go up in subsequent rounds, to speed up the elimination of players. As the blinds increase in no-limit tournaments, players are also required to post antes along with the blind bets.

At a casino, a staff member deals the cards, but for each hand has a notional dealer. The *notional dealer* has a small white button in front of them, and their position is known as being *on the button.* The two players to their left are the small blind and the big blind. (The player before the dealer is sometimes known as *the cutoff man.*) The betting starts with the player to the left of the big blind and works clockwise round the table, back to the big blind. In subsequent rounds, the first player on the dealer's left still in the hand bets first — typically, therefore, the small or big blind if either is still playing.

Starting hands

Every Hold 'Em player faces two critical issues that they need to come to grips with.

>> Knowing what makes a decent starting hand

>> Combining an understanding of a playable hand with the importance of your position at the table, because where you sit on any particular hand in relation to who has made a bet, and who is yet to bet, is critical

I start by looking at the possible starting hands and take it from there.

REMEMBER

If you're staying in hands at a pace of more than 1 hand in 4 in a nine-player game, you're either getting some great starting hands or playing way too many hands! You need to consider whether you, and the other players at the table, are tight or loose. *Tight* players are more careful about staying in hands; *loose* players have lower minimum standards. Most of the players you will encounter at a casino, and even more so in a home game with low stakes, are likely to be too loose and may play half their starting hands or even more. Play smarter than them by sticking to the tighter guidelines I list in this section. They may play more hands, but you will win the ones you do play.

TIP

The key to winning in Hold 'Em is selective aggression. Be very selective about the hands you choose to play before the flop, but when you play a good hand, play it aggressively.

Top-of-the-line hands

Any large pair (aces, the best hand, down to 10s) is the best possible hand with which to start. Even in the face of bets and raises, you should stay in to see the flop. With high-pair hands, you want to bet to reduce the field — you make it too expensive for other players to stay in with weaker hands and see the flop in the hopes of getting lucky. Any flush and straight beats your dominating pre-flop pair; why give other players a cheap chance to make those hands?

Next on the totem pole are any two high cards in the same suit. The strongest suited high cards are ace, king; ace, queen; ace, jack; and king, queen. Weaker hands in the high-suited category are all others with two cards, 10 or higher, in the same suit.

Other premium hands include strong *unsuited* high cards (two high cards in different suits). These hands can become high pairs or straights, and the size of your high kicker may split any tie in your favor. Unsuited ace, king and ace, queen are the best hands in this category.

WARNING

Hands without an ace look a lot better than they are when more than two players remain in the game. You're an underdog to any hand with an ace or pair. You have to get lucky to have a good chance to win, and you don't want to rely on luck to win in Hold 'Em.

Any middle pair — 9s through 7s — gives you a decent shot to have the best hand before the flop. But you need a favorable flop to improve your hand and have a chance to win.

Middle-of-the-road hands

Mid-level hands are playable only under the right circumstances.

Hands that don't crack the upper echelon include any two cards in the same suit, with one high card and one middle-rank card. Your best option is an ace with a middle card, but any two suited cards give you a chance to make a flush, and if the cards *connect*, or fall in consecutive order, you may make a straight. A suited ace and a low card also qualify. If the betting doesn't get out of control, you may stay in for the flop, but be prepared to drop if nothing comes up to help you. And remember that your chances of drawing two cards in your suit are only about 1 in 10.

TIP

The preceding hands listed in this section are relatively straightforward to play in that your next decision tends to be clear after the flop; if you get a favorable draw, you have a chance to win a big pot. If nothing comes up, you fold gracefully.

WARNING

Be careful when playing an ace with a low kicker. If another ace comes up on the flop, and you don't have a flush draw, you could be in trouble. You may think you have the best hand, but a player with an ace and a better kicker has you dominated.

You can also play the weaker unsuited big cards, such as king, jack and ace, 10. However, with the weaker hands in this category, such as queen, 10 or jack, 10, don't play if you think someone is likely to raise. If you're in a late position and don't face a raise, however, your straight possibilities, coupled with the chance of making the high pair, make such hands initially playable.

Handle any low pair (6s through 2s) with caution.

A small pair is far less promising than it looks. With a low pair, you lose out to larger pairs, and you're only slightly ahead against two high cards; in the latter situation, you figure to win no more than 50 percent of the time. Playing against two players with two higher cards, your chances are down to 30 percent. You'll only make trips from the flop about 1 time in 8.

Scraping-the-bottom-of-the-barrel hands

At the bottom of the barrel, you have hands where you have little justification for staying in and you need the right circumstances to persuade you not to drop (such as a cheap fee in late position when you're up against only a couple of players).

An ace or a king with a low card in the same suit gives you the start of a flush, but you have a long way to go against tall odds to make your hand. Suited middle cards or low connecting cards (cards of consecutive rank) need a good flop to improve, but they could turn out to be magic hands.

An unsuited high card with a middle card (such as a jack and an 8) gives you only a slim chance of a straight.

Garbage hands

You don't need me to tell you what to do with these hands, do you? Fold! The best way to save money is to drop out as soon as you can on bad hands. Particularly dangerous and unpromising are unsuited aces with low or middle cards.

WARNING

You lose more money by staying in hands with unpromising starting cards than in any other way. Calling the bet in middle position with a low pair in the face of action from the other players is a good way to lose money. Remember that, in any form of Poker, whoever has the second-best hand loses the most money. The key is to make your opponents play those second-best hands and to fold them yourself. It's far better to drop with a bad hand than to finish second.

Paying attention to location

After you decide what makes a good, medium, or acceptable starting hand, what drives you to stay in or fold? The answer for you and for real estate agents is location. Just as there are three types of possible starting hands, there are three possible table positions: You can be early to bet, you can be in the middle, or you can be late. This concept is called *position*.

The key difference is that the early bettors have to commit their money before they know what the late players are representing. The middle players get to see the early players bet or fold, but they don't see the players who come after them. The later players get the benefit of seeing the betting unfold, so they can drop out with marginal hands if the action gets too pricey; they can join in with mediocre hands if no one appears to have much to say; or they can bet hard to try to steal the money other players have committed with strong or mediocre hands.

The concept of position is repeated on the flop, the turn, and the river, which is another reason why you don't want to play too many hands from an early position. On every round of betting, early players are forced to act first, and the rest of the players can react to what they do.

>> If you have a choice of betting or folding, you should stay in only with a premium, top-of-the-line hand. You want to avoid committing money when you have the second- or third-best hand, and calling with a marginal hand before you've seen anyone else commit themselves is a losing proposition. Early players should stay in with any premium hand — and should raise with a high pair or strong, suited high cards.

>> If you in the middle positions, consider betting, if no one raises the bet, with either a premium hand or a mid-level holding. A limited number of players still have to bet, so middle-position players are unlikely to get blindsided. Middle players can take a more aggressive position as to when to raise.

>> If you're in a late position, you get to see everyone bet and can stay in with more moderate hands, as long as no one has raised. This is the prime position in which to bluff, which I discuss later in the section "Bluffing."

TIP

The fewer the number of players in the game, the looser your standards should be for starting hands. When you have five or six players, the hands I describe as minimally acceptable are reasonable to call on before the flop. With fewer players, you need to be more aggressive and call or raise with more hands, because the probability of many players having good hands decreases.

Strategically Speaking: Calling, Folding, and Raising

After you identify the potential of your hand and what seat you are occupying, you can fold, call, or raise. See Chapter 19 for definitions.

Betting before the flop: Call, fold, or raise?

If you're sitting in early position, your normal strategy in a game with many players is to drop with bad hands and call or raise with good or medium hands. Try not to become too easy to read by always playing the premium hands the same way, but you should normally get active with any high pair by raising — make the field pay if they want to stay in to see the flop and perhaps take your money in the process.

If somebody raises in early position, you must assume they have a reason. Don't assume that they're bluffing — in a big game, bluffing from an early seat is a truly dangerous play, so don't stay in with a marginal hand. The weaker premium hands aren't worth playing if you have to *call a raise cold* — if you haven't called yet and have to put in two bets to match a call and a raise. However, if you've already called and someone raises after you, you should almost always call in a limit game. In a no-limit game, you have to make that decision based on the size of the raise and how much money you have.

If you're late to play and no one has called the big bet, feel free to call or raise with any vaguely suitable hand. You may be able to steal the blinds, and you have some chances to win if the other players stay in. The more players who fold or just call before the flop, the better your chances of winning the hand with a bet. I cover this strategy in more detail later on in the section "Stealing blinds."

Unless you suspect a bluff, don't call a raise without a hand that you may have considered raising with.

WARNING

If you raise the bet and face a re-raise (particularly if someone checked initially and then raised the bet — a *check-raise*), be very careful before continuing. Make sure the pot odds are in your favor (see the section "Calculating pot odds" later in this chapter).

When one player raises the blind and another player re-raises, what the re-raiser is saying is that they believe they have a great hand — as was the first player with their raise. If you raise and another player re-raises, you should just call unless you know you have the best hand. If you raise with a hand that's not winning, and someone re-raises, take a long hard look at your hand to see if it's worth calling and paying off or if you should fold.

Drawing in appropriate situations

Of course, your decision as to whether to stay in the hand before the flop depends on how likely you think you are to improve your hand by the flop. So you need to look at the mathematics of Hold 'Em in some detail.

One of the most common calculations you have to perform in Hold 'Em is figuring your chances of your improving your hand with a favorable flop, turn, or river. You also have to try to calculate what hands your opponents may have, and whether they can make their hands. However, when first beginning to play, stick to considering only your hand's odds.

The following list gives you a feel for the calculations you may need to work out at the table (in your head, of course; unless you don't shy easily). For all the calculations that follow, it shouldn't surprise you that your chance of making your hand on the river (the fifth community card) is about half of what it is when going from the flop to the turn (the fourth community card). The logic is that after the flop, you have two chances to draw a magic card; after the turn, only one.

>> **If you have a pair,** the chances that you'll make three of a kind (trips) on the flop are 1 in 9. If you don't make it on the flop, you have 1 chance in 12 of making trips on the turn or river.

>> **If you hold two cards to a flush in your hand and the flop comes up with two cards in that suit,** the chances that you'll complete your flush on either the turn or the river are just better than 1 in 3.

The flush odds are very similar to the chances that you can complete an *open-ended straight,* where you have four cards in sequence after the flop, and you can complete the straight with two different cards on the turn or the river (7-8-9-10, for example). The odds here are just less than 1 in 3.

>> **If you're drawing to an *inside straight* — one that you can complete only with a specific draw (7-8-10-J, for example),** the odds are 1 in 6 that you'll make your straight on the turn or the river.

Phil Gordon, one of the Hold 'Em gurus you see on television, uses the following simple formula to approximate your winning chances:

1. **After the flop, count the number of cards available that will give you a winning hand.** With 7-8-9-10, you need a 6 or J, eight winning draws, or *outs*.

2. **Multiply the resulting number by four to give you a percentage chance to win the hand.**

In the example above, the eight cards give you a 32 percent chance of winning. If you have four cards to an ace-high flush, for example, your chances of getting a fourth heart (of which there are nine) on the turn or the river are about 36 percent. If you're already at the river, multiply the nine by two to get 18 percent.

Staying in a hand until the river when your chances of winning depend on drawing to an inside straight (also called a *gutshot*) is a common rookie error. You generally throw good money after a bad draw.

Also, be careful when drawing to the bottom end of a straight — for example, when the upcards are ♠2, ♣10, ♦9, ♥3 and you have ♠8, ♠7. Yes, you have an open-ended straight and can win if a 6 comes on the river. However, if a jack comes on the river, you'll lose to anyone who has a K, Q or Q, 8 in their hands. Equally, with the same hole cards, if the community cards are ♠K, ♣10, ♦9, ♥3, you'll lose outright to anyone who has a queen if the jack appears on the river.

The mathematics of the draw on the turn or the river are especially important when you have to evaluate what your chances of winning the pot really are, and how much you can afford to gamble on the chance.

Calculating pot odds

After you understand your chances of turning garbage into gold by improving your hand on the flop, the turn, or the river, you can apply your calculations in the middle of a hand.

The mathematics of Hold 'Em become important when you haven't completed your hand but hope to draw to do so. For example, say you're in a pot of $60 and three players are left. The way the betting has gone so far, you figure that both opponents have one or two pairs. The last bet was $20, and your hole cards are ♠A, ♠J with the community cards coming ♣K, ♦9, ♠10, ♠2. Should you stay in or fold?

To stay in the pot, you need to calculate that your $20 bet will take the pot up to $80. Therefore, to stay in, you should compare the bet you need to make, and the size of the pot after you make it. Since the bet is $20 and the pot will be $80, you need odds of 20 ÷ 80, or 1 in 4 to remain in. The odds mean that if you win once and lose three times, you put up four bets of $20 but get back a pot of $80 when you win, for a break-even.

REMEMBER

The calculation goes like this: There are 46 cards remaining (52 excluding the six you can see), and you believe that you'll win if any of the remaining nine spades come up or if any of the three other queens appear — note that you've counted the ♠Q once already, so you can't do so again. These 12 cards (the nine spades and three queens) are called your *outs* — if you get one of them, you'll win the hand. You have 12 chances in 46 to win the pot — more than a quarter — and it costs you one quarter of the pot to stay in. Therefore, you should call the bet.

With the same hand but with the flop having the ♦10 rather than the ♠10, you couldn't make a flush. A queen to make your straight is your only out — chances of 4 in 46, clearly not the required odds.

WARNING

Don't use the argument that you may get lucky, so you should buck the odds. The way to win in Hold 'Em is to *follow* the odds. The way to lose a small fortune (out of a large one!) is to *ignore* the odds.

With a close or marginal decision, you may decide to stay in when simple mathematics says to drop. However, I advise you to do so only if the last bet is relatively small compared to the pot size *and* if it can only cost you one bet (that is, no one can raise to see the next card). With more than one other player still in, you can make a lot of money on the remaining bets if you hit your hand, improving your payoff beyond the required percentages I discuss in this section, because your winning hand isn't evident to the other players who continue betting or see your bets. (You're particularly under-the-radar when drawing successfully to a straight or even to a flush, using both your downcards.)

Staying in or dropping out after the flop

With most hands, the flop is going to crystallize your hand into either a good or bad hand. When that is the case, you do not really need me to tell you what to do. But what if the flop leaves you in the gray area? Then you need to have some basic elements of strategy at your fingertips. And here they are!

When you have only three cards to a flush or a straight, don't hold out hope to get lucky; your chances of completing your hand are negligible. To continue winning ways, start planning the next hand — or even better, watch the behavior of the other players at the table — and drop out. To stay in, you should have a good hand or have a good chance to draw a good hand.

TIP

If you start with a high pair or high cards for your hole cards but don't improve, you may want to stay in if nothing on the board suggests others have drawn well enough to beat you. For example, you may call the big blind with only an ace because of your position at the table. If your hand doesn't improve on the flop and other high cards hit the board, along with bets from other players, you don't want to be looking for reasons to stay in the hand. However, if nobody bets and the board has all low cards, you may want to bet, because you may have a hand that nobody wants to call.

Bear in mind that more often than not, the flop won't bring the cards you need. If you have completed a straight or a flush, you'll surely stay in and raise the betting. But consider some more complex positions.

Facing tough post-flop decisions

If you have three of a kind with a pair in the hole and one card on the flop, you're in great shape. If you have only one card of the three down and a matching pair on the board, you're still well placed. However, if your other hole card is low, a player with the fourth matching card and a higher kicker beats you. Still, you want to bet strongly until you're convinced that someone has a better hand than you.

With two pairs, your position can vary enormously; with what you consider to be the two top pairs (pocket aces — meaning both cards are concealed — and 10s on the flop, for example), you may still be beaten by anyone who can make three of a kind from the pair on the board. If you have two pairs but can see that someone may have a higher top pair, be cautious. For example, you have two jacks in the hole, and the flop comes ♦Q, ♠7, ♥7. Anyone betting strongly either has a 7 or a queen — or wants you to think they have! Queens are the *top pair* here. Your chances are better if you have half of each pair in your hole (J, 7 in the hole and J, 7, Q on the flop, for example); to beat you, someone has to make a premium hand, with much less help from the board.

Even if you only have a pair, your chances are good if you have a high pair as your downcards — especially any *overpair*, or a pair bigger than any card on the board. Imagine that you have a pair of jacks and raise the betting before the flop, and two players call you. The flop comes ♠8, ♦5, ♣2. At this point, unless someone has a higher pair or a pocket pair of 8s, 5s, or 2s, you can safely assume that you have the best hand at the table. Admittedly, someone could make a straight or two pairs, but it's unlikely — why would anyone stay in for the flop with a hand like that?

Matching the highest card on the flop (giving you *top pair*) is generally a good hand — especially if you have a high kicker. You should bet top pair with a good kicker strongly, unless you see obvious flush or straight draws around or if another player bets strongly. With top pair and a low kicker, you have a marginal hand without a straight or flush draw. And middle pair or bottom pair is even less appealing without draws to a straight or flush — although you might stay in when facing weak betting.

If you don't have a pair, but you have high cards compared to the board (also called *overcards*), you shouldn't stay in the game if more than two other players are betting, and be sure to fold in the face of confident betting. To win from here, you need other players to miss the board, or you need to have a very favorable draw on the turn or the river.

Be particularly careful when the flop looks good — but not for you! Danger signals are high cards that don't make a pair for you, three cards in the same suit, and three cards in a sequence. Just because you didn't make a flush or straight doesn't mean someone else didn't.

Staying or dropping after the flop

If you make the best hand on the flop, you know what to do. Don't drive other players out if you think you have the best hand all the way to the river; try to bet in a way that keeps them in the game. But if you can see a chance that someone may outdraw you, make them pay for the chance.

With a draw for a flush or straight, you only want to call other bets if the pot odds make it worthwhile. Raising (with a semi-bluff) is a possible strategy.

With a draw to a straight, you may want to fold if three cards in the same suit show after the flop — anyone betting actively may have the flush to beat your straight . . . and you don't even have that straight yet!

It isn't enough to look at your cards and work out your chances of making the best hand. It's equally, if not more, important to analyze your relative strength in the hand. Your opponents want to make their hands, too. Try to recall who bet what before the flop — their activity at that point in the hand may give you a small clue about their holdings. Be sure to reassess the situation after the flop drops. Anyone who raised before the flop is probably left hanging by unconnected small cards — if you have two low pairs, you're likely to beat their hand, which figures to be a high pair at best.

Betting after the turn

The turn provides one more piece of information in the jigsaw. The whole picture is very nearly visible now, but two rounds of betting still remain, so you need to plan your strategy carefully.

When the turn hits the table, you need to take a long, hard look at what you have. If you stay in on the turn, you'll have a hard time dropping out at the river. Maybe that's why you call it the turn — your turning point in the hand.

From this point on, the bets in limit Hold 'Em are doubled. The stakes go up, and you have only one more card to make your hand, if you haven't done so already. On the bright side, you've obtained more information about your opponents' hands, so you're in a good position to reevaluate your hand.

As a general rule, if you believe you hold the best hand after the turn, don't be afraid to bet or raise in order to protect your hand. However, if your hand is clearly behind, caution is the word. This is the prime time to fold your hand, before you start throwing your money away by calling the expensive bets. And if you're drawing to complete your hand, be sure to have the correct pot odds when doing so. Calculate your outs (as I discuss in the earlier section, "Calculating pot odds") to see how much it will cost you to remain in the hand, and what the calculation of risk versus reward works out to.

Consider these specific positions:

>> **With what you know or believe to be the best hand of pairs or trips at the table,** get active in the betting — unless you believe there's a great chance that someone else has a flush or straight to beat you. If you don't see any obvious threats, assume you have the best hand. Bet now to make the other players pay to see another card. If you don't scare them out, you at least get them to put their money into the pot. If you're not aggressive on the turn, your opponents may get lucky on the draw — and if they don't, they will fold anyway!

>> **With a draw to a straight or flush,** continue calling or betting if the pot odds warrant it; but be wary of the possibilities that the upcards offer for other players. Completing your hand is disastrous if other players have hands to beat yours. At the turn, the probability of making your hand is substantially lower than on the flop, and the number of opponents willing to call is less. Checking and calling are often the right things to do, but betting is mostly wrong (unless you think you can scare opponents off).

WARNING

Most players err on the side of playing loose. They always find a reason to keep playing a hand. A better approach is to consider first whether you should drop. Ask yourself what on the board can beat you? Will you continue to play the hand if the betting escalates?

Crossing one more river

Deciding how to bet after the river usually depends on the caliber of your opponents. If you're playing against poor opposition who will call you with inappropriate hands, you should bet with most better-than-average hands — known as a *value bet*. However, against good opponents, avoid raising unless you know you can win a showdown. You have little to win and plenty to lose, because 90 percent of the time you only get calls from players who believe they have your hand beat; and on a bad day you may get raised!

However, once in a while you have to make a *crying call* against a raise. A crying call means you call, knowing you're beaten if the player has the hand they're representing; however, the pot odds mean that even if you calculate only a small chance they're bluffing, you have to throw a little more bad money after good hands. Let the pot size be the determining factor.

TIP

Folding a winning hand on the river is a *far* bigger mistake than losing one additional bet when you believe you've probably lost the hand. Think about it: If the pot is $40, and you have to call a $10 bet, you only need to be right about 1 in 5 times to make calling the profitable decision. When in doubt on the river, call in limit Hold 'Em, especially if the pot is large and you have a reasonable hand. In other varieties of the game, the odds may be far less favorable because the final bet may be so much bigger relative to the size of the pot.

If you think you have the best hand, try to figure out your opponent's most likely holdings and bet the amount you suspect they would call. You may want to stick to small bets when you have the best hand, because you may entice players to call with weaker hands. You can also go big by working out what bet would look like a bluff to the other players, based on your past strategy of bluffing at the table.

An alternative approach is to check with a good hand in order to induce a bluff from someone who thinks you missed your draw. The logic here is that because the player probably won't call your bet anyway, you should try to get them to part with money in whatever way you can.

WARNING

If you think the river card helps your opponents more than you, you should check. Your conservative play may be construed as a sign of weakness, and in a way it is. But if you do make a bet and the other players didn't make their hands, they'll fold. However, if they don't fold, you're almost certainly beaten, and you'll probably face a raise. If your opponent bets after you check, you can call; this costs you the same amount as making the initial bet, but you face no risk of a raise.

Bluffing

A *bluff* is a bet or raise made in an attempt to win a pot with little or nothing as far as a quality hand goes. The goal of the bluff is to get your opponent to fold immediately, because you'll lose if they make the call. My advice is the same advice *Punch* magazine gave 150 years ago to young people about getting married — don't!

Bluffing is overrated in limit Hold 'Em. The other players can call your bluffs for the first couple of betting rounds without spending too much, which means they have a chance to catch a hand that beats the one you're representing. When players are on a draw or have completed a pair (even if it's the lowest pair possible), they often want to see what the next card will bring, especially in loose games (and even more so on the Internet). In other words, when playing in a loose game, punish the other players for staying in with bad hands when you have a good hand. Make them pay, not receive, for their natural tendencies. At no-limit, the opportunities for bluffing are rather better because you may be able to browbeat players into folding rather more easily. However, the penalties for failure are more expensive.

Don't bluff bad players — they don't necessarily know when they're beaten. Even though you may present a good case for holding a fine hand, they may simply not notice — a case of "you can't fool me, I'm too ignorant." And don't try to bluff when a large number of players are still in the game; the chance of them all dropping like flies is too small, because someone figures to have enough of a hand to call you. The best time to bluff is when you have only one opponent who isn't betting strongly.

You must assess how tight or loose the players left in the game are. The tighter the opponent, the more likely a bluff is to work. You have to know your opponents, which is why figuring out their temperaments is so important. If you're a tight player, it may not be so risky to bluff early on and get caught. Everyone else will remember it, and maybe they'll stay in on your good hands!

In comparison to a full-out bluff, a semi-bluff has more to offer. A *semi-bluff* is similar to a bluff in that you bet, check-raise, or raise without the best hand at the table, but you don't exactly have garbage. For example, a semi-bluff would be betting with ♥A, ♥5 in the pocket when the flop comes ♥Q, ♦10, ♥7. You represent yourself to have a good hand, when in fact all you have is a draw to a flush.

A semi-bluff has a couple more ways to win than a bluff does. With a semi-bluff, you can win if your opponents fold, or you can improve your hand to make it the best at the table.

Here's another example: Say you hold two, suited high cards in clubs and raise in late position before the flop. When the flop comes up with two clubs and an ace, you can bet again if circumstances warrant, representing a pair of aces but with the other clubs as outs for getting a flush.

One important function a bluff serves, especially in late position, is the stealing of the blinds posted by the first two players after the dealer and any players in early position that call with marginal hands, or *limp in*.

Stealing blinds

Although bluffing may not be such a great strategy for limit Hold 'Em, *stealing blinds* — a variation on the strategy of bluffing — can be a good way to increase your profits.

In a regular game of limit Hold 'Em, you generally get good enough pot odds (see the earlier section, "Calculating pot odds") to show a profit if your steal success is close to half your attempts. Even if another player calls your stealing bet to stay in, you still have a chance to win the pot: You may get a good flop, or your opponent may get a bad one, and you win the hand with a bet right there on the flop. The flop may also bring an apparently threatening card (usually an ace or a king). Now you can win the pot by betting and representing convincingly that you have a big pair.

Part of your edge in stealing is positional. In late position, if you don't win the hand outright, you get to bet late on subsequent rounds and are more likely to get called when you have a good hand if you've built a reputation as a bluffer.

Another reason to try steal blinds is because it adds an extra element of deception to your overall game. If you only call and raise with legitimately playable hands, you become easy to read and will never get any action from your bets, so you won't win as much as you could on your good hands. One bright side to becoming easy to read is that you can steal blinds with bad hands by switching your strategy. And if someone catches you in a steal, you're suddenly unpredictable!

The most obvious moment to steal blinds is when you're the dealer or small blind and everyone has folded to you. You raise from this position to induce the other blind or blinds to fold. If you get a call, you may have to rely on the flop to help you out. If you get a raise from one of the blinds, you should usually hold on to your hand, even if you're trying to steal with a poor hand. Unless you're playing no-limit (where calling a raise is essentially throwing money away if the raiser goes all-in after the flop), a re-raise from the blind often gives you enough pot odds to see the flop. And if you fold here, your opponents may start re-raising you more often!

If you raise and get called before the flop, you get a chance to see the flop. You can now decide whether to continue the bluff. Knowing your opponents is key here; it helps to have a feel as to how likely they are to call, no matter what they have — and whether you have a reputation as a tight or a loose player.

If you're the small blind, you can steal with almost anything. From the other positions, flush-draw hands are reasonable for an attempted steal. Good draws give you two chances to win — you may draw to complete your hand if you don't drive the other players out.

Seizing Opportunities to Play Hold 'Em

You'd have to be a hermit these days not to see Texas Hold 'Em wherever you turn. Hold 'Em is the most popular variety of Poker when it comes to tournaments, and thus is the game most commonly on television, played by both experts and celebrities. Online resources for Hold 'Em abound, as well.

» **On television:** The first characteristic about Hold 'Em you see on television is how aggressive and generally accurate the professionals are. They can read their opponents' body language and betting styles — but they still make mistakes.

Watching the World Series of Poker on television in the United States allows you to see plenty of the subtleties of the game that you need to think about. In addition to being informative, the games are fun to watch, with intelligent commentary aimed at players of varying skill levels.

» **In tournaments:** Tournament Hold 'Em games may differ from what you and your friends play at home or at the casino in two main ways: The game is often no-limit, and after you squander your chips, you're out of the game. This means you have different calculations to make, and survival is paramount. You also need to make sure you have enough chips to participate in a meaningful way.

To play tournament Poker, contact the nearest casino and find out when it runs events. Most big casinos have more than one tournament a week, and on weekends, you're almost guaranteed the opportunity to compete. With prizes often going to the top 10 percent of the field, playing tournaments is an opportunity to gain experience without spending significant amounts of money or to pick up a decent prize if it happens to be your lucky day. Be sure to check out *Poker For Dummies* by Richard D. Harroch and Lou Krieger for more details on tournament Poker.

» **Online:** The subject of Internet Poker is big enough to be addressed in a separate book, *Winning at Internet Poker For Dummies,* by my colleagues, Mark Harlan and Chris Derossi. I won't tread on their toes by telling you all the secrets they reveal, but they make the following recommendations if you're looking for a site to play. The sites on their shortlist include https://www.partypoker.com/, https://www.pokerstars.bet/?no_redirect=1, https://www.888.com/, and https://gamesgrid.com/.

Chapter **23**

Omaha

A ll Poker is a gamble, or course; that is what makes it such a thrill. But Omaha may be the game for Poker players who like to win. There can only be one winner on every hand, but Omaha may appeal to you if you like to combine the thrill of gambling with sound financial strategy. If you play Omaha well, you will win — if only because it is such a tough game that very few people play it properly.

BEFORE HAND

To play Omaha High/Low (also referred to as Omaha Hi/Low Split, Omaha/8, Omaha Split, or Omaha Eight-or-Better), you need the following:

» **At least five players:** Somewhere between seven and ten is ideal, but you can cope with fewer than seven.

» **One standard deck of 52 cards:** No jokers are needed.

» **A table and some chips or counters:** Ideally, you should use chips of at least two different denominations (different colors or sizes) to make the accounting easier. Money is a perfectly acceptable alternative to chips, and most of the time the chips represent a money denomination. In fact, the game is almost always played for money. If you play at a small betting limit table, such as $2/$4 (see Chapter 19 for a discussion of betting limits), you need to have at least $100 in chips.

Getting to Know Omaha High/Low

Omaha High/Low (I discuss Omaha High later in this chapter) is similar in many ways to Texas Hold 'Em (see Chapter 22), a popular game played live in home games and casinos, on the Internet, or on television. The two games have many points in common, but Omaha boasts some important differences:

>> To make your hand at Omaha, you're dealt four cards face-down (your *hole cards* or *downcards*) rather than two as in Hold 'Em.

>> The dealer places five subsequent cards face-up (on the *board*), but, as in Hold 'Em, not all at once. First comes the *flop* of three community cards, and then a fourth card (the *turn*), and then the fifth and final card (the *river*).

>> The flexibility in the number of cards you can use from the community upcards and your downcards is more restricted than in Hold 'Em. You must use two and only two of your four hole cards plus three and only three of the five community cards to make up your best five-card hand.

Just to make matters more complicated, you can use a different two hole cards for your high hand and your low hand (they can also be the opposite two or have one card in common) as well as using a different selection of three cards from the board. As you can see, all these options require you to think on your feet.

Because you must use two cards from your hand and three from the board to make an Omaha High/Low hand, your hand must *cooperate* with the board. You can think of it, if you prefer, as always needing three from the board, as opposed to two cards from your hand — but the result is the same.

Because the final hands in Omaha can be a little hard to read, the rule is that the cards speak for themselves, which means that when you turn your hand over in the showdown, you do not have to state what you have. The cards themselves make the claim — so that you will not be punished for a verbal misstatement.

Paying attention to the high hands and low hands

Omaha High/Low is a game with the possibility of two winning hands on any deal: the high hand and a low hand. However, not just *any* low hand qualifies. To be eligible, the hand must consist of five different cards all lower than or equal to an 8.

In practice, this condition means that often you have no qualifying low hand:

Imagine that three of the five upcards are higher than an 8 — say, the ♦9, ♣J, ♥7, ♠Q, and ♠4. If this is so, then even if all four of your hole cards are lower than an 8, you can't make a qualifying low hand because you may not use more than two of your hole cards, and because the three lowest upcards are 4, 7, and 9, you can't make a low qualifying hand.

Equally, if the five upcards have a low pair (say, ♦7, ♣J, ♥7, ♠Q, and ♠4), you can't make a qualifying low hand because all five cards in the low hand must be different. However, a low hand can qualify if it's a straight (in fact, A-2-3-4-5 is the best possible low hand) or a flush.

The pot is divided half each for the high and low winner, if there is a qualifying low hand. All the pot goes to the high winner if there is no qualifying low hand. Bear in mind that each half may need to be split if there are ties — and this is relatively common at Omaha High/Low. For example, whenever 3-4-5 appears on the board, it is relatively likely that more than one player will stay in with A-2 and be entitled to a share of the pot.

TIP

Hold your cards carefully. In Texas Hold 'Em, you can easily keep your cards hidden from your neighbor, but in Omaha games you need to practice holding all four of your cards in a manner where you can see them and your opponents can't. It's important — unless you have a perfect memory for suits — to check your hand to see if you have prospects for a flush when two cards in the same suit appear in the flop. If you do need to go back and look at your cards, make sure you do it the same way on hands when you know perfectly well what you hold, so no one can draw any inference from your actions.

TIP

Reading a low hand can be difficult. The best way to think of your low hand is as a five-digit number, putting the highest digit first. If your hole cards are 7, 7, A, 2 and the board cards are 9, 6, Q, 5, 2, your best possible low hand is 7, 6, 5, 2, A, or 7, 6, 5, 2, 1. A player with hole cards of A, 3 or A, 4 can beat you (by making 6, 5, 3, 2, 1 or 6, 5, 4, 2, 1, respectively), and a player with 3-4 can make 6-5-4-3-2.

Betting

Here's some good news if you've mastered the betting structure of Hold 'Em (see Chapter 22): Betting at Omaha follows exactly the same pattern. You don't typically have to place an ante, but after all players receive four cards each, face-down and one at a time, the two hands to the left of the dealer make an initial blind bet. The *small blind* to the dealer's immediate left puts in half of the *big blind*, which is what the player to their left must put up. A round of betting follows — which may feature both calls of the big blind and raising — before the flop. The dealer ceremonially takes the top card off the deck and puts it aside (this is called *burning* a card and has no real significance; it's just what's done). Then three communal cards are turned over, which triggers another round of betting, followed by an opportunity to bet after the fourth upcard (the turn) and then the final round of betting after the fifth upcard (the river). The dealer burns a card before turning over the turn and the river. In a *limit game* (a game with set betting limits), the maximum bet doubles after the turn.

Just as in Hold 'Em, you can play Omaha High/Low as a limit game, a pot-limit, or no-limit (a rarity in casino settings). (See Chapter 19 for an explanation of these terms.)

Playing out a typical Omaha High/Low hand

Figure 23-1 shows a typical Omaha High/Low hand. Player eight is the dealer, so player nine puts in the small blind of $2, and player ten puts in the big blind of $5, assuming a limit game of $5 to $10. (Remember these numbers refer to the size of the bets in the early and late rounds respectively, not the size of the blinds; see Chapter 19 for a discussion on limit betting.)

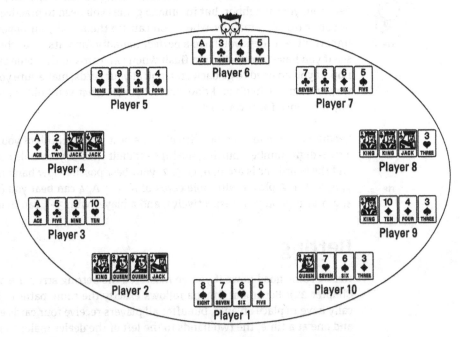

FIGURE 23-1:
A typical
Omaha hand.

Look at the ten hands in Figure 23-1 and assess them according to the criteria of needing either a flexible low base (including an ace) or the potential for high success, including an ace or a high pair with a number of suited high cards.

- >> **Player one** is first to act, with their pile of junk. Yes, they have the possibility of a straight and a slim chance of a flush, but they can only use two cards from their hand — so either of those possibilities is a long shot, and they have no realistic expectation of winning, even if they make their hand. So they fold.

- >> **Player two** has a number of high cards and suited combinations; enough to call the big blind's forced $5 bet.

- >> **Player three** has an ace — but that's about it. With no other real prospects, they decide it's not worth wasting a bet and fold.

- >> **Player four** has a decent low combination and a high pair. They call the bet. In a later position (if they sat toward the end of the round of betting as opposed to being in the middle), they may even raise.

- >> **Player five** has a great high hand — if they could use three of their hole cards; but, as you know, they can't. They fold — 9s are not the stuff of big wins; they're a good second-place hand.

REMEMBER

It may be counterintuitive, but remember that three of a kind in your hand is far, far, worse than a pair; you can only use two of them — and your chances of making a set decline dramatically if one of them is wasted in your downcards.

- >> **Player six** has a fine possibility for a low hand. With four working cards, they raise the bet $5.

- >> **Player seven's** low cards are just not low enough, and their high cards are not high enough, so they fold.

- >> **Player eight** stays in on the strength their kings. Their ♣J is a useful builder for a club flush, too.

- >> **Player nine** (with about as bad a hand as you can imagine) folds.

- >> **Player ten** has a couple of decent cards for a high hand — not enough to stay in, however. If their ♦Q were suited with a low card, they may have changed their mind.

So, after players two and four call the raise, with players two, four, six, and eight remaining in, the flop comes up: ♣A, ♣10, and ♥2, as shown in Figure 23-2.

After the flop, the betting is still at the lower limit of $5. There are two upcards still to come. Player two is first to bet now because players nine, ten, and one folded; they have fine chances of making a straight but worries that someone may make a flush. They bet $5, and player four calls with their top pair. Player six has fine possibilities for both high and low hands, so they raise the bet, and player eight, with a draw to the best possible (or *nut*) flush, stays in.

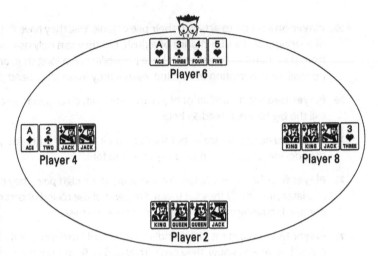

FIGURE 23-2:
The flop comes
with four players
remaining.

The turn card is the ♦4 — great news for player six, who has made the nut low hand (A, 2, 4 from the board and 5, 3 from their hand). Player two and four check, and player six bets $10 — the limit doubled up to $10 on the turn — and all the players call to stay in.

The river card is the ♣4, leaving players two and four with only two pairs. (Remember, player two can only use two of their downcards, not all three of the king-queen-jack.) Player six happily bets, and player eight raises because they made the nut flush, and because they have the highest club not on the board, the king. The other two players, two and four, drop out, and after a raise and re-raise, the remaining players split the pot.

Winning High/Low Strategy

Identifying what makes a good High/Low hand is critical to your success. You also need to decide what flops allow you to continue on in the hand.

Forming good starting hands

In order to avoid landing in the dreaded *muck* area of the table, where folded hands go to die, your High/Low hand generally needs more than one dimension; in other words, you should hold more than just one pair of promising cards:

>> **For a low hand,** you need either three or four low cards of different ranks, one of which should be an ace. The more different low cards you have, the

better your chance of using two of those four cards to make the best low hand. You want to maximize your chances of using what the board gives you. If one of your low cards shares the same suit as your ace, you're in an even better situation — you have a chance to make the best flush (and possible high hand), too.

Even when you have four cards below 8, there's a pretty fair chance that the board cards will consist of three or more cards above 9 (thus making a low hand impossible). And even if low cards hit the board, they may duplicate the cards in your hand.

>> **For high hands,** your best starting point is having high pairs that also match suits with the other cards in your hand. That augments your chances of making a flush, along with a set or a full house.

Another possibility is to try to combine a high pair with another neighboring high card (a *connecting* card) to introduce the possibility of making a straight.

TIP

Don't stay in a pot with only a high pair unless you have aces or kings. You need to have some flush chances (by having more than one card in the same suit as your high card) or straight chances as well, by having connected cards (such as A–K or A–Q). And even with a high pair of aces or kings, if you have no connecting cards, you can call a decent bet, but you shouldn't stay in a pot with only a pair if another player raises. Any low pair (2s through 8s) isn't a good high hand, unless you hit a *set* (three of a kind) on the flop.

Any time you can combine a high pair with suited cards or connecting court cards, your chances before the flop increase dramatically. Indeed, having any four cards 9 or better gives you some reasonable possibilities.

REMEMBER

The aim in Omaha is to *scoop the pot*, which means having the best high hand when no low possibilities come — or having a hand that wins both high and low.

The best possible starting hands combine high and low possibilities — such as beginning with an ace and 2. If you add any low card or cards to the mix, you're very well placed. On its own, an A-2 hand is a one-dimensional hand, although it's generally worth staying in for the flop. However, an ace-2 or ace-3 with a high pair is a splendid hand. An ace with any three high cards or three moderately low cards also gives you plenty of possibilities, and an ace with any suited card gives you additional flush chances.

If you don't have an ace, the best starting hands are 2-3-4-5 (or switch in a 6 or 7 for one of those cards), 10-J-Q-K, 9-10-J-Q, or a hand with two high pairs. For all the high hands in the last two paragraphs, having two cards in the same suit — or even better, two pairs of cards in the same suits — improves your hand by adding in flush possibilities.

Try to play premium starting hands only. Yes, you can mix up your strategy, depending on your starting position, and you don't want to gain the reputation of only playing great hands. But at the same time, if you play weak hands, you will get what you expect (and deserve).

Middle cards tend to be unhelpful to either high or low hands. Unless you get a lucky flop, 6s, 7s, 8s, and 9s sap your potential for almost everything!

Winning hands at Omaha High/Low

You may well ask why you need good hands in order to stay in for the flop, particularly by comparison to Hold 'Em (see Chapter 22), where you are encouraged to stay in on occasion with only moderate hands.

The answer is that the quality of a winning high hand at Omaha is far better on average than at Hold 'Em, because the strength of everybody's downcards is so much better. Because you are dealt four cards face-down rather than two, you have six possible permutations and combinations of those cards from which to try to form a suitable hand. Imagine, for example, that you receive ♠A ♠Q ♥Q, and ♥J. Before the flop comes, you may be going for a straight or a flush in two different suits, and you may be going for a set of queens; so many combinations, it's hard to keep track of them all!

But, as I emphasize throughout this chapter, you must have a good hand (and preferably a multidimensional hand) even to stay in for the flop. It isn't necessary to have both a good high and low combination, but you must have a good high hand or a good low hand.

Because everybody has so many starting possibilities, if you stay in before the flop with a hand that doesn't appear to have a good chance to win, you throw good money after bad cards.

Winning at Omaha High/Low

In Chapter 22, I suggest that selective aggression is the key to winning in Texas Hold 'Em. The idea is to play only the good hands, and to bet heavily with them. At Omaha High/Low, it may appear that you carry this idea to the extreme — to the uninitiated.

The key to winning at Omaha High/Low is twofold: First, only play hands that have very good high possibilities or that offer at least two possible combinations of straights and flushes. For the low side, only play hands with very good low possibilities; this generally means at least three different low cards. Aces are key;

although I would be oversimplifying, it would be fair to say that playing for a low hand without an ace is almost always a losing proposition, and almost all good high Omaha hands include an ace. Yes, you may have hands such as ♠Q, ♠J, ♥Q, ♥J, but these are very much the exceptions, not the rule.

Surviving the waiting game

The problem with playing Omaha High/Low is also, in a way, one of its attractive features: If you wait for a good starting hand and then play it aggressively, you find yourself sitting around for much of the game. The good news is that because everyone else is probably playing far too many hands, when you do get a good hand, you have a good chance to win.

In Hold 'Em, you find that you need to exploit a small edge frequently to win, depending on how good your opponents are and how high the betting limits are set. In Omaha High/Low, only playing good starting hands puts you at a big advantage. By the time the flop has been turned, you've seen seven out of the nine cards available on any hand. Accordingly, most of the uncertainty has already been decided. Yes, you can get badly beaten when the river comes up just right for your opponent, but if you only go to the river with suitable hands, believe me, the luck tends to even out very quickly.

TIP

Before you start to play Omaha at a casino or online, watch how often the players stay in for the flop. With a table of 10 players, you want to see more people staying in. The looser the game, the easier it is to win. If fewer than four players stay in for the flop on average, find an easier table!

Playing for position

Being one of the last players to bet in each round is a big advantage. You get to see the volume of betting before having to commit yourself, and you can also infer what the other players at the table are likely to have from their betting patterns. However, the quality of your cards is more important than position. Don't stay in with a bad hand for the flop solely because you're last to bet.

TIP

To determine your position, assume that the first third of the table to bet (which includes the big and small blinds) are in early position, the next third are in middle position, and the last third are in late position. The later you are, the more you should be inclined to stay in on marginal hands when no one has raised, and to raise with good hands.

Your position may affect your strategy before the flop. With good hands where you want to go only for the high hand, you should raise early. Because these hands tend to play better with fewer players in the pot, you raise to narrow the field. However, good hands where you want to go low tend to play better against a bigger field, as you figure to beat the field if the flop comes up right for you, no matter how many players are in. Thus you want the pot to be large and have many players in it; therefore, you tend to call early. However, when you're in late position and many players have already called, feel free to raise with a low-only hand. Because the players have stayed in for one bet already, they figure to call another bet. With a good two-way hand (where you are hoping to win both high and low), you may call early, but you should consider raising in late position.

Planning a strategy after the flop

The flop normally indicates to the table what sort of high hand is likely to win the hand — and whether a low hand is possible at all. Consider the following possible flops:

>> **If three unconnected cards appear,** say ♠Q, ♣9, and ♦2, the best high hands are those that can make a set, a straight or flush, or a long-shot four of a kind. Failing that, having a pair of aces or kings among your downcards or the connecting J-10 with a draw for a straight leaves you inclined to bet.

Don't stay in by calling with only a draw for a low hand if the flop comes with two high cards, and don't call with only a draw for a high hand if the flop comes with two low cards. It doesn't pay to chase drawing hands, especially in a big pot where other players may have unbeatable hands, even if you do make your hand. And there's nothing worse than making your draw and still losing.

>> **If a flush draw comes up,** consisting of two or three cards in the same suit, any time you have two high cards in that suit, you'll be inclined to stay in, and with the nut flush draw (the ace or perhaps the king of the suit among your hole cards), you should bet (especially if your two cards are A-2 through 8 so you can win the high and low). Two low cards in the suit aren't nearly so attractive, of course; the odds are that someone can make a better flush than you.

When trying to calculate your chances of winning after the flop on a draw, realize that every successful draw, or *out,* gives you about a 4 percent chance of winning the hand either on the turn or the river. For example, if you have six outs, you have about a 24 percent chance of improving — less than 1 in 4 odds.

>> **If a straight draw comes up,** be more optimistic if you have a high straight draw rather than a low straight draw, which may finish up second. When the flop looks like ♠10, ♦8, ♣7, having a 9 and 6 as your hole cards is good, but

having J, 9 is considerably better. Even in the latter case, you must beware of a jack or 9 turning up subsequently. For example, if a 9 comes on the river, a player with Q-J beats you.

>> **If a pair comes up,** four of a kind is likely unbeatable, but even a third card making a set leaves you well placed if the set is a high one, and pairing up to make a full house puts you in an even stronger position. Still, consider a flop of ♥9, ♥7, and ♠7. A ♣7 as a downcard gives you *trip* sevens (or a set of 7s), but another middle card may give someone else a straight draw, and more hearts may set up the possibility of a flush. The quality of winning high hands at Omaha High/Low is far better than in games such as Hold 'Em.

>> **If two or three low cards come up,** concentrate on whether you have the nut low hand. For example, if the flop comes as ♠7, ♦5, ♣3, with A-2 you may feel that you're in the pole position; however, if a 2 (or an ace) is turned up, your hand not only gets worse, but you also leave another player with A, 4 (or 2, 4, as the case may be) with a better hand than you. That doesn't mean you shouldn't raise the bet — indeed you should — but it does mean that you should be aware of the possibility that bad things may happen.

>> **If you are going for low,** the odds are rather against you from the outset, and an unfavorable flop can really dampen your chances. If it does, don't stay around for the denouement. Even if you do win the low hand, you're competing for only half the pot. Even worse, you may be against other players with A-2, in which case you have to split your share of the pot — sometimes referred to as being *quartered.* By contrast, if the flop contains two cards that cooperate with your A-2, you only need to hit one more helping card on the turn or the river to make your hand, so your chances of making the low go up to 70 percent — more attractive odds!

TIP

When you have a hand consisting of high cards and a decent flop comes, you should be more inclined to stay in than if you have a low hand and get a moderately good flop. Why? Because if the flop consists of high cards, the hand will probably produce only one winner, and you may scoop the pot. With the low hand, you always know the pot will be split with the high, unless you make the nut low straight or flush.

Flopping and dropping

As a general rule, after the flop turns up, you should stay in only if you think you already have the best hand — either high or low — or have a reasonable chance to make the best hand on a favorable draw or with a sensible two-way hand. In this context, a reasonable chance means better than 1 in 4, but the precise calculation depends on how many players are still in and how much is in the pot.

Don't stay in if you can see that while you have a decent (say 1 in 3) chance of improving your hand, it still won't be the best hand at the table. If you're waiting for a queen- or jack-high flush draw, how likely is it that someone else at the table can beat your flush?

Just as dropping before the flop is easier to do in theory than in practice, dropping when the flop doesn't fit your hand is also harder to do than it should be. If you go high and see low cards on the flop or go low and see high cards, don't stay in. The temptation to remain, hoping for miracles, is sometimes just too strong, but you can resist it!

TIP

In games where many people stay in to see the flop, a good rule of thumb is to assume that if a hand is possible, someone either has it or is drawing to it. If you don't have it, you should drop now.

REMEMBER

Bluffing in Omaha is something you probably shouldn't do as an inexperienced player. The hands tend to vary so much that the bluff stands a proportionately smaller chance of success than in games such as Texas Hold 'Em.

Playing on the turn

You generally know when you have the best hand (or the *nuts*) when the turn hits the felt. But if you're considering remaining in for the river, here are some strategies for betting and warning signals that may suggest dropping instead:

>> If you see a pair on the board after the turn, consider dropping unless you have three of a kind or better. Conversely, with the board showing three of a suit, drop unless you have a flush or better.

>> If you hit your flush or straight by the turn, you should bet hard, and you may even consider *check-raising* (checking when the action is on you and raising after another player's bet) if you're certain someone will bet (bet outright if you have any doubt). You could easily have a set or two pairs against you, and these players could make a full house on the river if you allow them to remain in the hand cheaply or for free. Make sure they don't get to look at the river for nothing.

>> If you need a draw to win the hand, and you have to decide whether to call a bet, calculate the number of possible winning draws, or *outs*. By doing so, you calculate how much it costs you to stay in the hand, and you see whether the odds justify your staying in.

Say, for example, you're playing pot-limit Omaha (where the maximum bet equals the amount of money in the pot at the time of the bet); the player in front of you bets the pot (say, $20 to make a total of $40 in the pot). Your hand is ♠A, ♥Q, ♦J, ♠10, with the four upcards coming ♣Q, ♠9, ♦10, ♥2. No low hands are possible, so the best high hand will win. If you put your opponent on a set, you need to hit one of the outstanding queens or 10s (of which there are four, assuming your opponent doesn't have trip queens or 10s) in order to make a full house of queens and 10s or any of the kings or 8s (of which there are eight) to make a straight. If you have to put in an amount equivalent to the pot to match the last bet, you need odds of 1 in 3 to bet because by making the bet of $20 you stand to win $60. Your chances of winning on the hand are only 12 out of 44 — there are 12 winning cards, and you can see 8 of the 52 cards, so there are 44 other cards. Given that your chances of winning are less than a third, you should fold.

Playing on the river

Generally, you should only stay in when the river drops if you think you have the best hand — be it high or low. With the best low hand and any sort of play for the high hand, bet heavily — who knows, you may force out the high players and scoop the pot. The same applies when you have the best high hand — you may be able to force out the low players, or no one may have a low hand. Conversely, if you have what you believe is the top straight, but you think someone else may have the same hand — causing you to have to split the high pot — you may want to take your foot off the accelerator.

TIP

If you hit your hand on the river, you may want to bet out instead of check-raising an opponent, because if you check, so may your opponent. By mixing your strategy here, you make your opponents fear the check-raise so that they may be afraid to bet on the river. This strategy lets you see some showdowns more cheaply in the future.

Omaha High

Omaha High is a simplified version of Omaha High/Low. As you may expect, you play the game in the exact way you play High/Low, without the low option.

REMEMBER

Because Omaha High players all start with four cards, if five other players stay in after the flop, the game is comparable to a Texas Hold 'Em game against 30 other players — because the five players each have six possible hands to choose from. So, you really need a good hand to win the average game; the fewer the players, the better chance you have with a marginal hand, of course.

If, for example, four suited cards hit the board and several players remain in the hand, it isn't a lock that someone has a flush. To make that flush, someone who has stayed in the hand has to hold two cards in that suit, not just one.

Low cards are irrelevant now, unless you get lucky with low straights, sets, or flushes. What you want are high pairs and suited hands — either singly, with two or three cards in one suit, or doubly, which means having two pairs in two suits.

The best starting hands are A-A-J-10, A-A-K-K, and A-A-9-10. In all cases, you want to be *double suited*. With the third hand, for example, you want to draw flushes in two suits, in which case you have the best possible flush, a draw for three aces, or even a draw for a straight with your 9-10.

Any other starting hands should feature high cards, preferably in pairs, or connecting cards, and should provide flush possibilities. Connected hands have more winning combinations; and the more chances you have to make a hand on the flop, the better your results will be.

WARNING

Avoid playing hands with limited promise, where one of the cards is irrelevant. For example, with a hand such as ♠10, ♥10, ♥9, ♦4, your fourth card is likely irrelevant, which reduces your chances of making a decent hand.

Any time you have two reasonably high pairs in a hand, such as J-J-9-9, you should stay in for the flop. Your chances of hitting a set aren't spectacular, but they're better than 1 in 4. Bear in mind, however, that three jacks isn't a guaranteed winning hand in Omaha High!

7

The Part of Tens

Do you want to know how to improve your temper, or temperament, or simply become a better player by sharpening your memory? Well, nothing is impossible, if you focus on this part of the book.

I can't promise you the earth, but if you read up on the tips in this part, you discover ways to improve your technique. I also provide you with a short list of places to go after you finish reading this book and catch the card-playing fever.

Chapter 24

Ten Ways to Improve Your Game and Have More Fun

P laying cards should be fun, so I don't want to catch you studying this chapter like you do a homework assignment. Just keep these tips and hints in mind as you play — you'll find yourself playing better and having a better time, too.

Treat Your Partner with Respect

When playing a game with a partner — like Euchre (Chapter 10) or Canasta (Chapter 5) — you may think at times that your partner is actually playing for the opponents. They may totally misinterpret what cards you want played, or they may blindly lead a card that the opponents have been waiting for the whole game.

No matter what happens, never criticize your partner at the table; they want to do as well as they can, too! If you upset them, you end up with a partner who may not be pulling their weight for your team, and you may relax your opponents. Why do that?

If your partner does something stupid but gets a good result, take that moment to let them know (courteously) that they may have committed a technical inaccuracy. If their action gets a bad result, don't comment on it unless they ask you to.

If you have a misunderstanding, don't correct it at the table unless the same problem is likely to come up again in the very near future. Make note of the incident, and discuss it later with your partner, if possible. Don't discuss the problem too soon; everyone has an ego and automatically becomes defensive, so wait for your competitive fires to die down before revisiting the scene of the crime.

Give Yourself a Reality Check

Almost all card games incorporate some element of chance, so bear in mind that you can't be perfect at a game; you should try your best, but don't get angry with yourself if you make a mistake, it tends to impair your judgment as well as reduce the amount of enjoyment you get from playing.

You can't win every hand. Many times in the course of a card game, you'll make a wrong move, or the dealer may give you the absolute worst cards in history. When fate put some obstacle in your way, just move on to the next hand without comment, if you can. Your ability to absorb bad results without comment may throw off your opponents. Besides, such behavior shows a lot of class.

TIP

If you are playing a game where you can have pencil and paper handy, or if you are playing on the Internet with the ability to keep a record, write down your mistakes and review them after the game. You can allow yourself to make mistakes, but if they bother you, and you really want to improve your game, writing down your moves can help you avoid making the same mistake twice.

Keep Your Celebrations to Yourself

At some point, you'll experience the thrill of victory — whether you win the game or just make a smart play. When one of these glorious moments hits you, you must resist the urge to proclaim your victory from the highest mountaintop.

Never gloat when you get a good result, no matter how aggravating your opponents are, and even if they've won every single game that night. When you celebrate a victory, you show that you lack control — which can be good information for your opponents to use against you in future match-ups.

Besides, gloating openly about a win doesn't give you nearly the same thrill as resting secure in the knowledge that you just pulled off something great. Irritating your opponents with a win proves infinitely more satisfying than irritating them with your mannerisms or comments.

REMEMBER

Record your opponents' disasters, too, if they seem relevant to you, so you can be sure that you don't make their mistakes.

Know When the Time Is Ripe

You can't be in top form all the time. Sometimes, you may not have enough time or energy to devote yourself fully to the game. Or maybe you just don't feel like playing.

TIP

Whatever the reason, if you can't give yourself fully to the game, don't play, particularly if the game involves money. If your heart and mind aren't in the game, you won't play well, and the people you play with won't have any fun.

If you're in the middle of a game and don't feel well, take a break in mid-session, even you only wash your face. Do anything that you can think of to break a sequence of bad luck.

REMEMBER

To be courteous to the other players, try to keep your break to around 5 minutes. You don't have to make excuses to take your break, as long as you aren't running away from the table after every hand. Everyone needs a break from time to time.

Cut Yourself Off

If you're playing for money, don't try to recover your losses by desperate gambling. Scrambling to get back to even only makes your situation worse.

If you have a set limit and you lose that amount, stop playing. Don't even think about going out to get more money and trying to recoup your losses. And don't play for stakes larger than you can afford to lose. If you do, the idea of losing makes you so uncomfortable that you don't play your best.

Even if you aren't playing for money, remember that the secret to a long life is knowing when it's time to go. If you're not having a good night with the cards, don't hesitate to call it quits.

Paint a Picture of Your Opponents' Cards

When you first start playing a card game, you may have your hands full just remembering the basics. As you become more comfortable with the play, however, you should start thinking about what cards your opponents may hold. You can slowly assemble a picture of the other players' cards by observing the clues that they give:

>> **Watch their body language.** Many less-tricky players openly show their disappointment about bad cards and don't hide their joy over good cards. If you know a certain player reacts this way, watch them closely. However, don't forget that a truly savvy player may try to throw you off the track by conning you with a false reaction (smiling when they have bad cards, for example).

>> **Listen to the bidding.** If your game has a bidding phase (such as in Bridge — see Chapter 12), take the opportunity to get information about your opponents' cards. Your opponents normally base their bids on the cards they actually hold.

>> **Watch for negative inferences.** Observing the cards that your opponent doesn't want can help you discern which cards they may be after.

REMEMBER

If you can, don't focus on the problems in your hand to the exclusion of other players' cards. One of the biggest challenges that I have when playing cards is that if I have a problem as to what card I should play, I can be oblivious to the other, seemingly irrelevant cards being played around me — until I suddenly realize that those cards weren't so irrelevant.

March to the Beat of Your Own Drum

You may have played with this person before. You know the one — they practically make you punch a time clock when it's your turn to play, and they start tapping their fingers on the table if they think you're taking too much time deciding what to do. What a drag Speedy is, not just to you, but to everyone at the table.

Play the game at your own tempo, not that of the dominant (in their own mind) player at the table. Many players get an edge from playing fast and encourage other players to match their tempo. Don't fall into their traps; keep your own time, unless everyone at the table is so clearly comfortable with a faster pace than your own that you can see that you are slowing everyone down.

If you are a fast player, you can play at that tempo and hope to persuade your opponents to err. But at the same time, don't try to rush your opponents by drumming your fingers or otherwise making them uncomfortable.

Talk Through the Cards

Mentally speak the cards you see to yourself as they're played. By verbalizing the cards (internally), you get a separate part of the brain working on the cards. The more ways you can set the cards in your mind, the better chance you have of recalling them.

REMEMBER

Don't move your lips as you do your mental inventory of the cards. Just as your first-grade teacher scolded you for moving your lips as you read, your fellow players will never let you live it down if they see you mouthing out all the cards. In addition, you don't want to give away how you've developed such a good memory for cards — the other players may catch on to your trick and start to do it, too, thus eliminating your advantage.

Count Down to Victory

Knowing how many cards your opponents have in a suit can help in some games, such as in Hearts (see Chapter 13). Count back from 13 if you're missing only a few cards in a particular suit. For example, if you're playing Bridge and you hold eight cards in a suit between your hand and your partner's hand, your opponents have only five cards. So as their cards in the suit appear, count back from five.

An alternative approach for a particular suit is to count the cards as they're played instead of adding in the cards in your own hand. This works well in games where you can't see your partner's hand.

TIP

Keeping a count on all the suits can be exhausting. Try to work out the key suits at the start of the hand and focus on those, not on all the suits. In some games, such as Hearts, you may need to focus only on the low cards, whereas in, say, Gin Rummy you may only need to focus on your opponent's discards.

Have Fun!

Whoever came up with the phrase "Winning is the most important thing" probably didn't get invited to too many parties. Nothing is more boring than playing cards with someone who acts like they're constructing a nuclear missile every time they play a card.

Keep in mind that you're playing a game, and don't take things too seriously, which not only cuts into the other players' enjoyment, but also hurts your game. The more pressure you put on yourself, the more tired and frustrated you get, and the worse you play.

Chapter **25**

Ten Places to Find More Information on Your Game

When you're new to a card game, you're sure to have questions about the rules, strategies, and nuances of play.

Even if you're just starting out with a game, don't be afraid to ask experienced players for advice; most people are only too flattered to be asked for help. If you can't find an experienced player to answer your questions, you may find the following ten sources of information helpful as well. Feel free to discuss the information you find with your new mentor!

The Internet

Almost all card games have a Web page or discussion group, and you can even play some games live on the Internet. Cyberspace gives you the chance to ask questions or debate a move with players all around the world, day or night. (I list websites for you to visit in many sidebars throughout the book.)

TIP

One of the best places to find the rules to every card game you can think of — and some you can't — is www.pagat.com. The manager of this site is John McLeod, the Technical Editor of this book, but even if he wasn't, I'd still recommend this site. The site includes an unparalleled reference section that points you just about everywhere you would want to go.

Here are some a few more sites devoted to card games:

» www.i-p-c-s.org, website of the International Playing-Card Society

» https://bicyclecards.com has official rules for a variety of card games

» https://boardgamegeek.com/boardgame/21804/traditional-card-games offers many useful resources for traditional card games, most of which can be played with a standard deck

Software and Live Sites on Computers

These days, you can play games of almost every sort against a computer or against a live opponent on the Internet. If you want to find the most challenging opponent or want to find the most economical buy, check out your options on the Internet.

Discussion Groups

Internet discussion groups exist under the heading rec.games for many different card games or under the heading rec.gambling. Go to Google groups, and type in **rec.gambling.poker** for example, and you can immediately locate the address of the site you need.

You can use these groups to ask specific questions about Blackjack, Poker, Bridge, and other games. After you subscribe to the newsgroups (which are free and the details of how to do so are easily accessible on the site), you can ask or answer questions or just read other people's questions. Another option is to try www.cardschat.com.

Gaming Bodies

You can contact the official governing body for your game of choice to ask for details about local clubs where you can play. You can often find these organizations listed in the phone book and on the Internet:

>> **For Bridge:** The World Bridge Federation, at www.worldbridge.org/.

>> **For Pinochle:** The National Pinochle Association, at www.npapinochle.org/.

>> **For online Poker:** Check out whether the IGC (Interactive Gaming Council) approves the site; www.gamingregulation.com/association/world/interactive-gaming-council/. There is, however, currently no governing body for tournament poker.

Books

Bookstores are full of books devoted to card games. Reading up on a particular pastime gives you a chance to get away from the table to work through potential problems in your game so errors don't cost you anything.

The chess and bridge bookshop in London is an excellent resource (try its website at https://chess.co.uk/ for more details). In the United States, you can start by looking on eBay (https://www.ebay.com). Or check out https://www.amazon.com for a bargain or two.

And don't forget about your public library. If it doesn't have any books in its collection, ask about shipping in the books you want via inter-library loans.

Newspapers and Magazines

You can read syndicated newspaper columns that feature the game you're interested in to discover the latest techniques, find the latest results, and hear about upcoming tournaments.

More and more magazines are also appearing on the Net — sometimes with a delayed publication date, sometimes requiring payment of a negligible annual fee before viewing. In fact, some magazines only appear online to save publication and distribution costs. The *Times* of London has a popular Bridge column. You can access The Aces on Bridge column online at https://bridgeblogging.com.

Playing with the Big Dogs

Playing with opponents and partners who are better than you at a particular game gives you first-hand instruction on improving your game. Taking losses may be temporarily deflating to your ego (and even to your bank balance on occasion), but the best way to get better in a hurry is to play against people who can improve your technique.

Tournaments

Playing with the experts is the ideal way to learn a card game, but sometimes world-class players only play with each other. Fortunately, you can still watch all their moves. Of course, you can watch the *World Series of Poker* on television, but if you prefer to play and can't afford the entry fee, you can enter plenty of satellite tournaments where the prizes involve both cash and an entry to the big dance. Check out www.wsop.com/ for more information on big tournaments. If you're interested in playing small tournaments online, you can head to any poker site and check out *Winning at Internet Poker For Dummies* (Wiley) for some valuable info. Or just head to the local casino to discover a host of tourney options.

Bridge tournaments take place all around the world, and you can go to a local, regional, or national tournament and compete against the top players in the world, often for a cost of $25 a day. Contact the American Contract Bridge League (ACBL) in the United States at https://acbl.org/, or the English Bridge Union (EBU) in the United Kingdom at www.ebu.co.uk/clubs. For Spades, check out www.premiumspades.com/spadewars. For Euchre, go to www.meetup.com/topics/euchre-tournament/. For Cribbage, check out www.cribbage.org, or if you want to find a game somewhere around the world, try www.meetup.com/topics/cribbage/.

Going Straight to a Gaming Source

Some vacation spots, such as Las Vegas and Reno, offer ample opportunity for you to practice and discover advanced techniques in many different games. These days, casinos are opening all around the United State, and you can easily play almost any gambling game, no matter where you live, if you're over 21.

Clubs

Of course, COVID has significantly affected live clubs, but assuming that one day we will be free of restrictions, there will always be a demand for live play as opposed to the Internet. Some card clubs are devoted specifically to one game, such as Bridge. However, most clubs offer more than just gameplay; they also offer some kind of instruction in the game. Don't be shy about looking up clubs in the telephone book or finding out details from sponsoring authorities. Most clubs actively recruit new members and are only too happy to accommodate beginners. Check out the section "Gaming Bodies" earlier in this chapter to find sites that point you to clubs in your area.

Depending on the area where you live, there may well also be clubs for games that are popular locally — for example Euchre, Pitch, Bid Whist, and Pinochle are all immensely popular in specific areas of North America. Try your phone directory or public library.

Index

Black Peter card, 58

Blackjack
  about, 271
  bank in, 276–277
  basic strategy for, 278–279
  betting in, 14
  burning the card in, 272–273
  Casino Blackjack, 279–286
  dealing in, 275
  Internet, 286
  placing bets in, 273–274
  setting game parameters in, 272
  Social Blackjack, 272–278
  splitting pairs in, 275
  starting over in, 278
  staying in, 275–276

blind bets, in Texas Hold 'Em, 323–324

blind nil, in Spades, 171–173

bluffing
  in Poker, 298–299
  in Stud Poker, 317–318
  in Texas Hold 'Em, 335–336

board, in Texas Hold 'Em, 322

body language, of opponents in Poker, 300

book
  defined, 14
  as a resource, 363

boss suit
  in Bridge, 189
  defined, 15

box, in Gin Rummy, 76–78

breaking spades rule, in Spades, 174

Bridge
  about, 189–190
  auction in, 13
  bidding in, 14
  boss/initial suit in, 15

competitive auction in, 13
  gaming bodies for, 363
  tournaments for, 364

Bridge Base (website), 190

Bridge For Dummies, 4th Edition (Kantar), 181, 186

bring-in, in Seven-Card Stud, 313

bug, in Poker, 292

builders, in Rummy, 70

building
  a Canasta, 93–94
  in Solitaire, 22

bumping, in Euchre, 155

burning the card
  in Blackjack, 272–273
  in Omaha High/Low, 341

buy a card, in Casino Blackjack, 283–284

C

Calculation Solitaire, 26–28

call
  in Poker, 294–295
  in Setback, 231

call a raise cold, in Texas Hold 'Em, 328

calling Rummy
  in 500 Rummy, 82–83
  in Texas Hold 'Em, 328–331

Canasta
  about, 85
  black 3s in, 93
  building a, 93–94
  calculating value in, 87–88
  discard piles in, 88, 89–90, 92–93
  end-game strategy, 95
  freezing discard pile in, 92–93
  going out, 94

Hand and Foot, 97–102
  history of, 86
  melds in, 86, 87–88, 90–92
  Modern American Canasta, 96
  moving around table in, 89
  picking partners in, 88
  red 3s in, 88–89
  Short-Handed Canasta, 97
  suits in, 86–87
  tallying scores in, 95–96
  unfreezing deck in, 92
  wild cards in, 86–87

Cancellation Hearts, 204

Canfield Solitaire, 28–30

card games. *See specific card games*
  about, 9
  etiquette for, 17–18
  playing, 14–18
  preparing to play, 11–14
  selecting, 18–19
  terminology for, 10–11
  tips for improving, 355–356

card rankings
  in Calculation Solitaire, 26–27
  in Canfield Solitaire, 29

cards
  deck of, 10
  history of, 10–11
  order of, 11
  pack of, 10

cashing winners, in Mini-Bridge, 184

Casino Blackjack, 279–286

center hand opponent (CHO), 12

Cheat, 55–57

cheat, in Solitaire, 22

Cheat Sheet (website), 4

S

safe bids, in Auction Pinochle, 218

sandbagging, in Spades, 176–177

scatter, in Hearts, 195

scoring
  in 500 Rummy, 81–82
  in Auction Pinochle, 220–221
  in Bid Whist, 136
  in Cribbage, 248–253
  in Five-Card Cribbage, 256
  in Hearts, 200–202
  in Mini-Bridge, 186–187
  in Pinochle, 208–209, 210–212
  in Poker Patience Solitaire, 37, 40
  in Romanian Whist, 143–144
  in Setback, 233–234
  in Spades, 173, 175–177, 179
  in Switch, 111

scraping-the-bottom-of-the-barrel hands, in Texas Hold 'Em, 326

Scum. See President

selecting
  card games, 18–19
  discards in Ninety-Nine, 146–147
  partners for Euchre, 155
  partners in Canasta, 88
  partners in Spades, 166

sequences
  in Cribbage, 247
  in Pinochle, 208–209

Setback
  about, 229–230
  bidding in, 231–232
  dealer in, 232
  deck for, 230–231
  Internet, 238

jokers in, 236

Partnership Setback, 238–239

planning strategy in, 235–238

playing cards in, 232–233

scoring in, 233–234

shooting the moon in, 234–235

Six-Handed Setback, 239

Three-Handed Setback, 239

winning in, 235

sets
  in 500 Rummy, 79
  defined, 14
  in Pinochle, 209
  in Rummy, 64

Seven-Card Stud, 312–316

seven-card trick, in Blackjack, 277

7s
  in Crazy Tan, 120
  in Fan Tan, 115, 116–117
  in Mau Mau, 107
  in Neuner, 108
  in Palace, 268
  splitting, 285

shooting the moon
  in Hearts, 200–201
  in Setback, 234–235

shooting the sun, in Hearts, 201

short suit, in Spades, 170

Short-Handed Canasta, 97

shuffling
  about, 11–12
  in Accordion Solitaire, 24
  in Spite and Malice Solitaire, 41

side pot, in Poker, 296

side-suit
  in Oh Hell!, 139
  in Pinochle, 207

silent estimate, 13

Simplified Snap, 48

single call, 13

singleton
  in Spades, 170
  in Whist, 128–129

six-card trick, in Blackjack, 277

6s, splitting, 284–285

Six-Handed Setback, 239

skunked, in Cribbage, 254–255

slamming. See shooting the moon

Slapjack, 50–51

small blinds
  in Omaha High/Low, 341
  in Poker, 294
  in Texas Hold 'Em, 323

smudging. See shooting the moon

Snap, 48–49

software, 362

Solitaire
  about, 21
  Accordion, 23–26
  Calculation, 26–28
  Canfield, 28–30
  Internet, 44
  Klondike, 30–31
  La Belle Lucie, 32–36
  Poker Patience, 36–40
  Spite and Malice, 40–44
  terms for, 22–23
  types of, 23–44

solitaire games, examples of, 18

space, in Solitaire, 22

Spades
  about, 165–166
  assessing value of high cards, 170
  bidding in, 168–169, 171–173

Internet, 125

jokers in, 136

leads, 128–130

playing hands in, 134–135

playing in, 125–126

remembering cards in, 127–128

Romanian Whist, 142–144

scoring in, 136

strategy for, 127–132

tallying score in, 126–127

Three-Handed Whist, 132–133

trump cards, 124–125

widows, in Auction Pinochle, 216–217

wild Canasta, in Hand and Foot Canasta, 102

wild cards

in Canasta, 86–87

in Hand and Foot Canasta, 100

in Poker, 292

in President, 265

in Rummy, 67–68

winning

in Cribbage, 253–254

in Five-Card Cribbage, 256

with high cards/trump, 15

in Omaha High/Low, 344–351

in Palace, 269

in Poker, 297

in Setback, 235

in Seven-Card Stud, 318

Winning at Internet Poker For Dummies (Harlan and Derossi), 301, 338, 364

World Bridge Federation, 363

World Series of Poker (WSOP), 290, 338, 364

Y

yourself, exposing, 13, 17

About the Author

Barry Rigal was born with a deck of cards in his hand. Having started with the children's games, Whist, Rummy, and Solitaire, he moved on to Bridge at the age of 12. After graduating from Oxford University (where he captained the Bridge team), he worked in accountancy. Highlights of his work career were learning how to play Piquet and Clobyosh in the Tax Department of Thomson McLintock. After 4 years with Price Waterhouse, supervising the partnership's Bridge team, he went into the world of business, working 7 years in the Oil Taxation department of Conoco. During that time he began a career as a journalist and commentator on card games. Over the course of the last three decades he has written newspaper and magazine articles and a dozen books on Bridge. Barry lives in New York and has traveled the world doing what he loves best.

Dedication

This book is dedicated to my late wife Sue, who made the whole project (and indeed everything else) worthwhile and has saved my life on countless occasions by fixing all my computer problems.

Author's Acknowledgments

My principal vote of thanks goes to Technical Editor John McLeod, who has provided invaluable assistance for just about every chapter in this book. John gave me essential information when I asked him, and he never got tired of my stupid questions. (You can visit his site at www.pagat.com.) In addition, I have used the assistance of many others who have created Web pages about card games, and who have been generous with their help and advice. Thanks are also due to the following people: Katie Sutton (for help on Canasta); Matt Schemmel and Erin O'Neil (Euchre); Melissa Binde (Fan Tan); Matt Ginsberg and Umesh Shankar (Setback); Richard Hussong, Jeff Goldsmith, and Bruce McCosar (Eights); David Dailey (Pinochle); Bruce Blanchard (President); Ernst Martin, Billy Miller, Tysen Streib, and Andy Latto (Poker); Michael Fosse, Dave Wetzel, and Pat Civale (Spades); John Hay, David Barker, and Alan Hoyle (Hearts); Carter Hoerr and David Parlett (exact trick games); Phil Gordon and Willy Ehlers (Omaha); Billy Miller (Hold 'Em). To everyone who answered my questions, thank you. And anyone I've accidentally omitted — sorry for not including you here! Special thanks to Carolyne Krupp and Mikal Belicove for getting me started on this project, and to Brian Kramer, my project editor, for helping me finish it. A tip of the hat also to my excellent copy editor, Josh Dials. Thanks also to project editor Lynn Northrup for her work on this third edition.

Publisher's Acknowledgments

Executive Editor: Steven Hayes

Acquisitions Editor: Kelsey Baird

Project Editor: Lynn Northrup

Technical Editor: John McLeod

Editorial Assistant: Audrey Lee

Production Editor: Saikarthick Kumarasamy

Cover Image: © Hu Xiao Fang/Shutterstock

Take dummies with you everywhere you go!

Whether you are excited about e-books, want more from the web, must have your mobile apps, or are swept up in social media, dummies makes everything easier.

Find us online!

dummies.com

PERSONAL ENRICHMENT

Staying Sharp	Facebook	Guitar	Investing	Beekeeping	Digital Photography
9781119187790	9781119179030	9781119293354	9781119293347	9781119310068	9781119235606
USA $26.00	USA $21.99	USA $24.99	USA $22.99	USA $22.99	USA $24.99
CAN $31.99	CAN $25.99	CAN $29.99	CAN $27.99	CAN $27.99	CAN $29.99
UK £19.99	UK £16.99	UK £17.99	UK £16.99	UK £16.99	UK £17.99

Meditation	Pregnancy	Samsung Galaxy S7	iPhone	Crocheting	Nutrition
9781119251163	9781119235491	9781119279952	9781119283133	9781119287117	9781119130246
USA $24.99	USA $26.99	USA $24.99	USA $24.99	USA $24.99	USA $22.99
CAN $29.99	CAN $31.99	CAN $29.99	CAN $29.99	CAN $29.99	CAN $27.99
UK £17.99	UK £19.99	UK £17.99	UK £17.99	UK £16.99	UK £16.99

PROFESSIONAL DEVELOPMENT

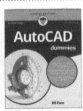

Windows 10	AutoCAD	Excel 2016	QuickBooks 2017	macOS Sierra	LinkedIn	Windows 10
9781119311041	9781119255796	9781119293439	9781119281467	9781119280651	9781119251132	9781119310563
USA $24.99	USA $39.99	USA $26.99	USA $26.99	USA $29.99	USA $24.99	USA $34.00
CAN $29.99	CAN $47.99	CAN $31.99	CAN $31.99	CAN $35.99	CAN $29.99	CAN $41.99
UK £17.99	UK £27.99	UK £19.99	UK £19.99	UK £21.99	UK £17.99	UK £24.99

SharePoint 2016	Fundamental Analysis	Networking	Office 2016	Office 365	Salesforce.com	Coding
9781119181705	9781119263593	9781119257769	9781119293477	9781119265313	9781119239314	9781119293323
USA $29.99	USA $26.99	USA $29.99	USA $26.99	USA $24.99	USA $29.99	USA $29.99
CAN $35.99	CAN $31.99	CAN $35.99	CAN $31.99	CAN $29.99	CAN $35.99	CAN $35.99
UK £21.99	UK £19.99	UK £21.99	UK £19.99	UK £17.99	UK £21.99	UK £21.99

dummies.com

dummies®
A Wiley Brand